GOGO MAMA

A JOURNEY INTO THE LIVES OF TWELVE AFRICAN WOMEN

SALLY SARA

Pan Macmillan Australia

First published 2007 in Macmillan by Pan Macmillan Australia Pty Limited
1 Market Street, Sydney

Reprinted 2007

National Library of Australia
Cataloguing-in-Publication data:

Sara, Sally.
Gogo mama: a journey into the lives of twelve African women.

ISBN 978 1 4050 3739 6.

1. Women – Africa – Biography. I. Title.

920.72

Typeset in 11.5/15 pt Baskerville Classico Regular by Post Pre-press Group
Printed in Australia by McPherson's Printing Group
Cartographic art by Laurie Whiddon
Text design by Deborah Parry Graphics

Papers used by Pan Macmillan Australia Pty Limited are natural, recyclable products made from wood grown in sustainable forests. The manufacturing processes conform to the environmental regulations of the country of origin.

In memory of Kate Peyton, BBC.

Killed in Mogadishu, Somalia, on 9 February 2005.

Aged 39 years.

A highly respected colleague who was renowned for her integrity, generosity and humour.

-Gogo *n. (isiZulu)* Grandmother
-Mama *n. (isiZulu)* Mother

Contents

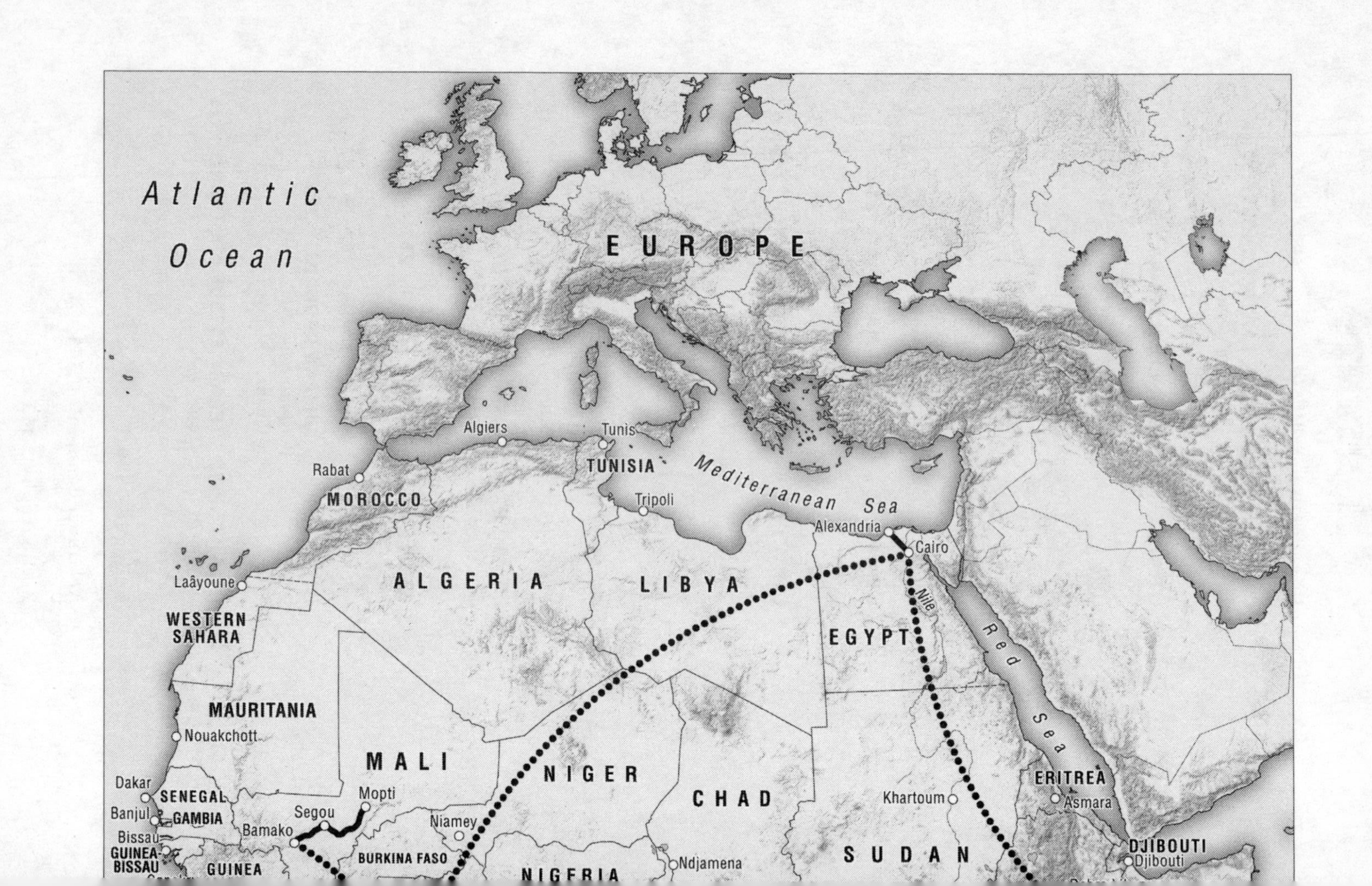

Atlantic
Ocean
EUROPE
Algiers
Tunis
Rabat
TUNISIA
Mediterranean Sea
MOROCCO
Tripoli
Alexandria
Cairo
Laâyoune
ALGERIA
LIBYA
Nile
WESTERN
SAHARA
EGYPT
Red Sea
MAURITANIA
Nouakchott
MALI
NIGER
Dakar
SENEGAL
Mopti
CHAD
Khartoum
ERITREA
Asmara
Banjul
GAMBIA
Segou
Niamey
Bissau
Bamako
GUINEA-
BISSAU
GUINEA
BURKINA FASO
NIGERIA
Ndjamena
SUDAN
DJIBOUTI
Djibouti

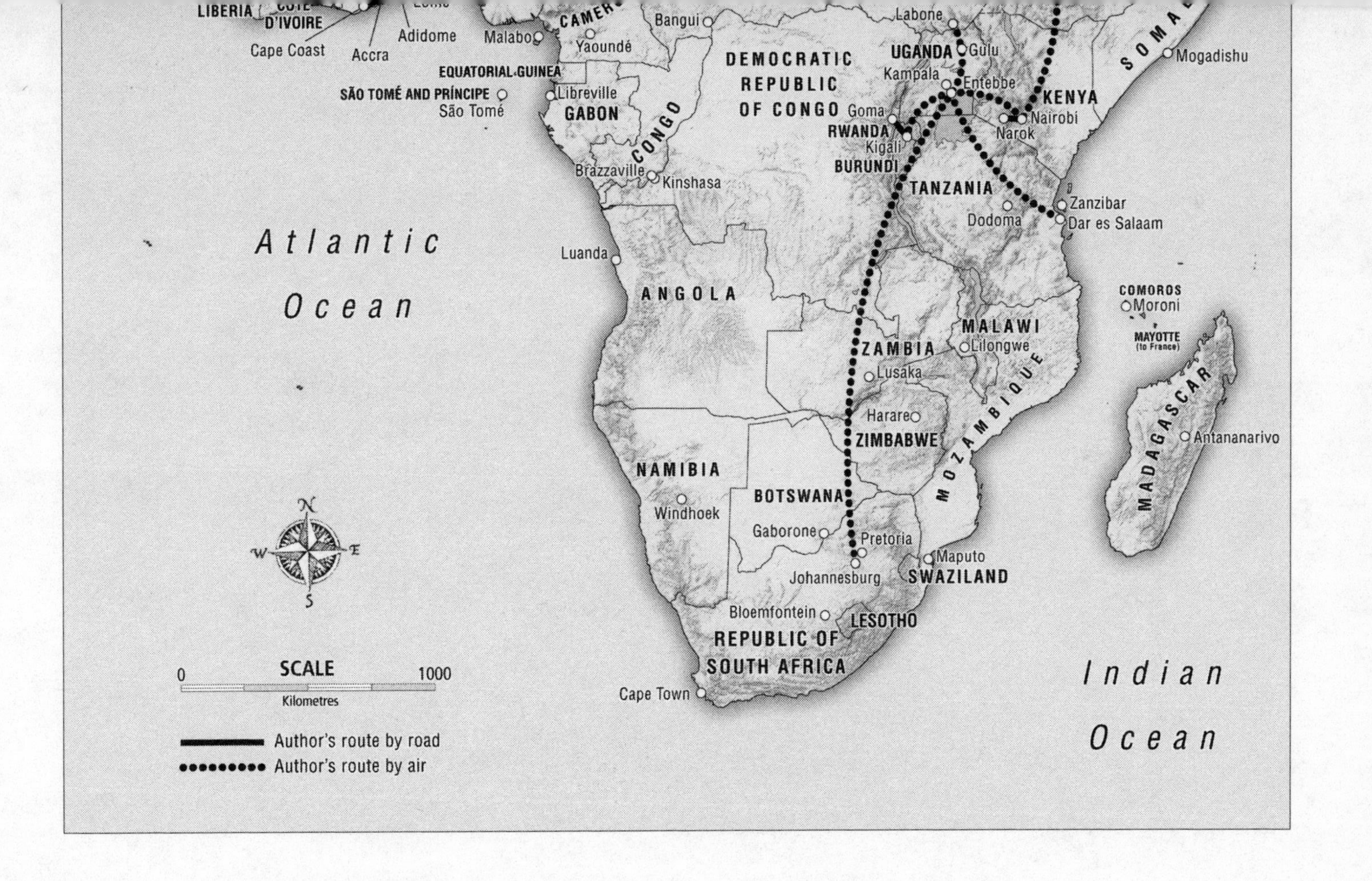

LIBERIA
D'IVOIRE
Cape Coast
Accra
Adidome
Malabo
Yaoundé
Bangui
EQUATORIAL GUINEA
SÃO TOMÉ AND PRÍNCIPE
São Tomé
Libreville
GABON
CONGO
Brazzaville
Kinshasa
DEMOCRATIC
REPUBLIC
OF CONGO
Labone
UGANDA
Gulu
Kampala
Entebbe
KENYA
Nairobi
Narok
Goma
RWANDA
Kigali
BURUNDI
TANZANIA
Zanzibar
Dodoma
Dar es Salaam
SOMA
Mogadishu
Atlantic
Ocean
Luanda
ANGOLA
COMOROS
Moroni
MAYOTTE
(to France)
MALAWI
Lilongwe
ZAMBIA
Lusaka
MOZAMBIQUE
MADAGASCAR
Antananarivo
Harare
ZIMBABWE
NAMIBIA
Windhoek
BOTSWANA
Gaborone
Pretoria
Maputo
Johannesburg
SWAZILAND
Bloemfontein
LESOTHO
REPUBLIC OF
SOUTH AFRICA
Cape Town
N
W
E
S
0
SCALE
1000
Kilometres
Author's route by road
Author's route by air
Indian
Ocean

INTRODUCTION

SOPHIE'S MOTEL, ENTEBBE, UGANDA
11 October 2004

I'm sitting in a $30 hotel room in Uganda wondering what the hell I've got myself into. This is day one of *Gogo Mama.* I don't even know all the names of the twelve women who will fill this book; only the journey will reveal them. I'm staring at places on the map as I sit cross-legged on my bed under a mosquito net, impatient to meet the women and nervous about whether I will even be able to find them.

This book started with a letter from a friend in publishing asking if I'd be interested in writing about my time in Africa. After spending several days thinking it over, I knew that I didn't want to write a 'foreign correspondent' book and I felt underqualified to attempt a grand political thesis. Slowly I came to the realisation that I wanted to tell the stories of the people I'd met. One in particular stuck in my mind, that of a woman from Uganda called Hellen Lanyom. She had had her lips cut off during a rebel attack and I admired her courage more than anyone else's I'd met in Africa. I thought, I want to write about women like Hellen – and that's how it began.

I've sent out emails to friends, interpreters and colleagues across the continent and have spent late nights researching by phone and internet to find the women I want to interview. Emails have been printed off, carried by bicycle to villages, interpreted into the local language and eventually answers have arrived in my in-box. The preparation has been exciting and frustrating as replies have emerged from the places I hope to visit.

My plan is to travel solo right across Africa from South Africa all the way up to Cairo and then across to West Africa, finishing in Timbuktu. I'll interview twelve different women in twelve different countries along the way. I'm deliberately steering away from some of the high-powered women on the continent; instead I want to tell the stories of others who deserve recognition. To give a sense of what life is like for many African women, this book needs to include some of the big challenges they face, including HIV/AIDS, poverty, lack of education, war, female genital mutilation and discrimination. But, above all, this book is about hope. Hope is the biggest lesson I've learned from Africa.

I will spend several weeks with each woman and I think the journey will take about six months. I'm doing the first stint of a couple of weeks during my holidays as a bit of a test run. I'm travelling alone, but I'll pick up interpreters and fixers along the way to help me find the women and conduct the interviews. Friends from aid agencies have offered to help me get into the more difficult locations, including south Sudan and Liberia. I'm carrying my backpack, my laptop, a notebook, a mini-disk recorder and microphone.

I feel excited but a bit apprehensive and quite alone. Under 'occupation' on my entry card I wrote 'author' when I arrived at Entebbe airport this afternoon and the old man at the passport counter asked me, 'How many books have you written?'

'None yet,' I replied.

'Oh,' he sighed with disappointment.

One way or another, this book is about to begin. *Hamba!*

CHAPTER 1

HELLEN LANYOM ONGUTI

Mutilation survivor

UGANDA

It was just after midnight when Hellen Lanyom woke to the sound of guns and the glare of torchlight as she and her family were captured by rebels in northern Uganda. The men were beaten to death and the women were mutilated, one by one. The rebels used a harvest knife to cut off Hellen's lips. She was left to die, but she survived and now lives as a farmer, sharing a hut with her orphaned nieces and grandchildren. Hellen is a survivor of the brutality of the notorious Lord's Resistance Army in northern Uganda.

SUDAN
Nile
SCALE
0
100
Kilometres
DEMOCRATIC
REPUBLIC
OF CONGO
River
Gulu
UGANDA
N
W
E
S
Lake
Albert
Mbale
KENYA
KAMPALA
Entebbe
Lake Edward
Lake
Victoria
Mbarara
TANZANIA
RWANDA

THE first time I met her, I didn't even know her name. She was just the lady without lips, the lip lady. The cameraman and I grimaced at each other before we set off to her house.

'Ay, Sally. How am I going to film this lip lady? . . . Ay-ay-ay.'

The cameraman shook his head and finished the sentence with sounds rather than words. It was his way of saying he was apprehensive. I was too. I had no idea this was about to be one of the most profound encounters of my time in Africa.

Hellen's story is the story of the war in northern Uganda. Her lips were cut off by child soldiers from the notorious Lord's Resistance Army, a rebel group which has terrorised the people of the north for almost twenty years. The war is one of the most brutal I've ever reported on – its syllables are not the blasts and bullet cracks of television wars. Much of the killing here is personal, deeply personal; it's done with knives, axes, sticks, bricks and machetes. Most of the perpetrators are children who have been abducted by the LRA. They kill for one reason – survival. They are told that if they refuse to take the life of another, they will lose their own. Hellen was one of their victims.

My first memory of Hellen was of her hands, not her face. She stretched her palms towards me and shook both my hands at once. I remember being surprised. Usually a two-handed shake is reserved for chiefs or elders in Africa. I was almost half Hellen's age and she was old enough to be my mother, but without any words she was offering friendship.

She could see by my slight embarrassment that I understood the significance. She looked me in the eye and didn't bow her head or turn away. But I was nervous. I only looked in glances at her mouth or stole a longer look when I was pretending to gaze at something in the distance. It was horrible: her lips were completely gone and her mouth had been stitched roughly. The scars in the corners of her mouth were X-shaped, a bit like the stitching on a rag doll. The skin was so shiny and tight, it looked as if it would split if she opened her mouth too wide.

I don't think about it so much now. I guess I've become used to it, it's just Hellen. She's one of my favourite women in this book; in fact, she's the reason I wanted to write it all. Now, more than a year later, I'm back in Gulu. As the light plane touches down, I can see a soldier running along the Tarmac flapping his arms, as if he too is attempting flight. But he's just chasing cattle off the runway. This airport is a lifeline for northern Uganda. Many of the roads beyond Gulu are dangerous corridors, because of the risk of rebel attacks. When the United Nations food convoys set off for outlying camps and villages, the UN staff are ordered to wear bullet-proof vests and the trucks are guarded by armed soldiers. But the locals who travel by foot and bicycle can only rely on their luck.

Gulu has been in the middle of this war for more than seventeen years. It's a worn-out town; its old colonial buildings have been lived in and worked in without repairs for decades and wear only a rash of flaky paint. It's as if they've been overinflated and let back down again. Nails have popped out of the roofing, plaster has cracked from the walls and windows are missing. Little tricks of wire and wood seem to hold things together.

There's no frontline to the war. A village can be peaceful for months or years and then one night the rebels will come, killing adults and kidnapping more children to fill their ranks. Sometimes they don't kill at all, they mutilate instead. The rebels may never come back or they could return the next week, there's no way to know and no sense to it; that's what makes it so frightening.

It's not a place to work alone. A young local social worker called Philip Lutara has agreed to be my interpreter. Philip is aged in his twenties, but has the authority and seriousness of a man in his forties. I met him when I was in Gulu more than a year ago filming a story on the war and we've stayed in contact ever since. He works for a group called the Concerned Parents' Association, which represents the parents of children who have been kidnapped by the rebels.

Although Philip is younger than me I treat him as if he's older, and I trust him absolutely. I think if I won a million dollars and asked him to look after it for me, he would have every last cent waiting for me when I got back, and probably also some stern investment advice.

Hellen's house is a fifteen-minute motorbike ride outside of Gulu. The town is busy even on a Sunday – most people are on foot as they balance buckets, boxes, baskets and bundles of grass on their heads. Mothers tie their babies on their backs with brightly coloured cradles of cloth and the babies bob up and down with each step as if they are nodding their heads in constant agreement. The flip-flop of thongs, the whir of bicycles, and grey smoke from motorbikes blur the edges of the busy market.

I stand near the gutter, while Philip starts the motorbike. The local women ride side-saddle as passengers; they look graceful and relaxed, but I feel like I will fall off. So I sit astride and hang onto the luggage rack on the back, stretching my fingers like claws as I grip on. We take off at high speed and ride past the waterhole where women are doing their weekend washing: they scrub the clothes by hand and then lay them flat on the grass to dry. Sheets, T-shirts and trousers are spread on the ground as if they are spelling out a giant message.

As we ride I lean over Philip's right shoulder so that I can see the obstacles ahead, but the rough road crunches my body from my teeth to my toes. I hang on without much elegance; my knees are turned in and my ankles turned out, like someone dancing the Charleston. I feel relieved when the brakes give a long groan and we turn off the track, snaking along the tyre marks between the fields while the grass swishes on my legs. Philip changes down several gears as we turn into a clearing and park under a tree.

I can hear Hellen's voice from a neighbouring hut. Children run in front of her as she walks down the path towards us. She's wearing a ragged skirt and a red top, her hair is in wild antennas of half plaits, half dreadlocks. She smiles and puts out both of her hands. Her grin widens as she rubs my arm and tells Philip that I have put on some weight: she grins with approval. She says she's been counting the days carefully, but she thought we were coming tomorrow. She looks a bit embarrassed and disappears inside to change her clothes. The children follow her. Even though it's the weekend, the boys come out in their school uniforms, which are the best clothes they have. Hellen emerges in a blouse and skirt, doing up the buttons of the blouse as she talks. Each button doesn't match the next and the fabric is scarred with patches and careful stitching. She washes her hands in a plastic bowl and greets us warmly again.

One of the boys brings out a woven mat and two home-made wooden chairs, and we sit down under a tree. It's the tail end of the dry season and oven-like winds blow heat and dust across the fields and through the shade. Squinting as the gusts interrupt the conversation, Hellen sits on the mat with her legs stretched out in front of her and her heels resting on the ground. Now I feel relaxed with Hellen, but during my first visit a year ago I didn't really know what to expect, or what she would look like. Would she have trouble talking; would she try to hide her face from me? I didn't know.

Hellen doesn't speak English and can read and write only simple words, but she's a smart, practical woman and she's tall and strong with a handsome body. Her hair is greying, but her skin is smooth; she has the dark, rich complexion of the Acholi tribe of northern Uganda. Hellen is aged in her sixties, but she moves like a restless child: her gait is quick and her body is rarely still. I don't think I've ever seen her wear shoes. Usually she's bare-foot and busy and I often have to add a little skip every few steps to keep pace with her. Her palms are rough from years of work. She only had three years of primary education that were inter-rupted by many missed years in between. Her father pulled her out of school to stay at home and help with the domestic chores and when the next term started, her brothers returned to school, but she was left behind. Her father refused to give her the fees to enrol; at first she hoped he had simply forgotten to do it.

'After one week I asked my father. He told me, "It is useless for a girl to go to school. From today onwards you have to remain home and look after the cattle."

'I realised that it was really the end of studies for me. I was very, very bitter with my dad. When I was studying, my ambition was to become a doctor. Almost for one week I could not even eat. I could only cry.'

Hellen uses her hands as she talks, flipping them back and forth in a gentle rhythm as her palms and her knuckles take turns in facing the sky. In the middle of the conversation, her youngest granddaughter, Aloyo, comes out from the hut. She's only three years old and was the last to finish changing into her best clothes. Aloyo is wearing an old skirt that is too big for her and over the top of this, Hellen adds a white petticoat with an elastic waist to hold it up. The clothes are torn, but Hellen proudly smoothes down the fabric as she talks, like a mother putting her child into a brand-new outfit.

Aloyo is small and stubborn. She has a cautious smile; her front teeth are brown with decay. Her name means 'I won' in the local Acholi language and it is given to girls to signify that the mother won the battle for the gender of the child. Aloyo's mother died from AIDS a week before Christmas. Hellen is caring for Aloyo and her orphaned sisters, and also looks after a grandson and two nephews. The children line up one by one in a serious procession to shake hands each time we arrive. They bow and curtsy, but they giggle when I pretend to squeeze their fingers. This is Hellen's makeshift family.

Hellen was married when she was eighteen to Janayo, a tall, muscular man she started noticing at church – he worked as a government official.

'It was me who chose him. I was already attracted to him. We used to meet when we go for prayers. He was brave enough. He used to come and talk to me at home. He would tell me all the good things and the plans he had for me.'

The visits started to bear fruit, and Hellen's parents decided that the young couple should marry. Janayo also spoke with his parents and the two families negotiated over the dowry, but Hellen was not allowed to take part in the discussions.

'I remember they came late in the evening. At the end of it I was told they had given my family six cows, two goats, and then six sheep plus 1400 shillings. At that time it was high value.

'I was one of the few respected ladies in that village. My name was never heard anywhere, like at the water pumps where people would quote that a particular girl likes men, any man. I could write and also say a few words in English. So I was of value. I was so happy because I knew I was a lady of character.'

Hellen says the words with quiet pride, but she keeps her gaze on the track as she talks. She and Philip always sit facing towards the track so they have some warning if the rebels attack. It's unlikely the rebels would strike so close to town during the day, but they have hit here before. It's quite eerie. The cassava plants in the fields are very tall and the wind is blowing so strongly it would be very hard to see or hear the rebels, should they decide to attack. Hellen and Philip say they don't want any surprises. I don't feel nervous sitting here – not because I underestimate the risk, but because I actually cannot imagine what it would be like to be caught up in an attack. I find it hard to believe that if rebels came they would kill me for no reason. But there is no doubt that they would. They kill for nothing every day. Only in my nightmares does my mind allow the reality to sink in.

The Lord's Resistance Army, led by Joseph Kony, is one of the most elusive, bizarre and brutal rebel groups in Africa. Kony says he wants to overthrow the government and rule Uganda according to the Ten Commandments, and warns he will punish the people of Acholi if they don't support him. But his ideology is so extreme he can't attract any recruits, so he kidnaps children to fill his ranks instead. Each year, thousands of children in northern Uganda are abducted by the LRA. Many are forced to kill within their first few days in captivity. The presence of child soldiers makes it an almost impossible war to fight for the government forces, the Uganda People's Defence Force. If they open fire on the rebels, the soldiers know they are actually shooting at children. When the UPDF helicopter gunships swoop over the bush, parents pray their children abducted by the LRA won't be the victims.

The modus operandi of the LRA is to terrify the local civilians into submission. The trademark of the rebels is to hack off the ears, nose, lips or breasts of local women; the mutilation is a warning to communities suspected of supporting government troops. On 4 October 1991, the war came to Hellen in the middle of the night. She was staying at her parents' farm, where all the relatives had gathered to help with the harvest. They spent their days in the fields and the nights sleeping in hiding places near the riverbank because they feared an LRA attack. Just after midnight, the rebels crept from the bush into the farmyard; they split up and started hunting for victims. The commanders were furious when they found the huts were empty. Eventually they discovered a small boy sleeping in the compound and they tortured him until he revealed where the rest of the family were. He led the rebels to the riverbank where Hellen and her relatives were sleeping under a low shelter made from sticks.

'I was deep asleep. I woke up when I heard a sudden bang. They kicked the shelter under which we were sleeping. There were torches and guns, there were torches all over our faces. That is when we realised it was the rebels. I thought they are going to kill us all. I just thought the whole family is going to be killed.'

'They started shouting, "We know Hellen is here, come out immediately." They said, "You have two brothers serving in the military, the government force. Where are they? You show us where they are. We want them now. If not, we shall kill you."'

The rebels rounded up the whole family and marched them back to the homestead, where they started attacking all the boys and men. Hellen watched helplessly as several of her relatives were beaten to death.

'I saw them being pounded with a club, they were groaning until suddenly the groaning stopped. That's when I realised they were dead. I saw it.'

When they left the riverbank, Hellen wasn't trembling; instead she was hoping that a miracle might save her family. But by the time they reached the homestead and the beatings started she thought everyone was going to be killed.

'It was terrible. It was like confronting something that would consume the entire family. I was just praying that the next one was going to be me. My hands were behind me. The rebels were kicking me, they were gun-butting me. They said, "Today is the end of you." One of the commanders shouted that, "Now, for these ladies, don't kill them. Cut off their lips so that their brothers who are in the army will come and see. Let the brothers come and witness what we have done to this family."'

Hellen was lying on the ground, ice-cold with fear. The commander ordered his child soldiers to take a knife and cut off Hellen's lips.

'They were just young boys, around twelve or thirteen years old. They were young boys. I could see them. I talked to them, I pleaded. I said, "Please, I am innocent. I have just come to visit my parents."'

The boys stalled, their eyes wide and frightened. They didn't want to carry out the order. But the delay infuriated their commander and he shouted a warning that they would be killed if they didn't start cutting.

'They grabbed me. I was the first among the ladies to be cut. They cut my upper lip first. Then they cut the lower one. They left me lying there. When they cut my lips, because of the pain and the blood flowing, I also collapsed. I only felt the first touch when they started with the upper lips. But when they were cutting the lower lips, I did not feel anything. I didn't know what happened.'

It was just after one o'clock in the morning. Hellen passed out as the child soldiers cut off her niece's lips and her sister-in-law's ears. She was unconscious for several hours, eventually being woken by the cold breeze of the early morning. She awoke piece by piece, as if she were finding someone else's body instead of her own. Her arms were twisted and tied behind her back and she lay slumped on her side. Beside her she could hear the sobbing of the other survivors.

'At first I heard the sound of people crying. It was the other ladies whose lips were also cut. One said, "Hellen is going to die forever." But the other one said she could still see my heart was beating. They were weeping and crying. I tried to straighten my arms, but I realised I was still tied. I struggled and then I sat up. I started pushing myself backward so I could get somewhere to lean because I was weak.'

When Hellen opened her eyes, she could see that most of the men were dead and the women had been mutilated. The rebels had left no-one untouched.

'I saw the dead bodies there and the other ladies who had been cut. I joined them, weeping. Then I realised there was cold wind blowing through my mouth. That is when I knew that my lips had been cut. I also started crying. "What am I going to do? I am really going to die." They were the words I was using to cry with. My hands were paralysed because of the length of time I was tied up. I asked people to help me to lift my hands so that I could feel it. But they just told me, don't feel it.'

Hellen doesn't use dramatic language to describe what happened. She doesn't say she was 'butchered' or 'sliced', she just says she was cut. Her words are plain and deliberate. If anything, her voice becomes a little softer, the way people talk about a terrible tragedy that happened a long, long time ago, as if their quiet and respectful tone might stop it from ever happening again.

If Hellen had been attacked and had her lips cut off in Australia, her case would have made national headlines. But this kind of attack is a daily reality for those who live on the outskirts of Gulu. Her scars attract pity and attention, but no longer the sense of shock which gripped the community at first.

Hellen goes into her hut and comes out with a knife similar to the one that the rebels used to cut off her lips. It's a home-made dagger called a *pala killi,* worn and smooth, and not much longer than Hellen's hand. The knife is sharp and strong; it's made by local blacksmiths and is normally used for harvesting rice. Hellen runs her finger along the blade and the wooden handle, showing it to me like a saleswoman demonstrating a product. She is very matter-of-fact about the knife, which she uses to harvest her own crops.

Aloyo comes and sits on the mat as Hellen is talking about the knife. She wants to look at it and join in, but her presence stops the interview. Philip gives her some coins to buy a packet of biscuits from the market. Aloyo's face comes to life; she grins and then runs down the track to tell the other children. Continuing her story, Hellen is calm and reflective when she talks about her attack. She looks down the track as she speaks and turns back to Philip at the end of each answer. Hellen finishes her sentences with a pause and then quietly says 'ay' in a voice that is gentle and clear. The loss of her lips hasn't affected her speech, but it has left her mouth jagged and unfinished.

'I realised my injury was severe when people came to see what had happened. The majority of people were just weeping and crying. Some would look once and then turn away, while holding their heart like this. People heard that we were injured, but they didn't know what kind of injury. When they saw, they could not just believe it. It was a total shock to the whole community, that is why they were crying. If it was normal injuries, that was normal. But the lips, that is what reduced people to tears.'

Hellen was one of the first women in the district to have her lips cut off. At that time the war was still in its early stages and this brutal mutilation was a new tactic by the rebels. She wasn't sure what her wound looked like; she was in shock and could only get some sense of it from the response of the bystanders.

'When I saw the reaction of people, there was nothing I could do. I just sat back and I was speechless. My senses were not working. People asked me questions, but I could not respond. I was not talking, I was only looking on. When I went to the hospital, my brothers said don't mind of what happened, just know that your lips, lower and upper have been cut.'

Now, Hellen keeps her medical records in a small plastic bag buried in the fields. It's not safe to store important documents in the hut because of the risk of attacks by rebels or thieves. Out in the fields is a makeshift filing system of shallow holes covered with soil: bank books, passports and photographs are wrapped in plastic and hidden in the earth, while bigger possessions are stowed amongst the crops. Hellen camouflages her cooking pots, plates and cups amongst the foliage and retrieves them in the morning.

She gets up from the mat and crouches behind the hut, digging up the bag that holds her hospital charts and opening it carefully. The words are scrawled in blue pen; it's the busy handwriting of doctors and nurses – short and clinical.

Lanyom, Hellen.
5th October 1991.
Cut wound with panga on upper and lower lip.

Hellen was taken to Lacor Hospital in Gulu, where doctors operated to clean up the wound. But there was little they could do. Hellen's lips were completely gone and the surgeons could only stitch the rough edges of flesh.

'After one week, gaining some strength, I could walk around. I started looking around for a mirror in the hospital. I saw myself. It was the nurse's office. There was a mirror on the wall. I was full of worry because I could not imagine how I was appearing. When I saw myself, it got me more worries. I cried. I just went back and started crying immediately. I couldn't imagine me Hellen, now looking like that. I was very beautiful, but when I looked at myself it was a different Hellen. I knew people are not going to accept me. The first thing I thought of was suicide. I said it out loud. My people, they just stood by me. They said, "Hellen, you are not born like this. Just carry on, even if you think you are useless. The people have confidence in you. Just carry on."'

Hellen decided to steal some drugs from the nurses' station and take an overdose. She didn't want to live. But her relatives were relentless, visiting her almost every day during her two months in hospital. Their message was simple: she had to keep going; there was no choice. Hellen felt a strong sense of loyalty and responsibility to the relatives who supported her.

'I thought, if I think of suicide I will not be the Hellen who grew up being honest. It would mean that I downplay the moral support my relatives . . . have been giving me.

'I had made up my mind. Whoever accepts me, fine. Whoever rejects me, it's up to them. Some people would laugh, some would cry. For those who laugh, I would just ignore them as if I had not heard.'

But she was nervous. She was one of the first women to go back to the community after losing her lips. People were curious, and afraid because the rebels were escalating their campaign of mutilation. Some of the LRA's victims were asked if they wanted to smile or frown. Those who chose the smile had their lips cut off, those who chose the frown had a padlock put through their mouth. It was a gruesome tactic. It not only added to the fear, it meant the victim was often rejected or ridiculed.

'I was on my way back from town. I was walking on foot. One of my relatives was on a bicycle following me. A boy started laughing. He said, "Look at that one, they have cut the lips. Look at the teeth. Look at the lips." When my brother who was following heard this, he hit the boy. He grabbed him and they started fighting seriously until people came and stopped them and took them to the local authority. The case ended up in court. I had to go to the court several times as a witness. After that, the boy was given imprisonment for seven years of hard labour.'

The boy was sentenced as an example to others, and in handing down the sentence the magistrate warned that anyone else who tried to ridicule victims of rebel attacks would also be jailed. Hellen felt embarrassed.

'It was not a good experience. I did not want to punish him. That was the first and the last physical confrontation. After that, the court ordered that whoever does this, they will be punished. Ever since then, there has never been any such incident. People maybe do it. But they do it silently. I don't mind. I don't care about them talking behind their hands.

'Some people are nervous. I see from their reaction. There is some uneasiness because of the loss of my attraction powers. Appearance attracts someone and creates that warm interaction. But if you have lost it, people sometimes show on their face.'

I turn off the recorder and ask Helen if it's okay to take some photographs tomorrow. She nods. 'No problem.'

I feel a bit apprehensive, I don't want to embarrass her. I remember feeling the same way more than a year ago when we filmed Hellen for our television report. I found it agonising when the cameraman drew in close to film Hellen's face. But he kept asking her gently if it was okay, and she nodded. She seemed to understand it was a necessary part of the story. I was very grateful, and struck by her dignity and generosity.

Philip and I start walking down the path to the motorbike and Aloyo runs behind us, telling Philip that she wants to come with me back to Australia. She's packed up all her clothes and her sleeping mat in the hut, and she clutches the few coins left over from the biscuit expedition. She runs up to the motorbike and shows Philip that there is space for her to sit on the petrol tank. She is serious and has a sense of urgency as she tries to find a place. I ask Aloyo how she knows that Australia would be better than Uganda. 'I know it is,' she tells Philip defiantly. Hellen laughs, but Aloyo's words sadden me. It's confronting to see a child who is not yet old enough to go to school but who already has such a strong sense of survival and vulnerability. I get on quickly as

Philip starts the motorbike, and we turn sharply around the tree and ride off down the track. We can hear Aloyo crying and yelling in protest as we go.

When we return the next afternoon, the children are waiting for the sound of the motorbike. They run up the path and Aloyo takes my hand. I'm not sure if the gesture is because she's forgiven me for leaving her behind yesterday or if it's to smooth the way for a second escape attempt.

Hellen is waiting by the hut, prepared for the photo shoot. Her hair has been tamed – the wild plaits have been brushed out into a smooth beehive. She's wearing a brightly coloured dress with red, green and yellow patterns. She looks quite different. I wink at her and she smiles back. I have to get the camera fairly close to her face to take some of the shots. Hellen is very gracious and patient. I show her the pictures on the screen of my digital camera. She's curious to see herself and doesn't seem to be uncomfortable.

But after her attack, Hellen was worried that her husband, Janayo, might abandon her. She was one of two wives: Janayo had married another woman who was several years younger than her. Polygamy is part of Acholi culture in northern Uganda; many men have several wives and women are expected to accept it. Hellen and her co-wife were good friends. They kept separate houses and Janayo lived between the two. When Hellen returned home from hospital she wasn't sure whether her husband would leave her for the second wife. But Janayo didn't push her away.

'After the attack that happened to me, he never changed because he used to stay with me for a long time, two or three weeks before going to the second wife. He would bring me household needs like soap, salt, sugar. He even used to give me money like he used to do, to keep myself. And he would also come and dig my garden, help plant the food crops and at time of harvest he would bring some food from the other woman and also help me harvest.

'It also helped to make others accept me. If he had ignored me, the rest of the people, even our children, would have started behaving the same way. His constant love bound us together and that gave me the strength to carry on.'

Hellen talks about her husband with gratitude. She's genuinely thankful that he stuck with her. I'm struck by her modesty: imagine being grateful for a few visits and a bit of soap from a husband you share with another woman. But for Hellen it was the difference between acceptance and isolation.

Hellen stops and looks at the broth of grey clouds in the sky. Drops of rain thud into the soil and bend the cassava leaves one by one, indicating that heavy rain is only minutes away. I follow Hellen and the children as they run inside the hut. The walls and floor are made from grey mud and wooden beams hold up the thatched roof. The design is starkly simple. A single wall divides the cooking area from the sleeping area. There are no beds or other furniture and clothes are kept on wooden racks in the ceiling. The mud floor is moulded to make a small fireplace for cooking.

We watch the rain through the doorway and I notice that the door is propped open with a base plate from a mortar launcher. Hellen says one of her brothers gave it to her. The rain starts splashing inside; soon it becomes obvious that the downpour is too heavy for Philip and me to ride back to Gulu on the motorbike, so we wait. I point to an empty space on the floor and joke to Hellen that it will be my sleeping place for the night. She laughs but shakes her head and says she doesn't know what the rebels would do if they found a white woman here.

It's often not safe for Hellen and the children to sleep at home so they walk for almost an hour into town. Each night tens of thousands of people do the same. Most of them are children. They set off just before sunset carrying old maize bags to sleep on – they don't have any blankets, instead they spread out the bags wherever they can find shelter. Thousands sleep in the grounds of Gulu's hospital, curled up in doorways and alongside the hospital buildings. In the morning, they wake up, pack up and walk all the way home.

I remember being shocked the first night I spent in Gulu. As the sun set, the roads were crowded with so many children walking in search of a safe place. I don't know what was more shocking, the sight of so many children too afraid to sleep at home or the acceptance of it. This has now been going on for a generation.

'When the rebels are at large we normally go to town and sleep. I used to go and sleep in the government hospital on the verandas. But sometimes if we go late, when the whole place is crowded, we just go under shops, the verandas of the shops, and that is where we spend our night. It is very cold and sometimes you get drenched by rain. That is the way we have been living.

'They have attacked us here twice. At night they came and captured us. They took us to the trading centre. I was carrying the youngest girl on my back. When we reached there and they looked at us they said, "Take this woman back home. Just leave her to go." They just sympathised with me. But I think if I get a wrong group they will just kill me because they will think that I will portray them as bad people who have injured me. They will just kill me.'

Hellen sighs as she looks out the doorway of her hut as the children sit around her on the floor. She hopes the heavy rain will keep the rebels away tonight.

'I now don't care. I don't bother about them. If they come and abduct me again, I don't care whatever they will do. Because what I have experienced with them is already too much. There is nothing more they can do to me. I am just an ordinary woman. But I find extra courage.'

The war has been going on so long that daily life has been moulded around it; walking several hours just to find a safe place to sleep each night is part of the routine. Some children in northern Uganda don't remember ever sleeping in their own beds. As childhood has changed hands since the start of the conflict, parents who grew up sleeping under the verandas each night now send their own children off to do the same. The parents can't afford to make the journey themselves, as it would take up too much of their working day.

The Lord's Resistance Army has imposed its bizarre rules on the people, declaring it illegal to ride bicycles. It is a crime punishable by death, but bikes are the main form of transport for many Acholis. Janayo and three friends were riding their bikes back from election meetings in 2000 when they were caught by the LRA.

'The rebels had passed a warning that anyone caught riding a bicycle would be killed. When they ambushed them and captured them, they were beaten. They first beat them with axes and then clubs until they were unconscious. Then in the morning they finished him off with the axe. I could not imagine the torture he underwent.'

A boy from the village risked his life by riding a bicycle to deliver the bad news to Hellen.

'I was washing clothes. It was early morning. When I saw him I knew something was wrong. He was not talking and he was trembling.'

Hellen took the boy inside and he told her that Janayo had been killed. She wanted to weep, but she knew she had a long journey to reach her husband's village and she didn't want to make the trip more difficult for the boy who was escorting her.

'I could not cry. I could only sob quietly because he had to carry me on the bicycle and we go back to the village.'

It was just before Christmas 2000. Hellen sat on the back of the bicycle as the boy pedalled towards the village. For her, the journey was a blur.

'It was like I was lifeless. My first thinking was that, God, did you send this war to wipe us out? After humiliating me and mutilating me, then you send them to kill my husband. I did not know what to say. In my heart I was very bitter. I had nothing I could do. The people around me they helped me because after long time, they said, on this earth you cannot punish someone for the injustices they have done. But let the Lord decide what to do with them because there is nothing much you can do.'

Hellen and the boy knew they were at risk travelling by bicycle, but it was too far to the village to go by foot. They hid in the grass several times when they saw the rebels' tracks in the dirt. The LRA was hunting for more victims, even during the burial of Hellen's husband.

'It was the most tragic burial I have ever seen. At the time when we were about to bury, the rebels again stormed the place and we had to run away and leave the dead body there until the following day. For us it's like a curse. That is not a decent burial for someone who has been important in society.

'The anger I had I could not compare. If I had to act by it I would be mad or even dead. I could not imagine. It was like they were not human. They should have given us peace to bury the dead body.'

It's one of the few times during the interview that I see Hellen show any anger. Her jaw tightens and she kneads her thumbs against her tightly clenched fingers.

'It was lonely. When I came back, people realised it was going to be a tough time for me. In our community so many ladies have been widowed by rebel activities. So they used to come and sit and give me some advice on how to live. Most important were the children I had around me. My grandson and then my granddaughters. When I was sad or isolated, when I was just about to begin mourning or grieving, they would come and sit near me. It made me strong and brave until a time came when I could actually live.'

When her grief was still raw, the rebels struck again. Less than a year after the brutal murder of Hellen's husband, they raided the village where her eldest daughter, Christine, was living. They ordered Christine to go with them, but she refused. They used machetes to slash her body from her temples to her legs and bayonets to pierce through her ribs. They hacked her to death.

Hellen uses her hand like a knife to simulate the attack. She shows where the rebels slashed the flesh of her daughter. She remembers the exact position of all the wounds on the body. Finishing the demonstration, she looks up at me.

'My life of sadness has been more than of happiness. I have been left to fend for myself. I thought it would be the end of me, I would never be strong again. I had to pick from whatever courage I had. Now I have managed to live and keep even more children in my house. That is something which is great. I think it was just by the mercy of God, who give me all the courage and the ability to carry on like that.'

The next day, Philip and I stop at the market, following the flies and the smell to find and buy some beef as a gift for Hellen. The butcher shop is deep inside the tangle of stalls and alleyways. A piece of beef sits on the windowsill. The butcher hacks off a large chunk and puts it in a black plastic bag, which I stow in my backpack.

The market is full of large Acholi women: black, shiny and strong. Many are well over six feet tall; their produce keeps them plump and powerful and they look like wrestlers as they lift crates with their large hands. Some doze through the afternoon with their faces resting on bags of millet and rice. We walk past baskets of tiny dried fish, spices and vegetables and back to the motorbike in the street. Some people laugh as we ride out of town. I haven't made much progress as a Ugandan biker chick; in fact, I almost lose my shoe and my balance as we pull up behind a truck.

I hand the beef to Hellen when we arrive at her house and she clasps her hands and smiles.

Meat is a luxury – some families can only afford it twice a year, once for Independence Day on 9 October and once for Christmas Day. The rest of the time they live on maize and cassava, millet and vegetables. Sometimes there is enough money to buy a handful of tiny dried fish that look and smell like cat food.

The children are running around outside, chattering and laughing. Philip explains that they're celebrating because they ate rat for supper last night. A neighbour set a trap and caught a rat the size of a house cat. Smoked rat is a local delicacy, and Hellen says any meat is better than nothing.

'Sometimes I go for months without eating meat. The edible

rats are difficult to come by because they are expensive. People sell them expensive when they get it. If I have any chance of money I buy, and we enjoy it. You wash it, then boil it to get the fur off. I cook it in a smoked way. That is how we prepare it. The children really enjoy it.'

The children are rat-fuelled to their eyeballs, chasing each other through the cassava field and giggling. Hellen smiles as she watches them.

'When I prepare it, you see, they take a long time to eat it, to enjoy it. Then they demand for more, more, more. They get excited about it. They also tell their friends. The children really enjoy meat because if I cook, you can see them playing excessively. They are full of energy. They play so hard that later some of them just fall asleep.'

Hellen is self-sufficient, feeding herself and her orphaned grandchildren, nieces and nephews with what she grows. Any extra is sold and used to buy other household items like salt, sugar and soap from the market. Hellen shows me the cassava crops. When the ground cracks at the base of the plant, she says, the cassava is ready. When the rains come, Hellen plants maize, beans and potatoes and she also grows pumpkins to feed the children for breakfast. There's a mango tree to deliver sweet fruit when it ripens. Everything has a purpose. Hellen planted an acacia tree to give shade, and the boys use the branches to make chairs for sale at the market. They also collect fruit called *tugu* from the palm trees. The *tugu* look like orange coconuts; they are pounded until the children can suck out the flesh, then the seeds are planted and produce soft roots than can be eaten, too. Outside the hut there's a cluster of bamboo for making roofs and a patch of grass to soak up the rain during the wet season. It's simple and clever all at once.

'I think I am living a purposeful life because of the children I have around me. When I am sad, working with them makes me forget about my worries. It is a company that I have formed around me that I cannot live without. They help me a lot. When they come back from school, if they find me doing anything they just say, "Mummy, you just stop, we are taking over." They are the reason I live. Life would not be the same without them. I think it would be a meaningless life.'

All this is why Hellen stays here, despite the risk of rebel attacks. If she moved away she would be safer, but she needs the land to feed her family. It's the same dilemma that faces thousands of other families – more than one and a half million people are living in camps in northern Uganda because it's not safe for them to live and work on their own land. They go hungry within view of their abandoned fields.

'I know everything has a beginning and an end. But this war has been going for almost twenty years. I happened to physically meet the President. When I asked him, "How are you going to end the suffering and the war?" the president told me, "Very soon I have the means and ability to end the war and it will end soon." But up until now it continues. Maybe if there is a change in government there will be a change and our children can live in peace. Our children need peace. They have to be peaceful.

'The level of brutality that Joseph Kony is committing on his own people, it is demonic and I can't understand. Traditionally in Acholi society, in any war situation, right from our ancestors, women are not killed. But Joseph Kony has turned his gun to his own mothers of Acholi. The mothers who breast-fed him, who cooked him food until he grew, the mothers who were carrying him in the womb for nine months. For him to do such a thing is a curse.

'The very people who committed the atrocities are coming back into our community. We have to live with them. When I meet some of them in the community, they just shake their head. It is a sign that they are ashamed of what they did. Personally I have no ill feeling, because I know they were sent to carry out orders. When the rebel commanders were returning, I went to see some of them. When one of them saw me, he just started weeping and telling me sorry. He said, "Mummy, forgive us. We did it against our will." I told him, "Don't fear me. I have no grudge against you."'

Hundreds of children who have escaped the LRA live in camps on the outskirts of Gulu. The camps are run by church and aid groups who help to rehabilitate the children and reunite them with their families. There's also a separate camp for former young commanders of the LRA, who are deliberately kept away from their former child soldiers because of fears they will further intimidate them. I remember going to one of the camps during my first visit to Gulu and watching small boys waving home-made wooden toy guns while they re-enacted kidnappings and killings. It was very disturbing. The boys laughed while they played, but they were well drilled and quick as they pretended to abduct each other. Teenage girls looked on; many had children of their own, the result of rape during their time in the LRA.

Children have become the currency of the war. The rebels abduct them, aid workers rehabilitate them, distraught families welcome them home and then often the rebels abduct them again. Some are abducted several times during their childhood. The camps are surrounded by sturdy fences and towering gates to stop the LRA from returning to abduct again, but there is little protection for most of the children of Gulu district. Each morning I see the hundreds who have slept in town for the night as they begin their walk back to the villages. They are barefoot and wiry, the boys wear baggy shorts and the girls wear ragged dresses. Some of the children walk up to 20 kilometres a day to make the round trip to sleep in Gulu, missing the first hour of school because the journey takes so long.

An eighteen-day ceasefire was declared a week ago. But the chidren are still too afraid to sleep at home. They start walking out of town just before dawn. Groups of brothers and sisters walk together, chatting and fighting. They laugh as they see me going for a morning run and shout to the next group ahead that a white lady is coming; the younger ones squeal and some of the older boys try to run with me. There are no adults to supervise the children on their long daily walk, only a few government soldiers making tea and eating bread on the roadside.

The sky is a soft pink and grey as roosters strut between the huts announcing the morning, and other birds wake up suddenly, squawking and fluttering as if the branches of the trees have been electrified. The sun has barely claimed its place on the morning horizon, but it's already hot. I'm red in the face and my arms are glistening with sweat when I return to the guesthouse where I'm staying.

I climb the stairs to my room and switch on my mobile phone to see if there have been any calls. I usually check it once a day: this morning it beeps full of text messages. I open and read the first one.

'*Kate(bbc) was shot and killed in Somalia 2day.*'

Kate Peyton was a BBC producer, friend and colleague. I squat down and listen to my voicemail, which is loaded with messages from grim colleagues. I stop, jarred by the unreality of it. The detail of Kate's death spills out from distraught friends. My voice curls up in a syrup in my throat, making it difficult to speak.

Kate was shot by an unknown gunman only a few hours after arriving on assignment in Mogadishu, Somalia. She was 39 years old and engaged to marry her African fiancé, Roger, later in the year. Kate was already caring for his young daughter, who had just moved into her house a few weeks before.

Kate was five years older than me, and her advice and reassurance had guided me many times when as a young foreign correspondent I felt overwhelmed. She was renowned for her integrity, compassion and humour, and she was one of my role models in Africa. The last text message on my phone was from Kate several days earlier, when I left Johannesburg.

'So sorry I missed you. I cant believe how busy my life has been. Then there's been work on top of all that! Would love to hear about your travels. Love, Kate x'

I go into the bathroom and sit naked in the bath, wrapping my arms across my shoulders. The taps are dry, so I wash myself with a bucketful of water. I pull my knees tightly into my chest. I sway and cry.

I eventually get dressed and go downstairs to meet up with Philip. We're scheduled to do the last interview with Hellen this morning and I can't leave Gulu without properly saying goodbye to her. Philip is calm and comforting when I explain what has happened. He takes me on the motorbike to the airline office to see if I can get a flight to Entebbe and get back to South Africa for Kate's memorial service. There is not another plane to Entebbe until tomorrow, but the man behind the desk changes my hand-written ticket and says not to worry. I will get a seat.

Philip and I ride to Hellen's house to say goodbye. The warm wind pushes past my face, but my eyes are red and tight and fixed in a stare. I feel uncomfortable about seeing Hellen. I don't want to bring bad news to her and, in a selfish way, I don't want to leave my safe place as an observer. For the past week I have been chronicling her grief, yet I don't want to share mine.

When we arrive, she already has the two chairs and the woven mat set up under the tree. I smile but can't make full eye contact with her. We sit down and Philip speaks in Acholi, explaining to Hellen that my friend Kate has been killed.

Hellen puts her long hands over her face: the tips of her fingers cover her eyes and her palms cover her mouth. She starts wailing in a long, one-syllable cry. I feel even more uncomfortable. The women from the neighbouring hut hear the wailing and they join in too; it's mournful and unmistakable and their cries are blown through the fields by the hot wind. Aloyo is playing outside the hut. She's only three years old but she already knows the sound of mourning. It is unnerving to watch her quickly comprehend that someone has died. Aloyo polices herself, sitting quietly and pulling her limbs close to her body in a rigid, unnatural pose as she bows her head. Her own mother died only a few months ago; I guess that's why she recognises the wailing.

Hellen takes my hands and talks softly as we sit under the tree. She doesn't hug me or hold me. She just touches my fingers. There are pauses as she speaks and Philip translates her answers. I apologise for bringing bad news, but she tells me there is nothing I can do to change what has happened, it was the will of God. As blunt as is it, it's comforting. I wonder what Kate would think of me sitting under a tree in a dusty field in Uganda, trying to make sense of it all.

There's no lecture from Hellen; she doesn't relish the familiarity of grief. She knows its scent and shape, but she doesn't welcome it with any flicker of drama or excitement. Rather, instead of taking me into her world of loss, she comes into mine. I hunch forward in my chair and listen to Hellen's murmured words and Philip's translation.

Her selflessness makes me feel embarrassed. Everything is upside down and I've found myself on the wrong side of the interview.

I don't have control when the grief hits me; I am washed around in the awfulness of it all. All I can do is look deep into Hellen's eyes. I am floundering in what she has already overcome. This is the kind of grief she's been talking about during our interviews over the past week, the grief of murder. It feels very different from what I thought it was. The realisation hits my empty stomach. The deeper I fall into the grief, the more I realise how far Hellen has climbed out. Her losses are beyond calculation. I have lost one friend, but Hellen lost her daughter, husband, countless relatives and her appearance. I can't even imagine the dimensions of that.

The senseless loss fills me with anger. As I feel the rage bellowing in my chest, I stop and look at Hellen again. There is no anger in her face. None. Her years of grief could have easily settled into deep furrows across her brow. But when I look at her, I can see she is free, she has forgiven. She doesn't show much bitterness or self-pity. Being free is a difficult thing to fake. I've interviewed people before who claimed to be free, but there was still anger in their words and awkward flashes of satisfaction in their eyes as they received sympathy from others. I've never seen that with Hellen, who just tells her story with such naturalness. She has earned her freedom through genuine forgiveness and doesn't carry much anger anymore.

Hellen stops talking. She makes a soft clicking noise as if to say sorry and shakes her head. As we say goodbye, I hold her hand and thank her. We walk to the motorbike and she touches her butchered mouth before speaking softly.

'Everybody who is born, is born without a scar. They just happen in the course of life. Whatever way I appear, just know I was not born like that. People who attach too much importance to appearance are shallow thinkers. They are shallow. We should accept people the way they are. Let us not despise whatever God has given.

'I am a woman full of courage and strength. I am very strong physically. Look at me, I'm in Uganda. I'm worse off than you. But I am carrying on.'

In September 2006, the Ugandan Government invited Hellen Lanyom to speak at the official peace negotiations with the Lord's Resistance Army. She came face to face with LRA leader Joseph Kony. He attempted to have her removed from the talks because of the severity of her appearance, but Hellen courageously told her story and refused to be intimidated.

Hellen's granddaughter, Aloyo, started school in February 2007.

CHAPTER 2

MASINDA MAFIANO

Batwa Pygmy villager

DEMOCRATIC REPUBLIC OF CONGO

Masinda Mafiano is a Batwa Pygmy who lives at the base of a volcano in the Democratic Republic of Congo. When it erupts, the lava can reach the Batwa village in less than fifteen minutes. Masinda, her husband and six children live in a grass hut built on the volcanic rock. The Batwa Pygmies are among the poorest people in the Congo.

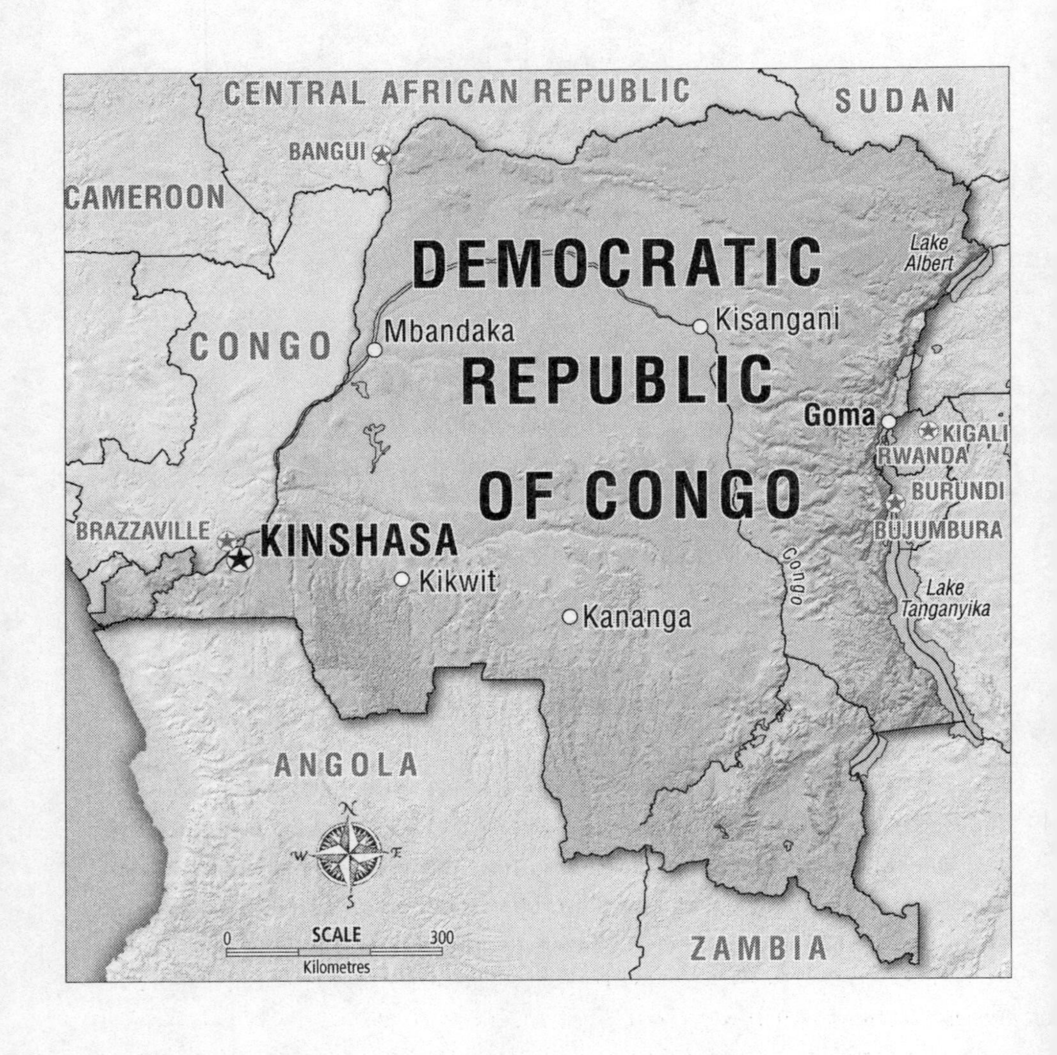
CENTRAL AFRICAN REPUBLIC
SUDAN
BANGUI
CAMEROON
DEMOCRATIC
REPUBLIC
OF CONGO
Lake
Albert
Kisangani
Mbandaka
CONGO
Goma
KIGALI
RWANDA
BURUNDI
BUJUMBURA
BRAZZAVILLE
KINSHASA
Kikwit
Congo
Lake
Tanganyika
Kananga
ANGOLA
N
W
E
S
0
SCALE
300
Kilometres
ZAMBIA

A tiny woman walks up the track with a hoe over her shoulder and a baby on her back. She is strong, dirty and quick-eyed, and her bare feet are caked in soil from the fields. She sits down on the ground next to the bench. Her name is Masinda. We've driven for more than an hour to reach her village near the base of the volcano Mount Nyiragongo, in the Democratic Republic of Congo. The village is not very far outside the town of Goma, but there's no proper road so we had to drive across the volcanic rock, which was so jagged I was sure it would rip the metal belly of the car. The village is called Mudja and it doesn't have a road because no-one here has a car. There wouldn't be any signs announcing the name of the village, either, if it weren't for the aid agencies which put up big notices outlining their projects here. But the signs are faded and many of the aid groups are long gone. The poverty, however, remains.

I've never been to a Batwa Pygmy village before and I'm not sure what to expect. The people come out of the fields and children stop playing their games to run up the track when they hear the car arrive. The children are small, muscular and lively; they wear torn clothes with collars and sleeves that have frayed into one big hole. Each child has a special movement to keep their clothes from falling off: one shrugs his shoulder to move a torn sleeve back in place, one hangs on to the broken zip on his shorts, another runs his hand down his chest to straighten a T-shirt that is too big and keeps slipping back over his skinny shoulders.

I'm surrounded by villagers. I feel ridiculously tall – most of the adults are only the size of Australian children and the children are tiny; ten-year-olds are the size of three-year-olds in Australia and three-year-olds look too small to walk. The whole village is in miniature. The huts have short doorways, and rounded roofs made from grass and banana leaves. The villagers move aside as we walk through because we have the district chief with us. He has given his permission for my visit and is accompanying us to make sure the first day runs smoothly. Without the chief, I may not have received cooperation from the villagers. Chief Mutumayi Kiza has been in charge of this district for 30 years and people move carefully around him, bowing slightly when they shake his hand. He is tall, and dressed in a pin-striped suit and a shiny black hat; he looks like a character from the 1940s or a jazzman. The chief has a well-fed belly and friendly eyes, and his grey moustache is neatly trimmed.

The chief orders several boys to go and get the women from the fields and to rally the men, because he wants to speak with all the villagers. The boys run off obediently, scurrying from field to field to spread the message, but it's a slow process. It's as much an exercise in reinforcing his authority as anything else; he doesn't get to Mudja very often, so he makes sure people remember he's the boss. When two teenagers walk past without acknowledging him, he calls them back and asks them a string of questions about who they are and what they are doing. They fidget uncomfortably until he eventually lets them go and they walk off with heads bowed.

Masinda watches the whole scene and jokes with some of the other women who have also arrived from the fields. Occasionally she glances at me. I think some of the jokes are at my expense, but I just smile at her.

Masinda is the leader of the women in the village, which is why the chief has chosen her to do the interview. He announces his decision to the villagers and, when he's finished speaking, nods his head. There's no discussion; the chief 's word is final. Masinda and I look at each other awkwardly.

The other villagers are deeply suspicious of the arrangement. They think that I will give Masinda some money, so they demand to sit in on the interview. We walk up to a broken-down wooden building with tiny windows and a dirt floor that is jagged with volcanic rocks. Masinda and I sit on a wooden bench next to the wall and close to twenty villagers sit in a group facing us like an audience. There is mumbling, then silence and arms folded. All eyes are focused on me.

'Right, I'll get my microphone out.'

Masinda doesn't seem intimidated. In fact, she is happy that the interview is being done in public, so that it doesn't stir up jealousy. She is plucky and confident. I ask Masinda what her name means and she replies that her mother had eleven children who all died before she was born.

'The name Masinda means grave. All eleven of them died by disease. We could have died, all of us, but fortunately I stayed alive. Thanks to God.'

It's difficult to tell how old Masinda is: her face is weathered on the edges and her teeth are brown, but her body is strong. She doesn't know when she was born. The volcano is the only definite measurement of time in the village – the previous two eruptions were in 2002 and 1977. The interpreter asks Masinda if she remembers the eruption in 1977 and she nods. He asks her to point out a child who is the same age as she was when the eruption happened, and she points to a teenage girl. 'I was this big,' she says.

The interpreter and I try to calculate how old she is; if Masinda was a teenager when the volcano erupted in 1977 she must now be in about her late thirties or early forties. She was born in this village and she has spent most of her life here. Her earliest childhood memories are all about survival. As a small child she could see that some people were going hungry, and she watched her mother and the other women as they worked their fields. She carefully observed the way they planted and cultivated the crops and decided to try to sow a field of her own.

'I was training to feed myself. I was growing beans. I was growing potatoes, when I was very young. I decided to cultivate because I was very hungry, I didn't get any food. I said, "Let me do what they are doing." The others were encouraging me and telling me to continue working so that I could get something to eat, to feed myself.

'My first harvest was very little. It fed me for only two days. But I was very, very happy to get that harvest. Even if it was a small quantity, I was eating something coming from my soil. We were living like birds.'

Masinda is one of the smallest women in the village. Her shoulders are the same height as my hips and she is about the size of an Australian six-year-old. Her childhood was spent helping her mother and she was never given the opportunity to go to school.

'I didn't make very much noise. I was very quiet. I was not a troublesome child. It was God who wanted me to be that way, to have that mood, instead of being a troublesome lady, someone who has to harass other people. It is God who did it. And I am very glad.

'My mother was a woman who was welcoming people. All visitors who were coming in our village, they were being welcomed by my mother. She was someone who could approach anybody. Up until now I am still following the same way that she led me. Anyone who should come, I should take care of him.'

But my welcome seems to be running out. Masinda starts swinging her legs back and forth as she sits on the bench, and she looks away impatiently. Her answers are interspersed with comments to the other villagers listening in. I don't know if she is arguing or agreeing with them, but the interview starts falling apart less than half an hour after it started. Eventually it stops altogether and the shouting starts. Masinda says she doesn't want to talk about her childhood because she thinks it's a waste of time. The villagers add their dissatisfaction, pointing and shouting at me. We are minutes away from a mutiny.

The interpreter speaks loudly above the villagers and bullies them into a temporary peace. I'm not sure what has caused the anger but the interpreter explains that it's all about one thing. Food. If Masinda spends her day talking with us rather than working in the fields, her family will have nothing to eat. Getting food is a daily battle for the villagers, who have nothing in reserve: if they have an unsuccessful day in the fields or the forest, they go to bed hungry.

I reassure Masinda. I look her in the eye and promise that we will bring some food from Goma when we return tomorrow, and eventually she nods in agreement. Calm is restored among the villagers. Masinda is smiling again; her mood softens once the business of food has been addressed. The villagers leave us to get on with the interview and I feel relieved that trust has been established. Masinda laughs and says that when she was a child, she ran away in terror if white people, nicknamed *muzungus*, came to visit.

'During that time we were hiding ourselves. The skin of white people, if you compare, it's very, very different. We thought so many things. We thought the *muzungu* would eat us. We were hiding and running away. We couldn't even face a white man. People were afraid. They were saying white people could kill us with a hammer. Now we are thanking God very much because God has put away that ignorance.'

The Batwa Pygmies still face a lot of discrimination. They are seen in the Democratic Republic of Congo as the lowest of the low. There is little protection for those who are on the bottom of the rung of a country which is itself on the bottom rung. Some Congolese don't even regard the Pygmies as fully human, preferring to stereotype them as uncivilised, stupid and dirty. In some communities, villagers refuse to sit next to them or allow them to use communal wells, and Pygmy women trying to sell goods are often pushed to the edge of marketplaces. Their treatment at the hands of European colonialists wasn't much better. The Pygmies were compared to apes and openly described as subhuman. In the early 1900s, one Pygmy man, Ota Benga, was put on display in the monkey house at the Bronx Zoo in the United States and attracted large crowds. He later committed suicide.

The Batwa Pygmies lived for centuries in the forests of central Africa, but they were forced out to make way for logging and national parks during a wave of expulsions which peaked in the late 1960s. The Batwa were expelled from many areas in the name of conservation, even though they had lived in harmony with the environment for generations. International conservation groups worked with the government to remove them, especially in forests inhabited by rare mountain gorillas. Batwa men who prided themselves on being hunters and gatherers were suddenly regarded as poachers if they were caught in the forest.

The Batwa lost their traditional land and lifestyle. They received no compensation or alternative housing. Thousands of families were left to fend for themselves with little knowledge of farming and few business skills; as a result, many resorted to begging. They were not welcome in many villages and were only able to build their shelters on the land nobody else wanted. That's why Masinda and her family live in the path of the volcano. Life outside the forest has been unforgiving.

Masinda and her relatives have lived in this village for as long as she can remember. They were forced out of the forest a long time ago; she doesn't know exactly when. Her mother used to tell stories about life in the forest, but the village became home. The Batwa Pygmies started farming and only returned to the forest to look for extra food to top up the harvest.

'In the forest we have big quantities of traditional potatoes, designed for pygmies only. Not other communities. That is our own property that God give us. We go into the forest and we have the knowledge to extract them from the soil. Other people cannot know, only pygmies can know where to dig them. God give us the knowledge.

'I was going with my mother and she was telling us, "Hey, when you go you must dig here." When you are digging, even if there are some rocks you still have to go deeply. When you dig deeply you are going to find our traditional food, which is designed for pygmies and is very, very sweet for us.'

Masinda speaks about the potatoes with a lot of pride and a hint of defiance. She shrugs her shoulders and looks me in the eye as if to say she doesn't know why God made the special potatoes exclusively for the Pygmies, it's just the natural order of things. I get the feeling she doesn't get many chances to be smug, especially around foreigners. Masinda proudly describes herself as a Pygmy. Many of the Batwa Pygmy groups also use the same term, but others believe it is tainted by years of negative stereotypes. The United Nations and aid agencies also have differing views on what is appropriate. For Masinda and many other Batwa Pygmies, the real issue is land.

'Without the land there is no life. You have to safeguard it, you have to protect it strongly. Through that field you can feed all your family. Even those people who come after you, they have to be filled, your son, your grandsons, they will be feeding through that field. It is a good thing in the world if someone has a field, that field has to be protected.'

The soil is dark and fertile. It was born in the volcano. The village is only 12 kilometres away from the crater of Mount Nyiragongo, which is cloaked in cloud and mist. Masinda can see it from her grass house when she opens the dirty curtain door every morning. Should there be an eruption, there would be barely enough time for the villagers to gather their children and run up a nearby hill to get out of the path of the fast-flowing lava.

During the 1977 eruption, the lava started sliding towards the village just after ten o'clock in the morning. Masinda was in the fields; amidst the chaos she found her younger brothers and got them up the hill to safety: one was on her shoulders, one on her back and the other held on to her hand. The air was thick with smoke and white ash.

'All people were having the colour of the ash. They were

white. All of them thought they were dying. They were not black as normal. They said, "We are now dying." We were very, very surprised and we were running up hills for protection. We were following other old people. I was protecting my younger brothers. We had already prepared some food, but that food turned into ash.'

Masinda and the rest of the villagers slept on the top of the hill. The night sky was glowing as the lava formed red rivers that burnt though the fields and the jungle. They watched it slide though the village, swallow the grass huts and take their crops too. Everything else was covered in poisonous ash.

'All of us were very, very hungry. We couldn't get any vegetables, any bananas, because all things were burnt. We start like living in the desert, the ground was hot. When we came back, all our fields were already damaged, either by the lava or the ash. When eating we were becoming ill and the diseases were taking people to death.'

Mount Nyiragongo is a volatile neighbour. When the Batwa were forced out of the forest, they were left to settle the land that no-one else wanted, the low land in the path of the lava, directly between the crater and the town of Goma. The volcano has forced its way into the culture. Masinda believes the eruptions are messages from God.

'When the volcano is bursting, we usually think God is angry. When he is angry, that is the kind of way of punishing people. It means he is taking the cane and caning people. The punishment can come through the volcano.

'If it bursts now, if it bursts we have to go. The children who are at home, they have to take their direction. I have to take mine and anyone else has to take his. It means it's not easy. We are like people who are in the tomb. Because we don't know when it will erupt. We don't know the time of eruption. It can happen any time.'

In the neighbouring village there is a volcano warning sign, with a coloured flag. Green means the volcano is safe, yellow is active, orange is a warning to prepare to evacuate and red is extreme danger. The yellow flag is flying as we drive past. It's late in the afternoon and we need to take the chief back to his house on the outskirts of Goma. We haven't eaten all day, so we offer a biscuit to the chief to keep him going for the journey. He takes the whole packet and sends crumbs flying as he tries to feed himself with one hand and hang on with the other.

Vehicles are a big novelty in the village, so the children jump on the back bumper bar and take a ride. The driver stops and tells them to get off because they are weighing down the car and making it even more difficult to drive over the rocks. But they ignore the warnings and the disapproving stares from the chief. The driver yells dozens of times without effect. Suddenly, the interpreter leaps out of the car, chasing the children through the grass until he catches the ringleader. He hands the boy over to one of the village men to be punished; the child wails in protest, but the chief mumbles and nods in approval.

People wave to the chief as they see him sitting in the front of the car. Some of them even flag us down in order to explain their problems. He winds down the window to deliver advice and judgements as we drive across the volcanic rock and along the dirt tracks that link the villages. It's a slow journey. The driver is barely able to get over the big rocks and up and down the bumpy path, and I grimace every time I hear the loud noise of the underside of the car scraping against the rock.

The chief hangs on to a handle above the passenger side window, his round body bobbing from side to side. Women walk along the rocky track carrying large bags of charcoal on their backs; the bags are tied on with pieces of cloth strapped across their forehead. They are hunched over with the weight of the loads that are heavier than their bodies, and as they walk slowly and carefully their faces are etched with pain and deep concentration. The women are doing the job donkeys would do in most other places.

Other women are digging amongst the rocks on the side of the road where they have planted beans and potatoes in makeshift fields. The beans are set out in mounds of heaped soil that look like covered graves. While the mothers hoe the fields, their babies sit under trees, cared for by older siblings. Further along there are also eucalyptus trees, growing on the roadside with long, straight limbs. Young men work in teams, cutting the branches and piling them together by the roadside ready for sale, while other men walk along the track herding goats to market. It's a procession of labour.

As we drive along I worry about returning to the village tomorrow. We must bring some food to compensate Masinda for giving up her time in the fields to be interviewed, but the other villagers are also desperate – if we only give food to Masinda she will be in danger from her hungry neighbours. So we need to bring something for everyone; enough to feed about 80 people. We decide to buy rice and dried fish. Even though rice is cheap, it's a luxury for the villagers in Mudja. The interpreter goes to the market and comes back with two large bags of rice and enough dried fish for each family.

I don't sleep well during the night. I have visions of angry villagers fighting over food: my fear is that if the rice and fish aren't distributed properly, things could get out of control. I've seen food distributions go wrong before and the ensuing chaos can be very dangerous. But it's clear that we cannot arrive empty-handed. It's unfair to expect Masinda to be interviewed at the expense of gathering food for her family each day. So we set off the next morning with the rice and fish covered in the back of the vehicle.

The villagers are impatient when we arrive. We ask the head man to bring us the list of everyone who lives in Mudja. But the list is missing. As we wait for more than an hour, people start becoming annoyed, and once again there is shouting and arm-waving. Masinda is the leader of the discontent; she loses her patience with me, ties her baby to her back with a piece of cloth, puts her hoe over her shoulder and starts storming off to the fields. I call after her, but she ignores me.

The list is found, just as Masinda leaves. We call her back, but she ignores us again until eventually one of the young men brings her to us. Once we have the list we can get the fish and rice out of the car and start distributing it family by family. The interpreter tells the crowd that Masinda will receive more because she is giving up her time to do the interviews. He asks for their agreement and they nod. There is some pushing and shouting as the distribution starts but in the end it is done without any major problems. I feel relieved and surprised; I had been predicting disaster all morning. Within minutes most of the villagers have gone back to their huts. There is quiet, except for the gentle sounds of cooking.

Masinda is grinning and chatting. The promise of food has been kept. We walk up to the main hut to do some interviews and this time there is no angry audience: the other villagers are happy to leave us in peace and Masinda seems relaxed. She is relishing a break from the daily search for food. Each morning she doesn't know what she will feed her family that evening. She usually tends to her fields or works in the fields of other people from other villages. Her husband and some of the other men walk to the forest.

'The husbands usually go very far in the forest to look for honey. There are some small bees who are growing the honey. We can use it as food with some bananas. If I've got something from my work or getting some vegetables from here or there, I bring, we eat. It means we can eat honey and what I have prepared. If the husband never found something, he has to be pleased to see what I have prepared. If there is nothing, we just sleep without eating. Like yesterday we didn't eat anything. We didn't have food.'

It is an almost cashless existence. If Masinda can find work on a neighbouring farm, she is usually paid in beans or flour – a day's work returns barely a day's food, nothing more. There's rarely any leftover food in her hut; it's the way she has lived all her life.

'A pygmy woman like me, I wake up early morning, in the dark. I sweep in my house. I try to get something for my children to eat, maybe some porridge. Then afterwards I go to work somewhere. We spend a whole day working for half a bowl of beans. We feed ourselves like that but no-one is full. When it comes, we eat immediately and it's finished. In the afternoon I have to leave and go looking for firewood. We have to go also to look for water. You have to go very far up to the lake to get some water. Many kilometres. After that, we prepare food for the evening.'

Masinda's husband, Muhima, is the head man of the village. He's an old, thin man, who sometimes just stands staring into the fields while people get on with their business around him. He is slow and quiet. When he was a young man, he chose Masinda. But she didn't want to marry him.

'My parents were saying that is a good man, a good husband for you. But I refused because I was still a little girl. I could not face a husband at that time.'

Masinda wasn't given a choice. As she wouldn't get married willingly, her parents arranged for Muhima to ambush her. It was the standard practice at that time for girls to be abducted and raped with their parents' consent.

'If the daughter refuses, the parents can just create an ambush somewhere. When the girl is out, they take her. The girl is raped, they bring her to the house of the man and she must accept to stay there by force. That is what happened to me.'

Her mother helped to organise the abduction. Masinda was ambushed just outside the village.

'It was in the evening. About 5 pm. I was just walking with my mother, here. Then they took me. I resisted. I refused strongly. But they beat me. They beat me by hands, by cane. I was beaten so that I couldn't go back to my family's house. The only solution was to go to the husband.'

Masinda was taken to her husband's house, where he raped her straight away. She was then his wife.

'I was weeping. I couldn't stop him. I wanted to go back to my parents' house. But I was unable to go because he had already raped me. The husband sleeps with you immediately. There is no delay.'

Her husband's friends who had ambushed her then delivered two jerry cans of banana beer and meat to her family, to confirm that the abduction had been carried out successfully.

'They brought the beer to my family to announce that they

have taken me. My family received it. After that they went to hunt an antelope. They brought it to my family. I was very angry at the beginning, because he took me by force. I was not ready enough for marriage. But as soon as he took me, I couldn't do otherwise. When I tried to go home, my mother said, "What are you doing? You don't have any place here. Just go back to your husband." My mother chased me.'

In a strange contradiction, after the rape, Muhima was kind and gentle to his new wife, doing the domestic chores and waiting on her, while she rested.

'I spent a month in the house without doing things. My husband wanted me to stay and have a rest because I had worked much in my previous house with my family. During that month, I was eating everything in my house. My husband was bringing everything there. When I left there I was like a white woman. My skin was very clear because there was no contact with the sun.'

But the month of seclusion was also an opportunity for Muhima to obtain sex on demand. Masinda was on call, any time her husband was in the mood. After the rape she gradually became more relaxed about sex.

'My husband was wanting to have sexual relations with me at any time. It is not easy to refuse when the husband asks for his right. He is the number one of the house. When he asks, he needs to get something. I cannot refuse.'

At the end of the month, Masinda and her husband went to visit her parents, bringing them some more banana beer to show that the marriage was a success. It was all part of the tradition: Masinda was expected to forgive her husband for the rape, which she did.

'My husband was a very, very kind man. He was welcoming people. I was lucky. I said to myself, "I have found a man who is not a troublesome one. He does not fight against other people in the village. He is the one who is very quiet. He never talks." It was good. I found that I loved him.'

I don't see much affection between Masinda and her husband. I get the impression she's the hard worker in the family.

Muhima is mostly idle and disconnected as he sits quietly in the shade. But, as the head man of the village, he is treated with benign respect.

Masinda and I talk for a long time. I tell her I don't really understand how she could fall in love with a man who had beaten and raped her. She shrugs her shoulders, but says she's glad the tradition has gradually been abandoned.

'That is an old system. This system of taking people is not good. Girls at that time couldn't leave by themselves. Here, now as a leader of women, I say we are very lucky because that system is over.'

Masinda starts swinging her legs back and forth again, as she sits on the bench. It's late in the morning and she's hungry. We stop the interview and I follow her back to her hut. As we walk along the track I can see other women are already cooking: children squat next to their mothers, fidgeting with hunger. It seems the whole village is eating fish and rice.

Masinda takes me to her home, which is round and small like a children's cubbyhouse. It resembles an igloo made from grass. The grass is woven over a bamboo frame and there are banana leaves on the roof to keep the rain out. The whole house is only about the same size as a double bed and only about a metre and a half tall, yet Masinda and five members of her family sleep here. If you imagine throwing a blanket over your dining table and trying to live with your entire family in the space below, you get some idea of how small it is. There's no door, just a piece of cloth tied across the entrance. I need to bend over to crawl inside.

A bamboo wall divides the shelter into two tiny rooms. The front half is for cooking. A circle of rocks makes up a fireplace in the dirt, surrounded by worn-out pots – some with dried food inside – scattered on the ground. The back section is for sleeping and the floor is covered in old blankets and pieces of cloth. The family's possessions are stacked next to one of the walls: a hoe, a water container, some ragged clothes. The dirt is pushed up against the walls in mounds to stop flooding in the wet season. Masinda shakes her head as she shows me inside.

She says her husband built the shelter, but it doesn't keep the rain out.

'Pygmy men, they don't know how to build houses. They don't know. You have seen the house I am living in. Pygmy men don't have any money to buy wood, to buy iron sheets. They don't have anything.'

Masinda unties the cloth around her waist, takes her youngest daughter, Juditte, off her back and puts her on the dirt floor. I sit outside the door, because there's not enough room for me to stay inside. At night, the children sleep around the open fire, but it's too crowded for everyone.

'We have to arrange with another family so that our eldest can go and sleep in another [hut] which has space. Five people sleep in our hut. But it's dangerous. We usually prepare food inside. The fire is there and people are sleeping in the same place. If it caught fire, everyone could be burnt.'

The shelters were only supposed to be temporary: the simple design came from the era when the Batwa moved from place to place in the forest. But now, because the forest is no longer home, the shelters are permanent. The Batwa are living between the traditions of the past and the reality of the present. Masinda shakes her head when she talks about those who are still trying to live in the forest in other parts of the Congo.

'Pygmies who are living in the forest, they are not clever as we are. We are very clever and we have the knowledge because we are living with other communities. We know how to live with the government. Those who are living in the forest, they are not clever. They are like animals. They don't know anything about living with others.'

Mudja is surrounded by villages that house other ethnic groups. Masinda's neighbours live close by in similar poverty; in fact, it's hard to tell where one village stops and the next one begins – the huts and fields of other families are less than 100 metres away from the Batwa.

The other villages are also desperately poor. The charcoal women make the daily march to market while their children, wearing ragged clothes, play along the track. Education and health care are too expensive for most families. A severely deformed girl sits by the road each morning when we drive to Mudja: she can barely see, her nose sprawls across her face with a single nostril and large lumps of flesh that almost cover her eyes. There is no help for her.

Because the people here are living between the volcano and the lake, it can take most of the afternoon to walk to the lake for water and carry the jerry cans home across the volcanic rock. When it rains, rickety arrangements of pipes, gutters and buckets catch as much water as possible. But in the dry season, the people here have no choice but to make the long journey to the lake. They can only carry enough water for drinking and cooking, so washing becomes a luxury. Masinda pinches the collar of her blouse with her fingers to show me how dirty it is.

'A pygmy woman should be washing her body one or two times a day like others. But we never get water in this village. If there is no water, we cannot even wash. When it is dry season, in June, in August, we have to wait until November. In November when it rains, then we can get some water. But we cannot bring water for washing over that distance. You have to bring water just for cooking and drinking.

'You see our clothes, how dirty are they. We cannot even wash our clothes. Because we don't have water. That is not only a problem of pygmies. It is a problem in general for all people in this area. All other communities. We normally get water in ponds when it rains. We have to go very far to the lake, not here. Some can drown there.'

Later in the afternoon I ask Masinda if we can go to the lava flow to take some photographs, and she smiles and nods. As we walk slowly from the hut towards our vehicle, Masinda calls her eldest son and her daughters and they gather in a huddle to talk. Masinda asks if her children can come with us and I tell her it's no problem.

I open the car door and Masinda sits on the back seat next to me, nursing Juditte. Her older children and their friends crowd into the back of the four-wheel drive, giggling and whispering. Masinda smiles as she looks out at the other villagers and then she laughs excitedly. Juditte's head bobs up and down and from side to side as we bounce along the volcanic track. The driver puts on some loud salsa music, and the children in the back thrust their shoulders back and forth to the beat, grinning at each other. They point and chatter as we drive through other villages, and people stare back in response as the four-wheel drive packed with Pygmies cruises past. The villagers look puzzled as the salsa music spills from the open windows. Masinda laughs even more. Travelling by vehicle is a delicious mix of novelty and status.

When we reach the lava flow, I realise just how many people we've got in the back of the car. They climb out one after the other like a magic trick. The procession of passengers unfold their knees and elbows and spring back to their full size as they jump to the ground. People walking along the track stop to see what is going on. They start questioning the driver. 'Why are you letting dirty Pygmies ride in your car?' 'These people are not clean. Let them walk back to their village.' Some of the comments are so disgusting, the interpreter is reluctant to translate them into English. He looks at the ground, full of embarrassment. Masinda ignores the insults; she's heard it before. As an outsider, I find the rivalry and stereotypes difficult to understand. Almost everyone here is extremely poor, but amid the poverty there is a pecking order. It's an unforgiving hierarchy that allows those who are looked down on to look down on someone else.

Masinda and her relatives tried to join the congregation at a nearby church. But they were turned away by the locals, who said they weren't clean enough to come inside.

'When we were going to the church they were chasing us, other communities. They were saying, "Why are you pygmies wearing very dirty clothes? You should wear nice clothes. Why are you sitting with us in such conditions?" Because of that discrimination we couldn't support the church. We left.'

The church's rejection led to an unexpected change. Some

members of the Baha'i faith – an offshoot of Islam that preaches unity and tolerance – heard about the situation and asked Masinda and the others if they would like to join their faith instead.

'Some Baha'i came and built for us a church. So all of us believe in Baha'i. We are now praying in this church. We love it very much because they love us also. They teach us unity among people.'

The Baha'i temple is the biggest building in the village. Constructed from old wooden planks and with a rusty iron roof, it is big enough to hold everyone in the community. There are wooden benches inside that tip and tilt on the rocky floor, and small windows without glass. I interview Masinda here every day, sitting in the half-light. A few of the children try to peek through the gaps in the walls, but the interpreter pokes his finger into the holes, making the children yelp before they run off.

Some of the children are Masinda's. She shakes her head and says she wishes they were at school, but education is expensive. Masinda has never sat in a classroom. She cannot read or write. Most of the other women in the village are illiterate too; it's a source of regret and sadness. Masinda is embarrassed when she talks about it and it is one of the few times I can see some vulnerability in her eyes. She looks down, but she quickly hardens her gaze again.

'If I studied, I could develop my mind more than what I am now. I can ask so many questions. I'm not so proud about my education.'

Masinda and some other women from the village went to a Women's Day celebration in Goma several weeks ago. At the end of a march that took place in the morning, they were told the event was over and they should return to their village. Most of the other women were educated. Masinda says they left feeling unsure whether the other women were planning to continue the celebrations without them.

'Those women who studied, I don't know what they planned after the demonstration. If they organised a party or do anything, I don't know about it. They told us as soon as we finished, go back home. We didn't study, we don't know. I don't know what happened.'

None of Masinda's children have finished primary school, because the family can't afford school fees.

'All my children, they started studying but as soon as we missed money, they were being chased at school. One stopped in the third, the other one in the fourth, other one in the second grade. My eldest son is the one who had the opportunity to go up to the sixth grade, primary. I would like them to study up until the end. But we are moneyless.'

Masinda's eldest son, Imani, is polite and reserved. His six years of primary school mean that he is one of the most educated people in the village. He is the makeshift administrator; the village documents are kept in his hut. He uses a blue pen and a ruler to draw up neat handwritten lists of all the men, women and children in Mudja. Without Imani, the distribution of fish and rice would have been chaos: his calm instructions kept the crowd under control. The villagers listen to him even though he's only just out of his teens.

As Imani talks with our driver, he looks nervously up the track. The other men also become uneasy, breaking off their conversations to get up from the shade and walk quickly into the fields in different directions. I'm not sure what is happening, so I ask the driver, who tells me that there are soldiers coming. By the time the soldiers walk into the village, the men have disappeared. The troops are looking for porters and force the local men to carry supplies up to their camps in the mountains, an unpaid task that can take several days.

The Congolese troops guard the hilltops. It's an unstable area: Mudja is less than 20 kilometres from the border with Rwanda. The forests have been battlefields and burial grounds, sanctuaries and hiding places. The killers who carried out the Rwandan genocide – the rebels known as the Interahamwe – hid in these mountains, fleeing Rwanda in 1994 after killing almost a million people. They walked across the border, through the mountains and down into the fields. Masinda and the other villagers were in the middle of the harvest season when the Interahamwe arrived. The rebels had walked for hundreds of kilometres and they were running out of food.

'Those Interahamwe. We don't know what brought them here. We were harvesting many things. When they arrived they were just damaging anything. They were just collecting anything at random. Some of them were even raping our sisters, our daughters. They were doing everything here.'

The Interahamwe started ransacking the village and stealing the harvest. They ate the maize and vegetables that had already been picked and stripped the fields.

'All of our people were against them, because their way of living is very, very bad. They are savage people. They were killing people, even my brothers. They died during that occasion. When they were going into the forest for hunting, they were caught by Interahamwe rebels. They buried them alive.'

The Pygmies were forced to flee their village, walking empty-handed to the other side of the lake. Thousands of other people had also been displaced and they faced acute shortages of food and shelter. International aid agencies tried to supply some food and plastic sheeting, but there were hundreds of thousands of displaced people around Goma in the wake of the genocide. Many were the perpetrators of the killing, who fled to avoid capture or revenge attacks, but what they found in Goma was a putrid hell. Disease and hunger swept through the muddy masses. The skeletally thin bodies of the victims were simply stacked on the side of the roads. After several months, Masinda and the other villagers returned to Mudja.

'Our traditional chief was calling us to come back. We came back, but we found our houses were already damaged, demolished, burnt. All things were very bad now. We were suffering from starvation. We felt very bad, you feel like someone who all the organs are not fitting, not linking. You feel like you are going to die. You cannot do anything. You are very, very tired.'

Masinda arrived to see that her hut and her fields had been ransacked by the Interahamwe. There was nothing left. Her shelter, farming tools and few possessions were either missing or broken – even simple items like plastic jerry cans were gone. Such items are highly valued and difficult to get; each one usually has a story, perhaps it had been donated by an aid agency or bought with extra money from a good harvest. To lose such possessions is a big setback.

'We saw everything was damaged. I was very, very, very angry with that. We couldn't get anything to eat because all of our plants had been harvested by those militias. These times were very bad. Some of us wept.'

Masinda and her family had to start again. They rebuilt their hut and struggled to replace the possessions they lost; a slow process. Tiny savings were put aside, coin by coin, note by note. Masinda hid the money in their hut, judiciously buying seeds for new crops and the tools to work the fields.

In January 2002, after a 25-year hiatus, the volcano began to stir once again. The earth shook with tremors and the crater spat smoke and ash into the air. I was sent to Goma to cover the eruption for ABC News. I remember arriving just after midnight. A colleague and I had hired a minibus in the Rwandan capital, Kigali; I slept on the back seat, trying to shut out the swerves, tyre screeches and crunching potholes. We'd been told that up to half a million people were trying to escape the lava on foot. We were worried our van might be stopped by people desperate for food. But when we arrived I was surprised by how quiet it was. I could hear the water lapping gently on the shores of Lake Kivu.

When the sun came up, I could see the full scale of the humanitarian crisis. Thousands of families were camped on roadsides and under shop verandas in overgrown old colonial gardens next to the lake shore. Smoke rose from cooking fires as hungry children huddled around half-empty pots.

The volcano was shrouded in ash, smoke and cloud. It was eerie. The air was thick with gas, and the ground shook under my feet as wave after wave of earth tremors sent people running in fear. The tremors hit every few hours in a rolling tide; I could almost hear them coming across the lake. I was staying in a house with several other international journalists, and most of us slept outside because the tremors were powerful enough to throw furniture from side to side.

Parts of Goma were completely destroyed. The lava came through in wide rivers, filling the streets with liquid rock, high enough to reach the top of doorways. It was an awesome display of nature's power. Cars and bicycles were swept along in the lava flow; houses were buried. It was so hot, I could feel the heat through the soles of my shoes as we walked along the newly formed rock. The magma continued to flow below the surface.

It was one of the most extraordinary stories I covered. I was struck by the scale and intensity of the natural and humanitarian disaster. I had never seen anything like it.

Hundreds of thousands of people fled their homes. Families took everything they could carry, walking along the roads towards high ground. Masinda and her family took their possessions and climbed the hill behind the village, and then sat and watched as the lava crawled through the valleys. While I was reporting on it, Masinda was living it.

'We saw the crater was giving some smoke. What came before was earthquakes. We were fearing the earthquakes. We were fearing that there would be a hole and we would be buried immediately. When the earthquakes started moving, we said, "What is happening with the world? What is going to happen?" We were asking questions. We were looking for protection. Wherever we go, the place was moving. We didn't know what else to do. We were afraid.'

Masinda was sitting on top of the hill with her children. She warned them that the shaking ground was a sign of danger.

'When there are some earthquakes, I usually tell my children, "Pay attention, be careful of this time now. The eruption is going to happen pretty soon. Don't go separately. You have to be together." When the eruption came we were already prepared. We went up that mountain that you can see there. On top.'

The villagers camped on the peak and looked down on the chaos below as Goma was cut in half by the lava.

'We were seeing how the lava was going down to burn Goma. We couldn't do anything to help the people. But we saw some people in a plane. We thought they were taking something to drop in the crater, to stop the eruption.'

When the lava began to cool, the villagers climbed down from the hill to check if their homes had been damaged.

'We went back home through the banana trees. Our village was not damaged. It was safe. God did good things. He knew that Goma people had some vehicles so that they could run away. But for us, as we don't have anything, our vehicles are only our feet. We couldn't all of us run. We could not run as fast as the volcano lava. God protected us and our village was safe.'

It was a reprieve. While other communities lost almost everything, Mudja was spared. A few months later, Masinda felt her belly changing; she was pregnant again. She gave birth to a little girl, Irene, and carried the child on her back as she worked in the fields. She sat and breastfed Irene when she cried in hunger: mother and daughter were almost constant companions. But Irene started getting sick. Seeking medical advice, Masinda took her to the dispensary in a neighbouring village, but it was to no avail. Irene's small body couldn't withstand the sickness.

Masinda doesn't make much eye contact with me as she tells the story. Still, I can see a lot of pain on her face when she talks about losing Irene. Her voice becomes softer and slower; she doesn't rush through it, even though the memories bring her sadness.

'She died of headache. Very strong headache. Sometimes you can see a child, on the top of the head there is something that is making very big pains. It can also bring some blood. She went to the toilet leaving some blood, blood, blood. My little girl died when I went to the dispensary. They tried to take care of her. But unfortunately she died after three days. She died in my hands.

'I knew that she had died. She went in the heaven, with God. I brought her back to the village in my hands. I brought her up to my house. We couldn't get anything like a coffin. We buried her and spent two days. Three days mourning is for adults, but for babies, two days.'

A year later, Masinda had another baby girl, Juditte. The toddler rarely leaves her sight. Masinda breastfeeds her and gives her soft pieces of banana. When Juditte is old enough, Masinda says, she will show her where to find the wild potatoes in the forest; she will pass on her knowledge from mother to daughter. But Masinda says the Batwa are losing their traditions.

'We are running the risk of forgetting. We have already forgotten because nowadays going there is no good. When we go there we can be arrested, because we are considered as poachers. That is the reason why we never go there again. We have to forget and we have forgotten. What can we do? Even if we are angry. There is nothing at all we can do.'

It is the final morning of interviews and we have promised to bring a gift on our last day to thank Masinda and her neighbours for their cooperation. We ask Imani for a list as the villagers start gathering. We have bought one piece of second-hand clothing for each of them. The driver carries some large bags from the back of the vehicle, full of shirts and pants for the men and simple wraparound skirts for the women. I feel a bit sad when I watch the children receiving their clothes. They don't have any choice; they're just thrown whatever looks roughly their size and I can see the disappointment in their faces as they do their best to look grateful. The interpreter had spent most of the previous afternoon bargaining like a tyrant at the market to make sure we could get something for everyone.

It was cheaper to buy the fabric for the women's skirts in bulk and then cut it into individual lengths, but when the interpreter opens the bag, I realise that he has bought metres and metres of the same cloth. It will mean that all the women from the village will be wearing exactly the same design. I shake my head, but it's too late and, in any case, the women don't seem to mind. They are already singing joyfully, excited because it is Baha'i New Year the following week and now they will have new outfits to wear when they walk into Goma for the celebrations. I imagine the procession of identically dressed women hiking across the volcanic rock. It reminds me of *The Sound Of Music*, when the von Trapps were decked out in their outfits made from curtains.

The arrival of the new clothing triggers celebrations. Some of the teenage boys go to their huts and come back with sticks, buckets and jerry cans, which they use as drums in a makeshift band. Masinda ties Juditte on her back and starts dancing, and other women and children follow her, shimmying in a conga line. When the beat changes, they weave in and out, like a wild square dance, and as they dance, the babies on the backs of the women wobble up and down. The infants look bewildered as they whiz in tight circles, the women stomping and twirling, their bare feet kicking up the dust. The ground beneath them is hollow and it gives a muffled echo as they dance.

Masinda walks over to say goodbye. She is sweating and smiling. We shake hands while her husband sits quietly on a bench under a tree. I give him a two-handed handshake to show him respect as the head man of the village. Masinda waves farewell and walks up the track carrying her new wraparound skirts. She takes them to her hut and I see her folding them in a pile on the blanket bed in the soil; most of her possessions could fit in a single shopping bag. She comes back outside the front of the tiny grass hut and smiles as we drive off.

'It is God who only knows why he made pygmies so small. I don't know why he made us like this. It depends what happens in the belly. A woman can deliver some people who are tall, others who are short. It depends on God's miracle. I can be tall or I can be short. But I have to work. I need to work hard to feed my family. It is only God who knows.'

CHAPTER 3

MARTHA YAR GAK

War survivor

SUDAN

Martha Yar Gak survived Africa's longest-running civil war, enduring famine and bloodshed during ten years on the run. She walked hundreds of kilometres across southern Sudan trying to carry her children to safety. She has spent the past decade in a refugee camp, waiting for the war to end. Martha is one of three wives to her husband, who is a commander with the rebel Sudan People's Liberation Army.

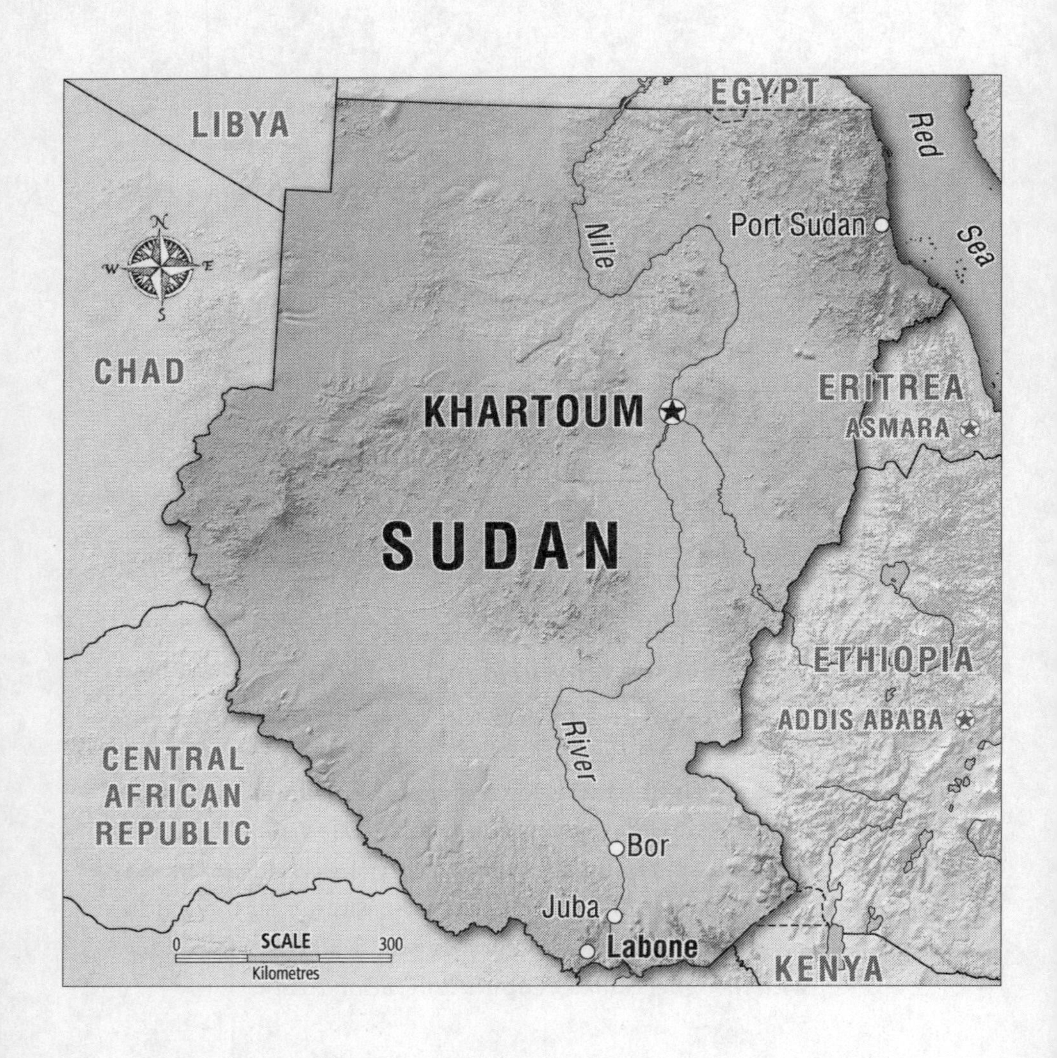

LIBYA
EGYPT
Red Sea
Nile
Port Sudan
N
W
E
S
CHAD
KHARTOUM
ERITREA
ASMARA
SUDAN
ETHIOPIA
ADDIS ABABA
River
CENTRAL
AFRICAN
REPUBLIC
Bor
Juba
Labone
0
SCALE
300
Kilometres
KENYA

I've only heard it once. At first I barely heard it at all – it was just a gentle aircraft noise in the distance, but it's one of the most dangerous sounds in south Sudan. It's the hum of an Antonov bomber. The planes come from the north, heavy with explosives. Sometimes the bombs are hand-made, packed into old oil drums, rolled out of the aircraft and on to the civilians below. The Antonovs fly high and they're difficult to see; they merely look like a passenger jet on the way from one destination to another. But their humming engines create almost instant fear. People in the village stop what they're doing and look up at the sky.

The first time I came to south Sudan, I was briefed by a United Nations security officer.

'If you hear the Anontov, run to the nearest foxhole and get down flat. Make sure you keep your mouth open, so the explosions don't burst your ear drums.'

We were told to carry a 'quick run kit', a small bag with food, water and a mosquito net in case we had to run into the bush during an attack.

Martha Yar Gak has been running from the war for more than two decades. When the Antonov flies over, Martha squints and looks up.

'You hear the sound is coming. Whrrrrrrrrrrrrrrr. People are very afraid because you don't know. Maybe it fall on you, on your children. Even our animals like dogs and chickens, if they hear the sound of an Antonov they run to the foxhole. Everything get afraid. It just go and hide somewhere.'

Martha is a small, sturdy woman with round cheeks and a piano-key smile of gaps and white teeth. She wears neat sandals, church-lady dresses with floral patterns and has a man's digital watch on her wrist, although she is rarely on time. Martha shakes hands carefully and speaks in a quiet but confident voice. I'm on my best behaviour around her.

She has lived in Labone for more than a decade. She walked hundreds of kilometres to get here, carrying her children across the battlefields of Sudan's war. She was among the gaunt millions who went so far into the abyss of hunger I don't really comprehend where she has been; she was one of the crouching women cradling children so hungry their faces were angry. The babies scratched at their mothers, unable to understand why their rasping cries for food were unanswered day after day. Now Martha's bones are padded, her arms are rounded and there's a crease on her plump neck.

The Antonovs have bombed Labone several times. The mountains surrounding the camp can't keep out the planes, but they have given some protection from the war. It's a valley that became a refugee camp and a refugee camp that became a town of its own. People have built huts, schools, shops and roads: they have been here so long, they didn't have much choice. There's almost no rubbish here, because there is very little to buy and it's not a place where much is wasted anyway. Makeshift shops sell simple wishes of soap, sugar and candles and there are few plastic bags or wrappers to throw away.

I first met Martha in February 2004 during a visit to Labone as a reporter with the ABC. I'd asked to speak with some of the women about the difficulties in the camp but, instead of an interview, the local officials arranged a full-scale meeting of almost 100 women. It took place in a long, mud-walled hut with a thatched roof and a dirt floor. It was dark and cool inside. The women sat in rows on home-made wooden benches and I sat at the front with Martha and a translator. It was hostile. For more than an hour the women stood up one after the other outlining their problems; some shouted and waved their fingers at me as if I were a visiting politician who had neglected them. They demanded more food aid and clean water.

'I'm sorry, I can't help with water and food. I am a journalist.'

'What can you do?'

'I can tell your story to people in my home country. Many thousands will see and hear you.'

'Will they help us?'

I confessed I didn't know. Martha looked at me with disappointment as I spoke.

'If you want the truth, many people in Australia don't even know where you are, some don't know where Sudan is on a map of Africa.'

The women shook their heads in disgust, but in some ways they seemed to appreciate the truth. When the meeting finished, they gathered outside and started singing a begrudging thank you. I could see many of the women thought the whole meeting was a waste of time, but one of them stepped forward and started dancing in front of me. She pointed at me and rubbed her lips back and forth with her fingers. I had no idea what she was doing, whether she was telling me to be quiet or bugger off.

'She is praising you,' Martha whispered in my ear. 'She says she once had a beautiful bull with pale pink lips like you. You remind her of this bull. It is a very high compliment.'

After the dance of the pink-lipped bull, my relationship with the local women seemed to improve and I also began to have long conversations with Martha about her experiences during the war. Now, after almost a year, I have returned.

The people are tall, thin and almost purple-black. Many have high cheekbones and gapped buck teeth. They are Dinkas. Once you have seen a Dinka, your eye will pick them from a crowd again. They are some of the most beautiful and distinctive-looking people I have seen in Africa: long-limbed and lean, some of the men with horizontal scars across their forehead, the markings of initiation.

Labone is one of my favourite places in Africa. It's not the dusty, dry Sudan of the imagination; it's a lush, green valley deep in the south of Sudan just near the border with Uganda, a crown of mountains surrounding the fields and mud huts. More than 35,000 people live in its fertile cup and in the wet season you can almost hear the maize growing in the fields: the valley buzzes with insects and promise.

It's a simple place. There's no telephone here and few newspapers from outside, and the missionary plane from Entebbe only flies in once a week. Evening meals are spent with the aid workers listening to the BBC World Service on the radio, and engrossed in deep discussions, laughter and debates as we absorb the news from the outside world. It seems so far away. One night we hear a story about women's rights. One of the Sudanese men says he wouldn't be caught doing women's work.

'I would be ashamed if anyone saw me sweeping the compound.'

'Why?' I ask.

'Because if people saw me sweeping, they would sing about me,' he says with great seriousness. 'This would be very bad.'

Another night we hear a story about obesity in America. One of the Sudanese staff members announces, 'You know, they have restaurants in America where you can drive through and get your food without even leaving your car. Those American people are very fat.'

The others shake their heads and giggle. Almost everyone around this table except me has been a refugee, and most of them have also been malnourished during the war. Their muscly, healthy frames were once withered with hunger but now they are the survivors. They have lived through more than twenty years of war in Sudan.

I'm staying in the compound of Catholic Relief Services, which is among the biggest aid agencies in the district. One of the local workers takes me to a round mud hut with a grass roof; it's called a *tukul*. It has flyscreens on the windows and a galvanised iron door. When I walk inside I find there is a bed and a desk. I hang my mosquito net from a nail on the ceiling.

A rooster and a harem of hens scratch and cluck around the compound. I can hear them in the morning when I wake up. There's also a large team of spiders that seem to roster themselves into positions in my *tukul* and in the long-drop toilet. I count them every evening and usually I see more than twenty.

Before dinner, young men from the camp come to the compound to play volleyball with the staff. It's a talent scout's paradise – some of the Dinka players are well over six foot six, their long arms and strong hands sending the ball over the net at high speed. Each point is celebrated with wild cheers and applause. The game is played with passion – it's a daily ritual at sunset, the best time of the day.

While the match unfolds, a man climbs up onto a ladder and stokes wood under a drum of water. When the sun goes down, the volleyball stops and we take turns bathing in the tiny concrete washhouses. We scrub away the dirt from the day, and flip flop in thongs back to our *tukuls*.

Late in the evening, the generator splutters its last noise for the night. Some nights I can hear drums and singing from the camp and the thud of leathery beats in the distance. It's the last noise before sleep and the first of the morning. The drumming and dancing go all night; the revellers don't go to bed. The different groups in the camp have their own night for dancing, so each evening the sounds come from a different direction. I don't know if they are dancing to celebrate, or dancing because there isn't anything to celebrate.

Martha has lived in Labone for more than ten years, but it's not her home. The war chased her here. Martha and most of the other refugees here are from the town of Bor, which is hundreds of kilometres to the north. They were forced to run when fighting swallowed the town. Their voices change when they speak of it: Bor is home. They grew up herding cattle and catching fish from the river, but now they grow crops in Labone; they're reluctant but capable farmers. They chew long and slow on the millet from the fields. It's sustaining but it's not the same as the fresh fish and milk from home.

Martha is one of the leaders of the women in Labone. The camp is highly structured, with different churches, zones and groups. Martha is one of the few women who can speak fluent English and has the confidence to do so. She liaises with the aid groups and the humanitarian arm of the Sudan People's Liberation Army on behalf of the thousands of women in the camp. She's also a nurse, which is one of the most respected positions in the community. There are no mobile phones in Labone, so one of the best ways to gauge Martha's importance is to follow her as she walks through the camp. She is stopped and greeted by dozens of women as she walks from her house, past the market to the hospital. Some greet her as a friend; others stop her to raise concerns about particular issues. She is one of the most prominent women in the camp.

Her confidence and courage come from necessity. Her childhood had barely begun when it was interrupted by conflict. Her first memory is of gunfire when rebels came into town and started shooting.

'I can remember when I was a small girl of six years, there was shooting in Juba town. I can remember that we hide under the bed and it just happened suddenly. Some people come and shoot. I think they were rebels, I don't know. That was my first time. We run along the river and hide in the bush. Even some children fall to the river. I can remember that.'

Martha ran with her mother and her younger brother, Solomon. Her mother told them to be quiet as they hid near the riverbank.

'My mother is a very strong woman. She lost three children before me. I was the fourth born. She said, "This child also will die like others." She feared to take care of me. So she refused me. My grandmother talked to her until she accepted to breastfeed me. My grandmother said, "God may leave this child to you, my daughter. So you breastfeed your child and take care of her. If God takes her, there is nothing you can do."'

Martha's mother didn't get a chance to finish school. She went quickly from girlhood to womanhood, married young and started having children. She gave simple, firm advice to Martha.

'She was not educated. But she say you follow your school to be an educated girl and you can help us in the future. Because she saw some other ladies that were educated, their life was okay. They were comfortable and their work was also not heavy like hers.

'I learn many things from her. When I was young she said, "Don't quarrel with other children; also, don't go and ask for food from the neighbours."'

Martha's father was a builder and her mother was a cleaner. They lived in Juba on the White Nile, before moving back to Bor further downstream. They were in the deep south of Sudan, which was ruled by the government in Khartoum, more than 1000 kilometres away.

Sudan is the largest country in Africa. Its simmering horizons stretch from Egypt and Libya in the north to Kenya and Uganda in the south. Much of the north is parched desert; the sands drift from the Sahara and camel trains still cross the hills, following ancient trade routes that link Arabs and Africans. The River Nile flows from the south, cutting through the scrubby land and the green valleys of south Sudan.

It is a nation on paper, but its borders circle people who have few bonds. The lighter-skinned, mainly Muslim people from the north and the black African Christians and animists from the south are brittle countrymen. They have been corralled into nationhood with very little in common and, to make matters worse, the tides of colonialism, war and slavery have washed over the harsh land they share. The southern battlegrounds are studded with rich oil reserves that have intensified the war and poisoned attempts at peace.

Sudan became independent on 1 January 1956, but the civil war, instability and poverty swallowed any chance of prosperity. The southerners continued their fight against the government, spending decades fighting for secession. But the north refused to let them go: the government didn't want to amputate half its territory, especially not when it held so much oil. Makeshift armies dragged generations into the conflict. The government used its troops and Arab militias, and the southern rebels recruited and conscripted their communities to fight back.

A southerner, Dr John Garang, was a lieutenant colonel in the Sudanese Army. He was sent to the town of Bor to quash a mutiny by southern troops who refused to be redeployed to the north, but instead of breaking the mutineers he joined them. Garang encouraged troops in other garrisons to do the same. It was a spectacular change of allegiance for Garang, who, after working his way into the command of the government forces, became the enemy. The Sudan People's Liberation Army – the SPLA – was forged by the rebellion at Bor in 1983. John Garang was the commander in chief, and he joined other southerners demanding independence and an end to Islamic Sharia law. Many non-Muslims rejected Sharia because of its harsh penalties and because they believed it was unjust to impose an Islamic system on non-Muslims. The unrest provoked the government into sending extra troops to stop Garang and the uprising. This was the beginning of turmoil for Martha and millions of other people in south Sudan.

Martha starts telling her story as we sit outside my *tukul* in the late afternoon. We can hear the cheers and shouts from the volleyball match in the centre of the compound. The man who lights the fire under the hot water drum is in silhouette as the sun starts setting. Martha has agreed to talk on one condition: that I bring English language textbooks for the women. Several of the other leading women from the camp come up to the compound to count the books as I unpack them from my backpack. Proper textbooks are so sought after, the other women gather to verify the number, to ensure none are stolen or stashed away.

'Nineteen.'

'Yes. Nineteen. Sally, you must tell the men leaders that you have brought these books only for the women, otherwise they will try to take them for themselves.'

It's hard to imagine such a fuss about a bag of books. The majority of them are designed for primary school English students, but most of the women are barely literate and they are desperate to learn English. Many, including Martha, had their education disrupted by the war. She was in Bor with her parents and her younger brother when the fighting started.

'It start in 1983, on May the sixteenth. The crisis happened. The shooting start from 5 am and then people run to the bush. We hide there. These were Arabs. We face thirst and hunger and some women were delivering. Some died of bleeding. They were crying, just crying for the difficulties they faced. Some even lose their children. The hyenas ate some of the bodies. People suffered a lot.'

As the war began, Martha's childhood ended. Her relatives wanted to find her a husband, to bring extra wealth to the family.

'In the village, the girls are the source of feeding. If you have a daughter you can give her to be married to give you dowry. So when I stay in the village, some of my uncles try to get for me a husband, which bring them dowry.'

But, even as a teenager, Martha already knew the dangers of early marriage. She had seen other girls married off to older men from the village.

'I remember, I said if I'm married to a village man I will get nothing. He will not allow you to do education.'

The girls who were married to the village men lost their freedom, their childhood and their place at school. But Martha started attracting the attention of a different man, Kennedy Khot Thuc, a commander with the Sudan People's Liberation Army, the rebel group fighting against the government forces.

'I like him because he is an educated man. I was married when I was eighteen years. He was 25. We talked and we made agreement. I tell him, "You take care of me and my relatives and I will take care of you and your relatives. We will stay together." He accept that.'

Martha took Kennedy on her own terms, but she was nervous. She hadn't been with a man before.

'I was feeling shy when I see him. That was my first time to go with a man. Even some days I hide myself in the house and tell someone to tell him I'm not around.'

Martha and Kennedy were married in 1985. She was sent to her husband's house, accompanied by a group of female relatives to help her settle in and manage the domestic chores.

'I go there with the daughters of my uncles, five of them. They escorted me and we stay there for seven days. They went back home and only one remained with me for one month. It's just cultural. If you are going to your house, you must go with your relative sisters.'

Within a year she was pregnant, her belly tight and heavy. Martha was trying to continue her chores.

'In the morning at seven, I wake up and go to my grandfather's house. On the way, labour started, but I didn't know. I was not sure that I am delivering. By six in the evening, I want to go home. But I was not able to walk. So my grandmother say, "You are not going. You will stay here. This is the delivery, you will deliver now."'

Martha's grandmother took her into the cowshed.

'I deliver inside the *luak*, the big house for cows. In the dry season, people live in the *luak*. So I deliver inside the *luak* and I stay there with my grandmother. She conducted my delivery carefully.'

Her grandmother was the midwife; she reassured Martha and told her how to squat for the delivery. It's a tradition in Dinka culture for the mother or grandmother to oversee the birth.

'I cry but my grandmother say, take care of yourself. If you are not sitting properly you may kill your child. It will be shameful to you.'

Martha obeyed her grandmother's instructions. There was no doctor or nurse and no medication.

'It was painful. I was squatting. She catch the child with her hands. When the placenta come out, she cut the cord. Everything. The grandparents, they name the child Achol. That is the name of my grandmother.'

It was a baby girl. Martha was grateful for her grandmother's guidance during the delivery.

'For someone who don't have a mother, it's difficult. When you are delivering, there are some tears. But she bless you nicely and tell you how to sit. It was so nice. It was good. I stay there for one month in my grandmother's house. My grandmother take care of my child while I'm resting. The child was so beautiful for me.'

Martha's husband was on the frontline. Messages were sent to him to announce the birth of the child and he was eventually given leave to return home.

'He came in May to visit me. He saw the child and he become very happy. He stayed for two weeks. When he left I was worried, but what can I do?'

Martha has spent most of the past twenty years raising her children on her own while her husband has been away fighting the war; sometimes she hasn't seen him for up to two years. Tattered messages and greetings delivered by other soldiers have kept some communication between the home front and the war front. Martha has accepted the long absences and extra responsibility of sole parenthood

She looks at her watch as she stops talking.

'Sally, I must go, I'm late for work. I am on night shift at the hospital. Come to my house the day after tomorrow.'

Martha invites me to lunch to meet her family. One of the Sudanese aid workers from Catholic Relief Services, Grace Aba, comes with me. Grace is a friend of Martha's and she can interpret when Martha's English falters. Martha lives on the other side of the camp; it only takes about ten minutes to drive there, but it's a long journey on foot in the heat of the day.

We park the four-wheel drive in a clearing near the church and then walk on the foot tracks between the towering millet fields, where a barefoot boy runs to greet us and then runs ahead to alert the family that we're on our way. Martha is peeling vegetables and letting the scraps drop into the foxhole. She laughs. The bomb shelter has become a giant kitchen bin.

'The bombing stop now so we just put the rubbish in the foxhole. We just close it. If the war stop and peace come, we not dig it again. But we don't know what will happen.'

Martha's family lives in a compound, where the mud *tukuls* are separated by bamboo fences. Martha has her own hut and she holds back a curtain over the door and invites me inside. It's immaculately clean; there isn't a grain of dust on the mud floor. It has been swept and cleaned with surgical precision as if every granule of dirt has been tweezered away.

The hut is round and small. Martha's bed is next to the wall, petitioned off by a blue and green curtain hanging from a wire stretched from one side of the room to the other, and the bed legs sit on blocks of wood so they don't sink into the clay floor. On the other side of the room there are home-made bamboo chairs and a table, each with embroidered covers. The brightly coloured round crocheted doilies that decorate the walls almost glow in the dark. I can see Martha's toothbrush above the door; she has put it in the thatched roof over the doorway so she can easily reach it when she goes outside to clean her teeth in the morning. It's the only personal possession that hasn't been hidden away for my visit. Martha is very proud of her family, the neat huts and the compound. She doesn't display any embarrassment as she shows me around. She looks at me and laughs when I pretend to take over pounding the millet with a long wooden pole.

'You, you are not strong enough. Your arms are too thin and your stomach is flat. The other women are wondering why your stomach is flat when you come from a rich country. You need to eat more to get the shape of an African mother.'

Martha asks me to sit down in one of the bamboo chairs. Neighbours come and lean through the doorway to peer at me and it is clear that there's a great sense of occasion. Martha proudly offers me a Fanta – it's a luxury. Then she goes outside and helps to carry in a procession of pots full of food: there's chicken, maize porridge, millet, greens and rice.

An old cassette player is warbling in the background. The song is about a Dinka man who says he would endure snakebites and mosquitoes to have the woman he loves. It's a rugged love story and Martha interprets the lyrics for me as her neighbours laugh. Most of the other songs are patriotic anthems recorded directly from the radio, interspersed with news reports about the SPLA's battles against Sudanese Government forces. It sounds like military music; some of the recordings are from the 1980s. Martha has kept the tapes for more than twenty years because she and the women like to reminisce as they listen to the old battle reports. The recordings are a source of genuine pride and patriotism.

But later, when the other women have gone, Martha's voice is softer as she talks about the personal cost of the war. It's one of the few times she struggles to make eye contact with me. She looks at the ground when I ask her about her second child, Dut. He was born in 1989, but died only a year later. It was 1990, one of the worst years of the war. Hundreds of thousands were struggling to survive without adequate food or shelter as the war swept through the south. Dut was only suffering from a simple fever, but there was no basic medical care.

'The child died because of dehydration. There was no hospital. I just cry. The child just get sick suddenly, I don't know what is the cause of it. If there was a hospital, my child could not have died.'

Martha nursed him in her arms and tried to tame the fever, but it was useless. His body was limp and cold.

'I knew the child is dead. I know because there was no breathing. The child was [not] breathing. We rolled the child in a bedsheet. If there was freedom, my child would not have died.

It was because of war. If we are in freedom, there would be no problem but because of war, I was very angry in my heart.

'I was crying. I was just crying, because people are dying and they don't come up again. I knew the child will be buried and I will not get that child again. It was God who took the child and there is nothing we can do.'

Martha sat with her son wrapped in the sheet. There was no-one to dig the tiny grave.

'In the village there is a belief that the father or the uncle are the one to open the grave. To dig it. At that time my husband was not around. The brother was not around. We stay up until 6 pm. We sent a message to the uncle to come and bury the body. If a person die and you stay near to the dead body, it's painful. They eventually came and the child was buried at night.'

They said prayers as they stood around the grave in the dark. When Dut was buried, other women from the village tried to comfort Martha.

'People prayed, they stayed for three days. After the child was buried we killed a goat. Me and the relatives, we also shaved off our hair. It's just traditional. If you have a death at home, the relatives and neighbours come and assist you. They come and help me. The pain reduce a bit. People come and they tell you, "Sorry". And they used to talk and encourage me. They say, "Leave that one. It's God who gives the child and he can also take him back. You will give birth to other children."'

Despite the reassurance from her neighbours, Martha was haunted by Dut's death; memories of him swirling through her thoughts.

'We used to remember him. Even dreaming come at night. I dream that I sleep close to the child. Like I'm breastfeeding the child. Like the child is playing around. Those are the dreams coming on me.

'Even me, I blame myself sometimes. I say maybe it is me who make the child to die or what. I say I will not deliver another child. I don't know if I can give birth to another child. It was painful to me so I just remember, remember until I deliver the third one.'

There was help available, but it couldn't get through. The Sudanese Government banned relief flights to almost all rebel areas from early 1990 until December 1992, stating that the bans were for security reasons, to ensure supplies were not being smuggled to the SPLA. Operation Lifeline Sudan, the largest humanitarian effort in history, was deliberately being blocked by the government.

'That was 1990. At that time, the Arabs come. So, people used to run night and day. We were scared. I was pregnant one month.'

Martha was running through the bush with thousands of other people who fled the fighting in Bor. She had malaria from sleeping in the open and struggled to carry the daily load of her youngest child, some pots and water containers.

'When I carry those things I sweat so much. When I put them down I feel shivering. I feel cold. My eyes become dizzy. I was unable even to walk. So one of the relative come with soup. Then he gave me and I opened my eyes. When I get that soup I say God is great. I will get a better day than this one. One day there will be peace.

'They were just bombing, they were just shooting at us. People were just hanging on the bush. We slept there two days, then I go back home. By then they burned the place. They took things and they even killed other people. We are just crying and we are blaming the Arabs, what they are doing to us. People were suffering because of hunger. People were hungry. You put the maize on the fire, but there is shooting around you. You can eat them while they are not ready or you can throw them down and you run. People just eat like animals. You eat unready food. You cook with dirty water. Sometimes there is no water. There are mosquitoes. There is cold and no blanket. We were naked without clothes on our body. An empty sack, that is the clothes you can wear. If you have that one, you are very lucky. So that is the way we were living.'

Martha recites the places she passed through when she was displaced: there are so many places it's a rhythmical list that falls from her lips. Some of the names come from the furthest reaches of her memory and she squints and concentrates to recall them. She stayed at some of the places for only a few weeks; others weren't villages at all, just patches of bush that offered some seclusion from the fighting.

Families were splintered and thousands of children were separated from their parents. Some older children formed large groups and walked across the country on their own in search of safety, many arriving on foot in neighbouring Ethiopia. But many parents lost their children in the panic and flurry of gunfire.

'If you go to fetch for water or firewood and people start running, you have left your children and you run alone. For those children who are able to walk they run and maybe you go and meet after some days or some years or some months. The relatives of my husband, they lose seven children. They found their children after two years. But other people's children, some of them are not found, some of them up till now. Maybe they are died or maybe they are what. Nobody knows.'

Even the children who were with their mothers were not safe. The hungry women could barely carry their infants, let alone find food to feed them. Martha was frightened of losing her children during the fighting and she held on to them as they walked through the bush.

'You have three children. You can take one on your neck, one on your back and you hold another one with hands. There is no food. So when people are running, children are crying. They want milk. That make children to die.'

The World Food Program was still being denied access to many of the worst-affected areas. Even when the planes got through, the scale of the humanitarian disaster was so large it was difficult to help the millions in need. Each Hercules C-130 aircraft could only drop enough food to feed 40,000 people for one day. It was dangerous and difficult to reach the most remote areas but some aid groups started arriving by road, defying the travel bans put in place by the Sudanese Government. Word spread into the bush that help had arrived. Martha followed thousands of others in search of food for her children.

'The aid workers opened a therapeutic feeding centre and that rescued our children. They did not die because of feeding centres. The international community, they help us. They put their heads on our problem. We were just crying to God. God is the one to help us in that suffering day because we had nothing. It was 1991.'

Up to 4 million people were displaced across south Sudan. Martha was one of them. She huddled in the bush with her children: they were naked, hungry and sick but government soldiers stole their clothes and anything else they had.

'You sleep on the ground. Nothing to cover yourself with. They took the clothes. Like if the soldiers come and find us here and they don't want to kill us. They just take our clothes, all. And you remain naked. You walk naked like that. Me and others also.'

Martha was boiling wild leaves and grass because there was nothing else to eat. Her once-round cheeks were sunken, her neck was thin and sinewy. The situation was getting worse; the hunger was so deep, people started tying cloth tightly around their stomachs to stop the feeling of emptiness.

'So you take some cloth and you tie your belly properly. If you tie it, you feel like somebody who eat. It's not much better, but it's better. I tied until I lose my clothes. By that time it was hopeless. I don't know if I can get food or if I get freedom.'

While the adults tied their bellies, there was little they could do to comfort the children, who cried with the relentless misery of hunger. Infants were dying from simple diarrhoea. Martha had nothing to feed her children so at mealtimes she would pretend government soldiers were coming as a way to distract them and keep them quiet.

'You just deceive them, slowly, slowly. You can say, "I will go and bring food for you" and then cry, there is something killing us here. Just keep quiet, keep quiet. You deceive them slowly, slowly and you are thinking how to get the food for your children. Even the leaves of wild fruits. You can go and collect and cook for your children. You deceive them slowly, slowly until you get the food.'

Eating boiled leaves made almost everyone sick, but there

was nothing else to eat. There were thousands of people in the bush, yet the Sudanese Government continued to refuse permission for aid agencies to deliver food aid to many locations because it believed the aid groups were simply providing supplies to the rebels. It was a stubborn stance, which drew condemnation from humanitarian leaders and generated widespread suffering. Hunger became malnutrition and malnutrition became starvation. Martha hadn't eaten for several weeks and her throat and stomach were shrivelled; she couldn't swallow properly when she finally received food aid.

'If you get food after some days, when you are swallowing here you can get a pain on the throat. So the best you do, you just take warm water slowly, slowly to warm your throat and open it. Then you take food that is light, like porridge. You take it for first time. Then you eat hard food.'

Martha holds her throat and tilts up her chin as she shows me how she used to drink the warm water to open her throat.

I feel quite inadequate. I've interviewed many hungry people in refugee camps before, but I didn't know about tying of the belly or what it is like to eat again after so long. Most of the time the people I spoke with were so desperate to get food, we were not speaking on equal terms. They were semi-naked and hungry while I was clothed and well fed. I was sharing the heat, dirt and flies, but not the hunger. No matter how long I talked with them, no matter how closely I sat with them, I could never fully understand what it was like to be hungry for months.

'That hunger, even for the growth of our children, it is there now. If you go and differentiate them with the children in town, the growing is not the same. They are growing slowly, slowly because they don't have enough food. If you grow, you don't know hunger, what is hunger? But we cannot forget it. It remain like a scar. You cannot forget the people that were there with you. We are still remembering the days of suffering that we left behind, up till now. We still remembering.'

Even now, there are few distractions to take those memories away, but once a week people come in from the fields or out of their huts to gather for a few hours of joy. Sunday in Labone is all about two things: church and wrestling. Church in the morning, wrestling in the afternoon. As the hours pass, the sounds across the camp become different and the steady beats of church songs are replaced by the shrill of whistles and the clapping of hands. The strongest young men change out of their congregational clothes, put on shorts and tie animal skins around their waists, paint their bodies with clay and draw squiggly patterns on their legs. Some of the wrestlers are close to seven feet tall, surrounded by scrums of relatives and fans. The supporters brag and shout about the abilities of their chosen fighter, and wave brightly coloured umbrellas, sticks and spears in the air. More than an hour before the wrestling starts, the fighters and their clans begin parading around the camp, jumping and singing their way between the huts.

More than 5000 people have gathered at the wrestling in a dusty open space near one of the churches. There are no seats; instead the spectators sit and stand around the edge of the makeshift arena. Dozens of boys climb trees for a better view, their skinny legs dangling as they sit in the branches. Soldiers armed with sticks keep the crowd in some sort of order. They allow only the wrestlers into the middle with a small group of supporters.

The young men leapfrog each other to warm up. It's spectacular to watch wrestlers the size of American basketball players propel themselves into the air while female relatives run in tight circles around them, ululating and squealing.

The wrestlers crouch down ready to start the bout. The referee blows the whistle and the wrestlers lunge forward, trying to drag each other to the ground. It's explosive: the crowd rises and falls with every contorted move. Sometimes there have been broken bones, although no-one can be absolutely sure because there is no X-ray machine at the hospital. The doctor can only make an educated guess about whether a bone has been fractured.

The larger wrestler finally flings his competitor into the dust. Hundreds of people run into the middle of the field, jumping up and down with their arms tucked at their sides in a victory dance. Men, women and children leap in unison like giant pistons, some breaking branches from the trees and waving them wildly in the air. But the celebrations only go on for just over a minute, then the soldiers move in. They swoosh their sticks at the spectators and force them back into the crowd, ready for the next bout to start.

It's exhilarating to watch. Each wrestling match only lasts a few seconds, followed by the roar of celebration and the scurry of supporters as the soldiers clear them out of the way. I have been given a prime viewing spot in the middle of the field, but when the spectators rush in I stand next to a tree so I don't get knocked over by the crowd. It's a dusty, loud afternoon. After the final bout, people walk back to their *tukuls*. The winning wrestler is surrounded by his singing, shouting relatives while, nearby, some of the supporters of the losing fighters chant promises of a better fight next week. It's a weekly sliver of exhilaration and freedom.

'Freedom' is the word Martha says with more feeling than any other. She says it with such stubbornness and longing; she's been waiting for freedom for twenty years. The war has splintered and separated her family and disrupted her education.

'Illiteracy takes us back. That is why we don't have freedom in south Sudan. Arabs used to take our things. And they used also to deceive us, because we were not educated. If we have freedom, our children and also us can be educated. We can know the benefit of our land.'

For Martha, freedom also means the little things.

'For me if there is freedom I can work as I want, I can plan as much as possible. I can get what I want to eat or what I want to wear. Anything you need in your heart you can get when you are free. We will not be dominated again, if we are free. Our leader went and bring guns and they volunteer to fight. Blood was shed, because of freedom. We have many widows and orphans now, because of the fighting. Even if we die, our children will be in freedom. And children of people who start the war will be in freedom. The widows also will be in freedom. And our land will be free.'

The SPLA troops guard Labone from attack. Skinny soldiers dressed in baggy second-hand uniforms and thongs have a large machine-gun post set up at the edge of the camp, overlooking a bridge. From here they keep watch. Other patrols go into the bush pursuing rebels from Uganda who prey on the civilians.

The local SPLA commander is Wilson Deng, a tall, muscular man who wears a neat uniform that includes a red beret and stiff rank slides that sit on his epaulettes. He carries a polished cane under his arm and is followed by a troop of bodyguards. Commander Deng has been in the SPLA for almost twenty years and gave up a place at university to join the fight. He answers my questions politely.

'Please, please. You are very welcome. No problem. No problem.'

He softens his voice when he's out of earshot of his troops. His words are those of an educated man and he speaks with a mixture of pride and regret – proud of the SPLA but regretful of the opportunities forgone in his own life. He is an intelligent man who had dreams of being an engineer but he's stuck in a camp in the backwater of Africa's longest-running civil war. He tells me he has a brother who is a doctor and who has emigrated to Australia. He lives not far from my parents' house in Adelaide and Commander Deng gives me his address. He sighs as he talks of his brother's new life in Australia; he knows it is out of reach for him. We talk for a while, then he shakes hands to say goodbye.

'I will see you this evening. There is a celebration at the Norwegian aid agency to welcome the return of one of their doctors. Everyone is invited.'

The night is as black as it gets and there are few lights. People mingle in the darkness and seats are set out in a big circle: there are lounge chairs for the most important guests and wooden ones for the rest. I'm ushered to one of the lounge chairs. Commander Deng arrives dressed in jeans and a T-shirt and his bodyguards follow him awkwardly. They're not allowed to bring their weapons to the party, so they wait patiently by the gate.

Aid workers, hospital staff, local priests, officials and community leaders are gathered, including Martha. The speeches are excruciatingly long and formal. People are thanked and introduced in a long procession, then the master of ceremonies declares the time has come for dancing. Any sense of spontaneity has long since dissipated. The MC announces the pairs.

'First of all, I can see Commander Deng and Miss Sally.'

My stomach lurches in nervous disbelief. I had come here to observe and report, not to make a spectacle of myself on the dance floor.

There is polite applause. I don't know if this will be some intricate tribal manoeuvre or a waltz. Commander Deng's hand emerges from the darkness and leads me to the centre of the circle. I've never jigged with a rebel leader in the pitch black before. The only consolation is that whatever dance we are about to do, I don't think anyone will be able to see us anyway. Somewhere from the edge of the circle the 'play' button is pressed on an old tape recorder. Commander Deng releases my hand and starts dancing back and forth like a teenager at a school social.

Relief. I can do this one. My fears of fumbling my way through a dusty bush ballet are unfounded; other pairs are also called into the circle – doctors and nurses, officials and aid workers are paired together for the dance.

Most people are a long way from their real partners. The war has left many people alone and taken the lives of a disproportionate number of males. There are not enough men to go around. Martha's husband has three wives, and most women in south Sudan live the same way.

'In Sudan we have polygamy. Even if you are the first one, he will marry after you. My husband went to the frontline and just married another one. He married the second wife when my second child was breastfeeding.'

Martha's husband didn't consult with her before he took a second wife, whose name was Druka. The two women met for the first time in 1990.

'The first time we meet I was not happy with her and also she's not happy with me. I was worried maybe she is coming to stay with my husband and my husband will chase me away. And she think I may come and fight with her. I just wait carefully. I wait for her to come and greet me and to see how her face is looking like.'

'Sometimes there are difficulties. Most of the co-wives are not good. Some come and chase you out of the house and remain with the husband. If she is stronger than you she always fight you until you pack up and you go. So people worry about that. Some husbands when they marry the young one, they just divert to the young one and he will not take care of you, maybe clothing you, feeding you.'

But the mutual suspicion eventually faded. Martha and Druka shared their husband and their homes. One wife didn't try to chase the other away.

'My co-wife was staying with me. I did not fight her one day, even. We stay carefully, nicely. If husband is there with other wife you don't think of it. He will come for you also. Your time will come. So I was not worried about that and I knew he would come back to me. We just stay like that. We are not quarrelling.'

Martha and Druka became friends. While their husband was away on the frontline for several years at a time, they ran the household together.

'I was very close with her in the same house. We distribute the work the same. When I go for the work she remain with my children. She love them so much. She went for treatment because she came and stay for five years without delivering any children. She have her *tukul*, I have my *tukul* but we are eating the same food. There was only my children, she did not have a child. She loved them and my children also love her.'

In 1996, the third wife arrived; she was Martha's sister-in-law.

'If the brother dies, your husband will also inherit that wife even if there are two or three. My husband inherited his brother's wife in 1996. The brother was killed during the crisis. The relatives talk that the wife will be inherited to my husband. I don't have any problem because this thing is always happening. Now she have two children from my husband.'

The three wives continue to share one husband. Martha shrugs her shoulders when she talks about it. 'Polygamy is not good but it is part of the culture. That is why people accept it. Culture cause us to have polygamy.'

While Martha's husband is away, she is the unofficial head of the household. She supports her entire extended family with her nursing wages. It's not a high-paying job, but it's one of the highest status roles for a woman in Labone. The hospital is the most important place in the camp and is the only facility of its kind in this part of south Sudan. People walk for days through dangerous terrain to reach the doctors and the feeding centre here. Most of the buildings are made from tin or mud, with thatched roofs and few windows, leaving most of the wards in almost total darkness. There are no waiting rooms, so patients with appointments for the clinic or the theatre sit on benches outside under the trees. Martha and the other nurses work long hours and then face a long list of heavy chores at home.

'I'm living at home with fourteen people. I get up between four and five, I start cleaning. Then I prepare breakfast for my children, a porridge. And then I go to the work. It's one hour to work, walking. I stay there. Then I go back home. I go to sleep at ten, maybe eleven.

'To describe myself, I am the responsible person in the family. Those relatives of my husband they take me as a responsible wife. They respect me and also I respect them. If we get freedom, my husband can come home and get salary. He will take the responsibility for the family. It's heavy for me, but what can I do? There is no other way. If I leave them they will suffer. So I get tired but where can I go?'

We stop the interview in the late afternoon. Martha has to go to the hospital to get ready for night shift, so I go for a run. I wear a T-shirt given to me by the aid workers: it's part of a polio eradication campaign. There is a picture of a baby on the back of the shirt, along with the words 'Have you seen a paralysed child?' in big yellow letters. I hope no-one answers yes because I'm not sure what I'd be supposed to do with the information.

Children start lining the track more than an hour before I run each afternoon. Some put little twigs on the track to see what will happen when my running shoes go over them. I stretch my legs outside the CRS compound as the heat of the day slips away into a pink sky. The light is exquisite. A gentle breeze bends the tall millet in the fields as I run on a red sandy track towards the junction. The track is powdery and each of my footsteps kicks up small puffs of dust. An old man is walking up the track towards me and he stops and squints, looking panicked when he sees me running in the distance. The only time people run in Labone is when the Antonovs are coming. A woman shouts out to reassure him, but his posture is still rigid with uncertainty. Chickens and ducklings weave their own mad path in front of me. Running in Labone feels almost extravagant; to have enough food in my belly and energy in my limbs to run at the end of the day is a luxury – to run nowhere in particular, turn around and come back is partly comical and partly obscene. Most people laugh when I go past. '*Khawaja*! *Khawaja*!' Foreigner! Foreigner!

The people here have walked halfway across Sudan, dodging the ever-changing frontline of the war. I feel a bit embarrassed as I struggle along the track and stop in front of the market to catch my breath. The sellers laugh.

'Madam. What is wrong, why are you stopping? Do you have malaria?'

'No, I'm just tired.'

Some of the teenage boys from the camp run with me. They are lean and muscular, and their thongs flip, flop in a crisp rhythm as they increase the pace. '*Yalla, yalla.*' 'Go, go.' I joke with them in Arabic, and they laugh and run faster. When we reach the finish, we smile at each other. 'Thank you.' I walk into the compound and they go back to the camp.

Martha doesn't have any time for running. She wants to stop and settle.

'We are tired of running, we are tired. It's so painful when you are running. You don't know where to go and stop. We want to go home. If we run from here there is no other place. If we run from here, we don't know where to go.

'If I go home I will go and do something that will be permanent for me. When you are running, you do something good and you leave it there. There is no benefit for you. So if I go to my home and I have a very big garden, I can benefit from that garden. If I have my chickens I know that those chickens, I will not leave them.'

Martha wants to return to her mother in Bor, but it's not safe to go. Rebels from the Lord's Resistance Army in neighbouring Uganda are prowling the bush on the other side of the mountains and the road to Bor is still littered with landmines.

'My mother, she is at Bor. Fourteen years I do not see her. Long time. We get communication through radios now. It make you to be relaxed a bit. But not yet completely. My mother, she is alone at home. She is becoming older, no-one taking care of her. So it's difficult. The little I have I send to her, but it is not enough.'

Martha looks away and speaks softly when she talks about her mother; there's sadness. Her mother was separated from the family during the fighting.

'She's now suffering alone. The feeling is so painful to me. When I remember her, my heart is just beating. Poom, poom, poom. I feel bad until I sleep. She is very far. Sometimes you can send something to her but it gets lost on the way. I love my mother because she took care of me when I was small, young. She prevented me from fire and from everything. So I love her so much.'

It's late in the afternoon. We finish the interview and Martha and I go over to the dining room. Tomorrow I am flying back to Entebbe, so the aid workers have organised a farewell. The chiefs from the camp are invited: they are tall, lean, handsome old men, most are well over six feet. Some wear cowboy hats, others wear second-hand suits, some have walking sticks. They are gentle and reserved and sit in the lounge hut drinking soft drinks. When the food comes out, they pile their plates with maize meal, millet and chicken. They chew over the bones, their old teeth chattering as they nibble gently in search of the last sinew and gristle, and suck out the marrow where the last of the chicken flavour hides.

After dinner, the aid workers put on a James Bond video and the chiefs sit, captivated, laughing and nodding with approval every time 007 kills an enemy or kisses a sexy woman. One of the action scenes is set in the snow and I wonder what the chiefs think as they watch this *khawaja* in a dinner suit flinging himself from one adventure to the next. They raise their walking sticks each time he has another conquest. When the video finishes, the chiefs say goodnight and walk home into the darkness.

The next morning I meet with Martha to finish our last interview. As we sit under the veranda of my *tukul*, lizards make random dashes up and down the wall, their big dark eyes peeking out from hiding places. Martha stares ahead as she talks about the future and her voice is quieter as she talks about wanting to have more children.

'If I can give birth to other children it would be good. If God is willing. In Dinka culture you have many children. Maybe eight or ten. If you become old, they will take care of you. That is why we need many children. A big family is good in case of everything. If there are people coming to attack you, you will defend yourself. And if one in the family is sick, another one in the family will take care of you. It is important in our culture.'

Martha is also desperately hungry for more education. It's an almost unattainable luxury, spoken of as though it is a dream.

'In ten years from now, if we have peace I can finish my school. The most painful thing for me is education. If there was no war and I continue my school, the life can be one hundred per cent.'

Martha stops talking and looks up at the sky. We can both hear the distant sound of an aircraft; it's not an Antonov, it's the missionary plane, to take me back to Uganda. The engine noise fades in and out as it bumps its way through the heavy clouds. I put my bags in the back of the four-wheel drive and we drive to the airstrip. Children run to the side of the track to wave as we go past. '*Khawaja*! *Khawaja*!' One teenage boy falls off his bike at the intersection as he tries to wave madly and turn the corner at the same time.

The airstrip is at the base of a hill on the edge of the camp. Women with babies tied on their backs plough the ground on either side of the runway, using hoes to work the soil. But they scatter as the aircraft bounces along the runway and pulls up in front of us. When the propellers stop, the young missionary pilot climbs out and we can see that the African sun has scattered freckles all over his pale skin. He puts my bag in the luggage compartment and holds the door open for me. I hug Martha goodbye and strap myself in on the back seat. The pilot puts on a flight helmet, like in *Top Gun*, and then turns around and starts reciting prayers before we take off. I smile at Martha through the little window of the aircraft.

The engine revs, sending grass cuttings and dust into the air. The pilot lets the throttle go and we go charging along the runway until we bounce into the air and start to climb. I can see Martha waving goodbye. She has given me a small crocheted mat as a farewell gift. She tells me to think of her and wish for peace.

'Our children, we don't want them to suffer again. Let these difficulties remain on us and let our children to be in freedom.'

On 9 January 2005, the SPLA and the Government of Sudan signed a peace deal to end more than 21 years of civil war.

The war claimed more than one and a half million lives.

Monday 31st January 2005

Hi Sally,

Greetings to you in the name of our Lord Jesus Christ Amen. I hope you are well as I am doing fine here with my children. Achol and David were sick in November last year but they are now ok. We had enjoyed Christmas and still enjoying a happy new year of peace.

Congratulations to the whole family on the marriage of your brother. Tell the members of family that now with here, the time of crying has gone and we are in the time of peace and happiness and preparing for development. For my going to Bor, it depends on the government's arrangements because I am working. I shall be going to Kampala next week so I will inform you when I am leaving.

And thanks, Martha

CHAPTER 4

Bi Kidude

Musician

ZANZIBAR, TANZANIA

Bi Kidude is Zanzibar's most famous living diva. As a teenager she ran away from an arranged marriage to learn music from Arab sailors. She performed in Swahili nightclubs across East Africa and spent time as a lady-in-waiting for Zanzibar's royal family.

Bi Kidude was rediscovered when she was aged in her seventies. She has toured around the world, from Europe to the Middle East and Japan. She has a reputation for being talented and rebellious. Despite her age, she still enjoys smoking, drinking and picking fights.

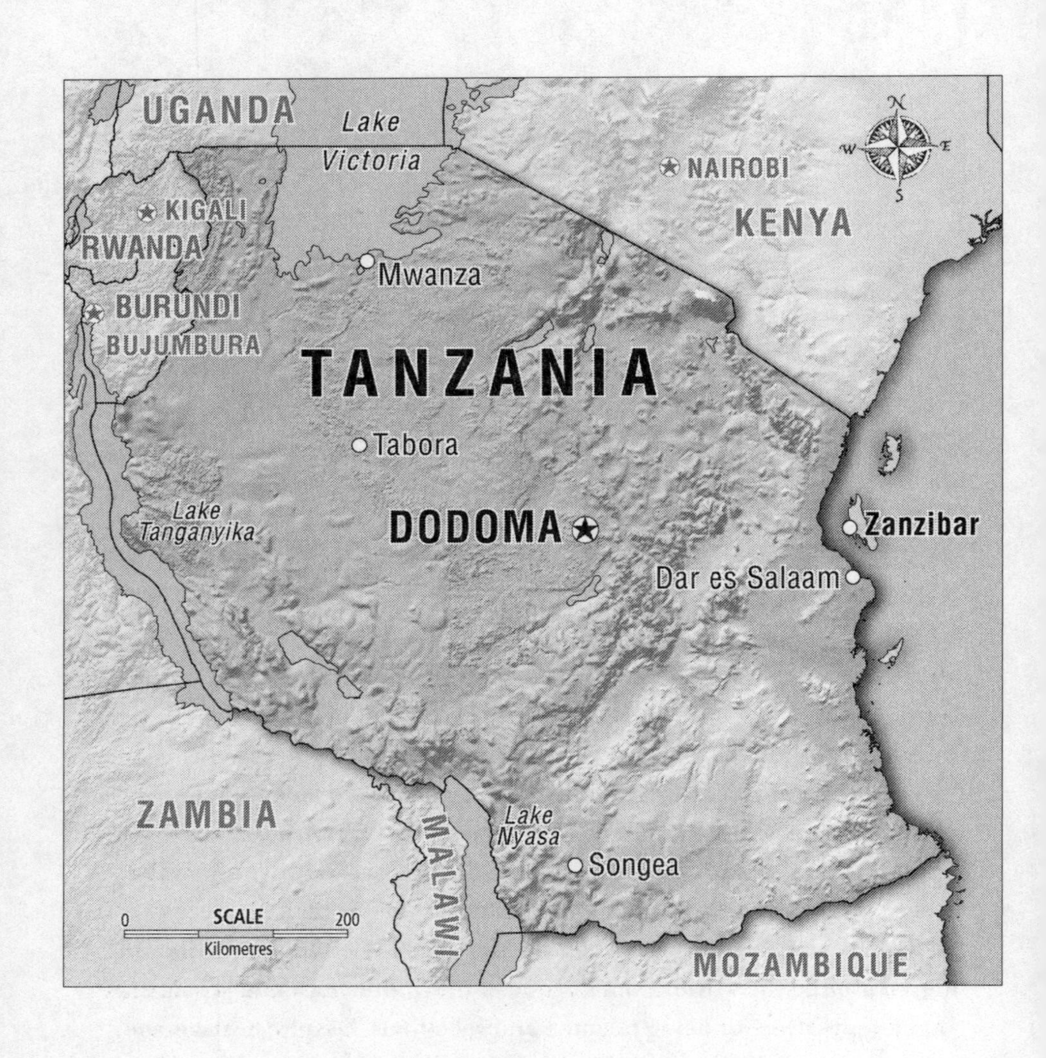
UGANDA
Lake
Victoria
NAIROBI
KENYA
KIGALI
RWANDA
Mwanza
BURUNDI
BUJUMBURA
TANZANIA
Tabora
Lake
Tanganyika
DODOMA
Zanzibar
Dar es Salaam
ZAMBIA
MALAWI
Lake
Nyasa
Songea
0
SCALE
200
Kilometres
MOZAMBIQUE
N
W
E
S

The journey to Bi Kidude's house begins in darkness; there are no streetlights. Ally, the interpreter, uses his mobile phone as a torch to throw small spoonfuls of light onto the sandy ground. As we stumble from the car to the front steps of the house, I can't see my feet or the uneven ground so I lift my knees in a clumsy march as I try to walk through the darkness.

We are in the back alleys of Zanzibar on a humid, sweaty evening. People sit outside houses that are too hot for sleeping in. There's no breeze to send off the heat of the day and even if there were, the streets zig-zag too much for it to blow much relief into the houses. The scent of the sea, fish and cloves hangs in the air.

Bi Kidude is one of the few people left who knows what life was like here almost a century ago. She is the most famous woman in Zanzibar, a singer, drummer and medicine woman. Her life has unfolded in the sandy lanes and old stone houses of the island; her raspy voice has bounced through this neighbourhood since she was a little girl. She is aged in her eighties or nineties, but she doesn't know for sure and there's no-one old enough to remember exactly when she was born. She grew up in a house just around the corner from here.

She tells me later: 'I was very naughty. I was a tomboy. I used to fight a lot with boys, just for the fun of it. Most of the time I was winning. I used to collect other girls and boys. We went to a place called Kizingo, where I arranged fights. I would say, "You fight this one, you fight that one. If you can't, then I will beat you." I was standing as a boss, watching the fights go on. Just for fun. But it was serious fights. I used to quarrel a lot. Even if you are a man, if you make trouble with me I just call you into the alley and I beat you. But I'm cooler now you see me. I'm old.'

I feel nervous about meeting Bi Kidude: she has a formidable reputation and I'm not quite sure how I'm supposed to approach her. There's something about her age that makes me uncomfortable, but also a little bit excited. I can hear the sand crunching between my shoes and the concrete as we walk up the front steps of her house. The house is made of grey bricks and is unfinished; one side has walls and no roof and the other side is lived in. It leaks light and voices – Bi Kidude is at home.

The door is open. It's a Zanzibari door, old and wooden with rows of the big metal spikes that are the same shape as orange squeezers. Inside the half-house there is a corridor with a cement floor. One of Bi Kidude's nieces greets us, and then goes into one of the rooms and comes back with a red-and-white striped mat and lays it down for us. We sit down on the floor with our backs leaning against the wall and our bare feet stretched out in front of us on the mat.

It's a fascinating house. There are pots and pans and coconuts on the floor, and something is boiling on the charcoal stove. Small buckets and containers full of home-made potions line the corridor and there's a wire-covered cupboard at one end. It looks like a fisherman's shed, dark and cluttered and interesting, the doors greasy from years of smudged handprints. I think if I had the place to myself for an hour I would explore it and open Bi Kidude's door, just a little bit, to see inside.

I can hear her voice. It's loud, confident and distinctive, the kind that spills into the neighbours' house and across the street. She's getting dressed to greet us. It's almost ten o'clock at night and she sounds sleepy; it's the Muslim holy month of Ramadan, when people fast during the day and socialise late into the night. The evening is the time to go visiting.

Bi Kidude comes out of her bedroom. She is a little tomboyish woman with brown skin and she wears a faded wraparound skirt. Her white hair is plaited into rows along her scalp and some of her teeth have gone; others are jagged. She's barefoot and the soles of her feet are cracked. She has the wiry body of a child, but the weathered skin of an old woman – her limbs are strong and lean and veins run along from her wrists to her forearms. She sits down next to me on the red-and-white mat, holds my hand and smiles. She is warm and enchanting.

Ally told me to bring a gift from South Africa. I wasn't quite sure what to buy for an elderly diva, so I give her a tiny basket with a beaded Zulu necklace and bracelet inside. Bi Kidude smiles kindly as she opens the tiny clasp of the necklace. I keep watching her hands; they are perfectly steady, she doesn't shake or hesitate. She puts on the jewellery and grins, and her arms ripple with sinews when she moves her fingers.

Her nieces sit quietly on small wooden stalls and tend the charcoal stove while she talks. Bi Kidude is the undisputed boss of this house – if she gives an order, it's followed. If she tells stories, her nieces listen even though they pretend not to. They've heard most of them before, but their grins widen when they know the punchline is coming. Bi Kidude's humour is rough and fast, her biting one-liners are devastatingly quick and are met with rounds of deep laughter. She speaks in Swahili, and Ally smiles and leans his head back with delight as he listens and passes on the stories to me in English. Bi Kidude watches for my reaction: she is genuinely welcoming, but intimidating if she wants to be. She grew up in a large family and learned how to stick up for herself.

'We were seven brothers and sisters. I was the last born. The last born is often naughty. It's true. That's nature. I was very naughty to the extent that my mother was very tired of it. We went to live in Pemba. There were two British kids, Barbara and Finnis. They were playing. Barbara cursed my mother. She said *Kumanina,* which is not a good word here, it means vagina. So I beat Barbara. I beat her very severely. My mother was so angry, she put me into a sack and threw me into the sea. I think she did it just to scare me. The sack was open. I swam out of it. Some fisherman came to rescue me.'

Bi Kidude smiles and has a wicked look in her eye when she tells the story. Her memories go back as far as Zanzibar in the 1920s. Her mother had married into an Arab family, but she eventually divorced her husband and married Bi's father.

'Most of the time my mother was a petty trader, cooking rice, banana, whatever. My father was a coconut climber. It was a profession here a long time ago. Normally he wouldn't go early to the farms, maybe ten o'clock he would go for the climbing of the coconuts, because he was a boss. The plantations were owned by Arabs. There were a lot of Arab settlers in the rural areas. I am taller than my father. He was small build and short. But he was strong.'

Bi Kidude lived in a house across the street from an Islamic school. She was forced to go to lessons and study the Koran, but she was bored. She didn't like the discipline and the routine.

'We had to go to Koran school. If you were late you got caned. I got caned many times but I had a trick. I put coconut husk here on my back. So the stick would not touch my body. Our teacher was a woman. She was not a strong caning master.'

Bi Kidude decided to escape the classroom; she waited for her chance and ran towards the waterfront. The bay was crowded with wooden sailing boats known as *dhows,* some of which had sailed all the way from the Arabian Peninsula.

'When I was ten years old I ran away from Koran school and go sailing on the *dhows.* There were some Arabs coming to Zanzibar, especially during the monsoon winds. These Arabs were the Laatubis from Yemen. I used to go to the Laatubis. I was alone and I was the only girl. We would sit. People used to play music. The Laatubis had a lot of instruments. I used to learn to play an instrument called the *dumbak*. When someone with a *dumbak* was tired I used to take that and started learning to play it.

'After the Laatubis finished practising on their boats they came into shore. There was a legendary singer bigger than myself. Her name was Siti Binti Saad. They went to Siti Binti Saad's place to sing with her. I would sit outside trying to learn what is being sung inside. I started learning. I would sing along with the Arabs and learn the Arabic songs. I would mimic Siti Binti Saad. I would sit and listen to her. And then I would start imitating her.'

Bi Kidude was captivated: she found the music irresistible. Her hands beat the leather skins of the drums and her voice followed the melodies of Siti Binti Saad. The music – a style known as Taarab – sounded more Middle Eastern than African, a blend of violin, flute, lute and drums. The lyrics were mournful and strong.

Siti Binti Saad was the queen of Taarab from the 1920s. The music was introduced to Zanzibar by the Omani sultans in the late 1800s; it came across the water from the Middle East and was the entertainment of Zanzibar's Omani elite. It was originally sung in Arabic and mostly by men, but Siti Binti Saad was a female pioneer and began singing Swahili lyrics. In her time she was a superstar, and her voice took Taarab all the way from the Sultan's palace to the back streets of Zanzibar.

Siti Binti Saad was a regular performer at the palace, singing for the Sultan's wife, Sayyida Maatuka bint Hamud al-Busaid. Bi Kidude was a relative of Maatuka and her family connection and musical talents gave her access to the palace. Bi Kidude served as a lady-in-waiting, a common practice for wealthy families, who 'adopted' poorer relatives. The royal family was surrounded by a circle of relations, servants, officials and hangers-on.

'I could go into the palace because of my mother's Arab family. It was fun going out with the lady, Maatuka. She would go alone in her car. We would be in another car with other dignitaries. I would be there. The Queen would always be wearing something to cover her body, a chador.

'We went to Kibweni palace, it is only about 2 or 3 kilometres from here. But at that time we thought it was very far. We had special clothes to go there. If you belonged to the Maatuka, the Queen's family, you should be wearing trousers, a colourful dress which goes down, four bangles and a necklace. Then people knew you came from Maatuka's side.'

The Sultanate moved its capital from Muscat to Zanzibar in 1832. The royal family siphoned a living from the riches of Zanzibar's trade in spices and slaves. They closed local slave markets in 1873, under pressure from the British, but slaves continued to provide much-needed labour in the banana and clove plantations. Although Zanzibar was officially a British protectorate, the Sultan remained in power.

Zanzibar is off the coast of mainland Tanzania in the warm waters of the Indian Ocean, only a short ferry ride from Dar es Salaam. The islands of Zanzibar are part of Tanzania, but they are semi-autonomous. Their recent political history has been dominated by hard fought elections and bouts of unrest. Up to 17,000 people were killed when the Arab elite was overthrown in 1964, and since then it's been a bitter contest for power.

The Sultan's extended family enjoyed a life of luxury in large Arab estates and they owned plantations across the island. The loyalty to the royal clan was strong; many of the courtiers were distant relatives, like Bi Kidude. She was fascinated by the dozens of servants who tended the royal family.

'There was a special cook, an Indian from Goa called Pishi. Before any food was served to the royalty, there was a doctor who came and inspected the food, both for the Sultan and the Queen. This was the routine almost. We had our own cook who was an African, not a Goan. The Goan would cook only for the royalty.

'There were antelopes inside the palace grounds and peacocks, turkeys. It was fun, the whole place had a lot of birds. If you were driving or passing through the palace and there was a peacock, you had to stop until the peacock goes through. We would be playing there, horse riding, enjoying the peacocks there. We would come back later in the evening. So it was a day out.'

Maatuka had an elaborate entourage. She was tended by her

personal staff. Bi Kidude was a junior member of Maatuka's court; it was an honorary position.

'I was a lady-in-waiting. Not the first one but the second one. The first one was called Dimalenu, she had one blind eye. She was the one who was serving the Queen directly. When Siti Binti Saad, the legendary singer, was singing there, the Maatuka would be sitting in the rocking chair listening to the music and she would be helping with making noise with the drums.

'If you wanted to offer anything to the visitors, there was a special tray called *khanshe* in Arabic. We would give an offering to a guest. It was fun. We were free to go in or go out. We would go back to our own homes for two or three days and then go back there. We were not tied there.

'We would be sitting around Maatuka. Chatting with her. She was a very free person. She was beautiful. We would normally greet her by saying "*Chei Chei*": that greeting is now reserved for smaller children greeting older people. We would never knock. We would assume we've been called. Then we would say "*Labeek*", as if we were saying, "I'm coming." We would say it three times, so she would know someone is coming. Then her assistant would come out and ask our intention.'

Bi Kidude loved the music and the rituals of the palace: it was a welcome relief from the domestic monotony of home. But her time working for the royal family was about to end. The Sultan took another wife and Maatuka became isolated.

'The Maatuka was followed by a second wife, by name of Nunuu. Maatuka said Nunuu became unpleasant. The Maatuka was not happy with that so she committed suicide. Maatuka died. It was so sad in this country. People were not allowed to put lights on. You had to cover everything to do with light at night until the mourning period was over. The whole country was sad because of her death. The mourning period was called *Zima Taa*. It was a very big burial ceremony. After that I couldn't go to the palace because it was the Maatuka who was my relative and she was dead. I had no reason to go there.'

Sayyida Maatuka bint Hamud al-Busaid died on 2 July 1940.

That was the end of Bi Kidude's time in the palace. It was back to the more familiar rhythms of walking barefoot, cooking fish over charcoal and sharing houses with relatives.

Bi Kidude tells her tales of the palace with little sense of self-importance, the words spilling out with varying enthusiasm: sometimes she likes sharing stories, other times she's bored. Late in the day she's restless, sitting down next to me on the striped mat, but her concentration is broken; she's fasting for Ramadan and she's hungry by sunset, when her nieces start cooking the evening meal.

In the afternoons, fishmongers take their place on the roadside to sell their catch. Flaky scales scattered across the area mark the spot. The fish are kept in baskets and buckets and people buy them as they walk home from work. It's a busy trade: customers stop on foot, on bicycle, moped and car. The afternoon is also time for football. Young men in mismatched jerseys play with great speed and intensity, sharing the pitch with grazing cattle, and dodging low-lying patches of black mud. The soccer fields are shaded by pine trees, parallel to the beach. Some of the customers at the fish stalls watch part of the game while they queue.

I run past the soccer fields late every afternoon. I weave through the skinny streets of Stone Town, past the tourist hotels and restaurants in Shangani Street and along the foreshore. Hawkers try to sell me Maasai paintings as I run past and they look surprised when each day I say no. The streets are tight, hiding the oncoming traffic until the last second – it's like starring in a video game where the obstacles appear with little warning. I hurdle boxes of fish on the footpath and dodge mopeds. The route takes me in front of the High Court, the clock tower, State House and the Lenin Hospital; I step off the footpath and run on the road when I get near the hospital entrance, to avoid the freshly discharged patients who walk with unsteady steps. Eventually I reach the soccer fields where the fish-sellers sit. I can smell the fish and the pine trees and the exhaust from busy motorbikes. I turn around and follow my tracks back into Stone Town, sprinting the last bit across the square near the guesthouse. The Stone Town run is one of my favourite in Africa.

The following day we take Bi Kidude to my hotel room to do the next part of the interview because there are too many interruptions at her place. Her voice arrives at the top of the stairs of the hotel before she does. The staff smile and greet her. She's wearing one of her best dresses and a colourful headscarf. She looks beautiful.

My hotel room has dark polished wooden floors and two beds with ironed white sheets. It's Spartan, starched and spotlessly clean with mosquito nets hanging from the ceiling. We push the beds out of the way and sit on wooden chairs near the window overlooking the sea. Bi Kidude stares outside like a child stuck in a classroom. It's raining and she leans on the windowsill with her chin resting in the palms of her hands watching the downpour. She looks tired. I ask her if she would like to stop and she says she wants to have a rest. Without hesitation she pulls back the mosquito net from my bed, climbs in, turns over and goes straight to sleep. I give a puzzled look to Ally; he shrugs back at me. I've got a Swahili diva napping in my bed. Bi Kidude sleeps for about an hour curled up on the crisp sheets. She looks even tinier when she's asleep in her veil – like an African version of Mother Teresa.

Ally and I talk quietly while she rests. Eventually she wakes up and quickly comes back to full speed, beginning with the topic of her first marriage.

'You didn't get to choose your husband. You didn't even know him. Not like today. At that time it was just arranged and you didn't even know who the husband is. This man came to ask for my hand. He went to my father. My father received a dowry and they arranged it without even my mother knowing. The dowry was two rupees. With two rupees you could even get a house at that time. It was the first time I saw the husband. But I didn't know it was him. The man spoke to my mother, he said he had proposed. I was married off. I just felt nice about getting married. I was not worried or troubled. Marriage is something nice.'

Bi Kidude had a reputation as a rebel; she was often loud, confident and argumentative. But social expectations were strong and it was difficult to abandon completely the Muslim values that were at the core of Zanzibari society.

'Even though I was a hooligan, I never had sex before I got married. That was a trend of the time. We were not raped. We were not harassed. When we were with the men we could lie between them, sleep between them. They were our security, in fact. People used to go very free. We did not get spoiled sexually. So my husband found me a virgin.

'According to Muslim tradition here, if you found a woman to be a virgin you must give her a gift known as the *Jazou*. I got a necklace. Marrying a virgin was still very important at that time. We put white sheets on the bed so after that [these are] taken to your family with a lot of celebrations. So your family is happy and there is a lot of fun.'

Bi Kidude was too young to treat it with much seriousness, and as the celebrations faded so too did her enthusiasm. Being youthful and impulsive, she decided to run away.

'I stayed with the husband for a short time, then there was an opportunity that I couldn't miss. I thought, why don't I run away, just for the fun of it? I just took off in a truck. I didn't want to stay in. I went into the truck. The people noticed. They said, "Do we have an extra person here?" I just kept quiet. I just ran out. It wasn't because of the marriage. I just ran out because there was some music going on somewhere in town. It was just part of childhood. Getting out.'

She ran away from the rural area and went into town to listen to music. She also missed her mother, so her husband reluctantly agreed to move into town. They rented a nearby house and Bi Kidude stayed there until her mother died several years later.

'My first husband was handsome. His name was Ibrahim. He

was a very talkative person. He was a specialist in renting clove trees. People would rent the farm so that they could pick the cloves. The reason for the divorce? It was just over. It was just fate that we separate. The first marriage, I just got rid of him. We were together for five years.'

Bi Kidude was young, single and unsettled. The flat, warm waters between Zanzibar and the mainland were enticing. Bi Kidude wanted to see what was on the other side, so she packed up her clothes and her few possessions and went looking for a boat that was sailing to the west.

'I went on the *dhow* to go to the mainland. I stayed there for five months. There was a family that took me there were Arabs. There was a man who came and saw me singing. He went to Dar es Salaam and said, "I've seen a singer from Zanzibar, her name is Kidude. She sings like hell, so why not bring her to our club, the Egyptian musical club?"

'I lived in Dar es Salaam singing for nine years. This was between the first and second husband. It was that period when I was free. I was going with Egyptian music club even to Congo and Kenya.'

The club entertained East Africa's elite. Julius Nyerere, who later became President of Tanzania, was a regular patron, and he would join in singing some of the old songs. Bi Kidude was one of the most popular musicians, performing until midnight and then going home to sleep until the middle of the day. She was paid well and enjoyed the freedom of life on the road.

'It was fantastic. We used to travel a lot. There were musicians and singers. I was being cared for. I got a sack of rice and some fish. I had a housemaid to attend to me. I was a star. If there was an Arab picture on at the cinema we would hire a whole wing. We would sit by ourselves. The Arabic pictures were very popular then. We would take the whole wing just for us.

'But I never had sex with any club member for all the time I was there. I have never been a hip-hopper, going to places with men. I never brought a man inside the house there.'

She eventually returned to Zanzibar and her arrival

attracted the attention of a local man who asked for her hand in marriage.

'The second husband was Juma Kombo. He was a fishmonger. It was many years later, I was a grown-up woman. It was about twenty years until the second marriage. We divorced because my husband was rude. He didn't talk nicely to me. He was always shouting. I lived with him for five years and then he left me. It was just over. I don't think I was a difficult woman to live with.'

Bi Kidude had to make a living on her own. She built up her musical career over almost a decade of professional performances on the mainland, but there were few opportunities in Zanzibar. She worked as a maid and spent her spare time singing at weddings and traditional gatherings. Her voice wound its way into the memories of many families on the island. She was famous for performing special music known as 'unyago' at initiation ceremonies for Swahili girls. Unyago is played on drums, and is often accompanied by dancing and games to teach teenage girls about womanhood. The elaborate but secluded ceremonies are usually held over several days. Bi Kidude not only performed as a drummer, she also gave advice on sex to young women preparing for marriage.

'As for sex, it's very tricky. If a girl says she doesn't want to go into sex, it means she knows about it. But if you don't have any experience, you think of nothing. Someone who is carefree you are assured she is a virgin. But if someone knows some shyness it means she has already been in it. Also if someone has had sex you can know by the buttocks, because the buttocks will be less firm. They become loose.'

Bi Kidude pauses. She leans forward in her chair and has an expression of great seriousness as she talks about sex, explaining that each young bride was assigned a *somo*, a traditional godmother who tended to her in the first days of marriage.

'A *somo* is someone who teaches you what to do. She is the one who goes with you when you are first married. The basic idea is to teach you the ways a woman is supposed to take care of the house and the husband. She even comes into the bedroom. The *somo*'s duty is to attend to you. She comes into the room. She cleans for you, she cooks for you because you are queen for that period of honeymoon. She stays with the married couple for seven days.'

Bi Kidude became a familiar part of weddings on the island. She was in demand as a singer, drummer, tattoo artist and adviser. It became her profession; she sang for newlyweds across Zanzibar. Mariam Mohamed Hamdani remembers Bi Kidude's performances. Mariam is a large, elegant woman with sparkling eyes and coffee-coloured skin who works as a journalist and music promoter.

'Bi Kidude is very important because in almost every house, 90 per cent of households in Zanzibar, she has played a role. Most of the people, when they get married, Bi Kidude plays music for them. So most people remember that. If not for themselves, for their sister, her mother, her aunty. Or people have attended a wedding where Bi Kidude is performing. She used to sing for the bride and the bridegroom while they were in the room. They always remember.

'Everybody knows her. She jokes that every man is her husband and every woman is her co-wife. She is jolly to everybody. She likes to make jokes. But she is also tough. If you know her, she has a way of answering you. She doesn't insult, but she has a way to hit back. I will put it that way.'

Bi Kidude lived with Mariam and her husband for four years, until she started earning enough money to build a house of her own. But she wasn't eager to move out.

'At first she refused to spend a single cent for the house, saying that she does not have children of her own, so why should she bother. One day she was really annoyed when I insisted and she called me an alligator several times! But when the house was ready, though it was not that good, she thanked me.'

Bi Kidude's career was a long way from her days as a young star in Dar es Salaam. She was popular, but she received little respect from the local music industry, being treated like a familiar old aunt, not a professional performer. As she got older, the opportunities to sing at clubs began to dwindle. Many Zanzibaris didn't want to see an older woman on stage. Mariam Mohamed Hamdani saw Bi Kidude perform at a local hotel.

'I remember one day I went to Bwawani Hotel, Bi Kidude was performing. People were actually making a joke of her. People were saying, "How can an old woman start singing, swinging?" They thought it wasn't proper. They made fun of her, the way she was dressed, the way they put make-up on her.'

But Mariam was impressed. She was approached by a record company in search of Taarab artists, and she told the producers about Bi Kidude. Initially they were reluctant, thinking that people would laugh at an old woman trying to sing, but they eventually agreed. The recording was a success and the artists were invited to perform in Germany in 1989. Mariam begged for Bi Kidude to be included; however, the organisers of the tour were worried about taking her on the road.

'They said, "Bi Kidude is very wild and we don't think you can manage her." I said there was no problem. I told them I wouldn't have any problem dealing with an old woman.'

Bi Kidude was aged in her seventies at the time. Some of the producers and promoters continued to question her talent and were scared off by her reputation. She didn't fit their expectations.

'Bi Kidude is somebody who really fought for women's rights. Even in the times when women were not supposed to sing, she was singing. She was fighting with men. They could not bully her. They could not even tease her. Because of that they thought she was wild. But she was just fighting for her rights. That was her life. If she could sing, why should men not respect her? As for the drinking, that is her pleasure. It's her own affair. But, of course, if she drinks too much she fights. She lifts up her skirt and says, "Do you want to see my shorts?"'

Her inclusion on the tour was a gamble. She started rehearsing with a newly formed Taarab group, the Twinkling Stars, and well-known singer and compere Mohammed Ilyas, but Bi Kidude was virtually unknown in Europe. Some government officials were worried that she would be an embarrassment.

Mariam Mohamed Hamdani says it was difficult even to get a passport for her.

'The ministry could have done that. It was their job. But some people were not interested for her to go. I said, "To hell, I will go with her." She didn't even know her age. The age in her passport is younger, because the person who signed for her age was younger than her. He couldn't sign that she was born on a particular date when he himself was not yet born then.'

News of Bi Kidude's planned trip started to circulate around the island. At first it was dismissed as gossip: many people didn't believe the old woman who had sung at local weddings would be going overseas. Bi was stopped in the street by friends and strangers alike who wanted to know if it was true.

She flew to Germany and prepared for her first performance. She waited calmly in the wings while the other acts performed, then it was her turn. Initially the audience members weren't quite sure what to make of this small, grey-haired woman who took to the stage. But when she started singing, her powerful voice left no doubts about her talent. The crowd screamed and cheered. Bi Kidude took off her headscarf, tied it around her waist and started belly dancing. Bi Kidude was in command of the audience and word of her success found its way back to Zanzibar. Those who were embarrassed that she had been chosen to go to Germany couldn't ignore her talent for much longer. Even before she returned to Zanzibar, her supporters outnumbered her critics. The popular saying at the time was '*Unastaajabu nini – Bi Kidude kwenda Ujerumani?*', 'Why are you surprised Bi Kidude is travelling to Germany?'.

It was a turning point. The elderly performer, who had been ridiculed for continuing to go on stage in her homeland, was receiving international acclaim. She soon became an unofficial ambassador; her talent and her age almost guaranteed publicity. Her fame also grew in Zanzibar, giving her the same feeling of excitement and status she enjoyed when she was a young woman performing in Dar es Salaam.

'When I sing I feel like a teenager. I work, I make my own

money. I get some gifts. It's better than going around on Friday asking for donations like a beggar. I'll never do that. I've been to many countries in the world now. People who come to my performances are amazed that a lady so old has so much talent and that I'm still able to keep up with my singing. I just stay on the stage and the crowd claps.

'I travelled by foot but I never had any sickness or ailments. I've never been affected by the cold when I travel to Europe. For example, I have decided to wear no shoes. It's all right. Going barefoot keeps you healthy. I also started smoking at a very young age. I think smoking has kept me moving and I've never been sick with smoking. I can drink four to six bottles of beer a day, in one sitting, and [smoke] one and a half packets of cigarettes.'

Her lifestyle has done little to dent her stamina; she drums and sings until the sweat makes her face glisten from the stage. But during her 2004 European tour, rumours started back home in Zanzibar that Bi Kidude had died.

'Myself, I received the death call, a phone call from Zanzibar to say I was dead. One of my nieces made the call. She was crying. We asked her, "Why are you crying?" She said, "My aunt has just passed away." The people I was touring with, they said, "Well, just speak to her. She's on the phone right here." I just treated it as normal, the whole issue.

'When I arrived at the airport, there were many people to welcome me back. I played drums. They gave me a T-shirt that said, *Amefufuka*, that means "risen from the dead". But I'm very much alive and very much back to my daily work.'

Now Bi Kidude's CDs are big sellers in Zanzibar and at music festivals around the world. She even has a restaurant named after her in one of the island's most luxurious hotels. Despite her success, Bi Kidude lives a simple, active life and she doesn't seem very interested in money. Money is about buying enough fish for dinner or maybe some new clothes. She lives barefoot in her half-finished house and talks about her success with indifference. She tells riotous stories about her travels. Her nieces writhe with laughter as Bi mimics Japanese bowing and talks of her adventures grocery-shopping in Germany. It's half mime, half stand-up comedy; she pretends she's busy doing chores as she gives the impromptu importance.

As she clowns outside, several young mothers are waiting inside, sitting patiently and laughing as they listen to the performance. Almost every day they come and sit in Bi Kidude's corridor because she is renowned as one of the best medicine women on the island. Her speciality is asthma medicine; she makes it from a special recipe of herbs and plants boiled in pots on the charcoal stove.

One of the mothers carries a sickly boy. Bi Kidude examines him as he sits in his mother's lap. She leans over and checks his eyes, then shakes her head in disapproval, lecturing the mother and son for failing to follow her treatment recipes. The mother bows her head in embarrassment but Bi Kidude quickly changes the mood, softening her voice and playfully teasing the children, nicknaming them monkeys. Some of them laugh, but others watch her carefully.

The home-made brews of asthma medicine are cooled in plastic buckets. Bi Kidude uses a funnel to pour the liquid into empty Coke bottles and the mothers pay with some small change. It's a cheaper alternative to the expense of going to the hospital or the pharmacy. Many Zanzibari families are living on modest incomes. Most neighbourhoods and villages are run-down; big, dull apartment blocks flank the road on the way in from the airport, and the roofs of Stone Town are a rusty patchwork of corrugated iron. But with the worn exterior comes great authenticity. Zanzibar is a real place, not a postcard. It doesn't have the blemish-free appearance of a resort but it has a vibrant life of its own.

Stone Town is the busy hub: a jumble of Arab, Swahili and European culture. The Muslim call to prayer echoes through the narrow streets, reminding me a bit of Arab neighbourhoods in Jerusalem. Other localities feel like an ageing corner of a European city. Balconies, uneven rooftops and heavy wooden doors break up the streetscape and many of the houses also have a *baraza*, a stone step used as a bench, where locals sit and talk. Despite the big earnings from tourism, many of the buildings are crumbling and the streets are barely clean, but Stone Town is full of atmosphere. The scent of cloves wafts through the markets and the warehouses near the waterfront. Spices have been part of Zanzibar's economy for hundreds of years. It's a lucrative business: clove smugglers avoid local taxes by illegally shipping their product to the Kenyan port of Mombasa.

In the evenings, craftsmen, hawkers and food-sellers set up stalls on the foreshore and smoke from the cooking fires swirls in the soft breezes that arrive as the sun sets. Maasai tribesmen from the mainland in their red robes and sandals sell jewellery to wandering tourists. Fishermen in wooden *dhows* return just before dark, their sails catching the last sighs of wind for the day. The *dhows* move slowly and when they finally reach the beach, the fishermen unload their catch as skinny cats with straight tails and hungry cries pester for some scraps.

Later in the afternoon when we return to Bi Kidude's house, it's all quiet; she's gone shopping. We wait. Her voice spills out from a small tailor's shop just up the street where she's organising some new outfits. She wears a black Islamic headscarf with an elastic chin strap – it makes her look small and frail, but when she takes it off, her white plaits and sparkly eyes frame her face again.

She goes into her room and gets changed so we can take her for a drive. Emerging in a blue dress she strides out to the car. She has even put on some shoes for the occasion. I open the door and she sits in the front, with the window wound down. I sit behind her, holding my microphone over her shoulder.

She gives Ally directions. We drive a short distance to a nearby sandy street: this is the house where she was born and across the road is the Koran school, just as she said it would be. We get out of the car and Bi Kidude sits on the corner of the old house while I take some pictures of her. As we drive through the neighbourhood, people wave and call out to her – she is every bit the celebrity. A policewoman stops us and says hello. Bi Kidude jokes with her and says if she patrols the back streets she will never be promoted.

As we drive into Stone Town, people look up with surprise when they see Bi Kidude. They greet her with humour and genuine warmth; she is the most famous woman on the island. She tells them she has got herself a chauffeur, they laugh and she soaks up the attention.

The drive is fascinating. Bi Kidude's memory is sharp and fast, she points to buildings and recalls detailed accounts of events and people. She doesn't stall or struggle as she recounts her memories: she remembers murders, fires, fights and accidents.

We drive through the thin, damp alleyways and along the waterfront, and stop at a roadside fish stall. She inspects the catch and orders up, knowing I will get the bill. The fisherman scales and guts the fish and wraps them in newspaper, I hand over the money and get greasy, fishy notes in return. The fishermen chat with Bi Kidude, and she refers to all of them as her husbands as they crowd around the car to speak with her.

As we drive alongside the fish market, young men shout and wave, trying to get Bi Kidude's attention. I'm sitting on the back seat, directly behind her. I love watching their faces as they glance up from their fish trolleys and see her passing by. I get the feeling it's the main story they will take home with them tonight. People shout out to her with the slang greeting of *Mambo*; she responds by saying *Poa*, which means 'cool'. She plays along with the joke, but on the way home she becomes quieter, more serious and detached.

'Things have changed in Zanzibar. In my time I would never see a woman cleaning in the street. It's only done now. In the old days it was not for a woman to go working in public. Now people are more desperate. People have to struggle with life.

'Moral standards have gone down a lot. There is no respect now. People now are hooligans. There is no respect. In my time, young would respect the old and the old would respect the young. But now, everyone misbehaves. People don't care about age. In the old days, a child or someone in the neighbourhood would be cared for by everyone in the neighbourhood. But now if you discipline someone's daughter or son, you will be taken to the police station. If that child does something evil you cannot say anything to him. I am just agreeing with what the world wants. If they greet me with *Mambo*, I say *Poa*.'

The conversation stalls for a few minutes. I'm a bit surprised by what she has said, but in other ways it makes sense. The more time I spend with her, the more I enjoy her solemn moments; beyond the clowning and the bravado there seems to be a sense of pain that she has outlived her generation.

Bi Kidude surrounds herself with youth and activity – it's rare to see many old people in her house. The corridor is constantly cluttered with a procession of visitors, relatives and friends. Bi Kidude directs the traffic: she summons those she needs to see and firmly dismisses those she doesn't have time for. Her business is done from her hip, she keeps her money tied in a knot in the corner of her wraparound skirt and sends her nieces on errands. She ties and unties the knot as she hands out money and the change eventually returns. Once a teenage boy came back from his mission empty-handed, and Bi Kidude told him off and grabbed him by the T-shirt, twisting the fabric that covered his stomach. She pushed him into another room; he smiled and he knew she was playing. But there was also a little bit of fear behind his laughter, as Bi Kidude had a vegetable knife in her other hand and she waved it around for effect.

'I can fight up until tomorrow. I will never injure someone. But if anyone annoys me, then I can become mean. I fight today, even, if it is by hand, stick, fist-fight. I'm still ready to do that. I fend for myself. Those girls at my house, I still fight them. I close the door if they anger me. Sometimes children tease me. But I just joke with them. Almost all of the time I have been happy.'

We drive the bumpy, narrow streets to Bi Kidude's house, to say goodbye. We go slowly past the mosque, where men and boys are waiting outside for evening prayers and women walk past in long dresses and headscarfs. It's the routine of Ramadan.

Late in the evening, Bi Kidude is quiet and gentle. She's lying on a patchwork bedspread on her big double bed, which has an old wooden frame above it, but no mosquito net. There is an ashtray by the bedside and the ceiling is stained and flaky. Faded pictures of Bi Kidude hang from the wall in ragged frames: one photograph shows her standing with the President of Tanzania. Suitcases and clothes are stacked up near the window, and a tiny ginger kitten sits on top of the luggage. It climbs down, shrieking and meowing. The kitten is called Ramona, and Bi Kidude strokes and cradles it with her hands before putting it down next to a saucer of curdled milk on the floor.

Bi Kidude says she has a gift for me. She grins as she reaches down and picks up a white plastic bag. Inside is a large piece of coloured cloth, blue, yellow and white with big red flowers. It's the traditional dress for women in Zanzibar and many parts of East Africa. I drape the fabric over my shoulder and one of her nieces comes back with a knife to cut it in half, so I can wear it as the local women do, with one half as a top and the other half as a skirt. Bi Kidude laughs and shakes her head as I try to wrestle with the material. Eventually it's tied properly and Bi Kidude smiles and nods in approval.

I feel very sad to say goodbye. I touch Bi Kidude's cheek with the palm of my hand and give her a gentle kiss on the forehead as she lies on the bed. She looks old and vulnerable when she is tired, but her eyes keep some of their sparkle. Ramona the kitten follows us to the door as we step over the ragged doormat and walk outside down the sandy path and back into the hot Zanzibari night.

The light from Bi Kidude's bedroom window shines a strip of yellow onto the dark street.

'Many people I knew, they have now passed away. I remember them and I pray them to God. But I miss them. Why have I lived so long? It's just God's will. It's called freedom. I am like an old coin. Everybody knows me.'

In October 2005, Bi Kidude's remarkable career was recognised when she won the prestigious World Music Expo WOMEX Award. She received a standing ovation at the presentation ceremony in the UK.

In 2006 a documentary film on her life, '*As old as my tongue: The myth and life of Bi Kidude*', was released.

CHAPTER 5

KATUMU MACCULAY

Former child soldier

LIBERIA

Katumu became a bodyguard to a rebel commander at the age of seven. She was small and energetic. She was given a pistol and the nickname 'Over Plus Active'. She grew up among the chaos of Liberia's civil war. Katumu was a child soldier and went on to become a commander. She was one of the feared female fighters who took part in the final battle for the capital, Monrovia.

She's now handed in her weapons and is trying to make a new life for herself and her young son.

SIERRA
LEONE
GUINEA
Zorzor
Gbamga
Robertsport
Tubmanburg
CÔTE
D'IVOIRE
MONROVIA
Zwedru
Buchanan
LIBERIA
N
W
E
S
Sass Town
Harper
0
SCALE
200
Kilometres

There's loud applause as the aircraft tyres touch down on the sticky black Tarmac.

'Sweet Mary. Mudder of Jesus.'

'Oh God, 'tank you Lord.'

The large black woman next to me thanks a range of saints and prophets, not so much for an elegant landing, but for the fact we landed at all. The pilot finally succeeded after two aborted attempts to bring the aircraft down through a late afternoon storm. Fire trucks with flashing lights are lined up next to the runway. Some of the passengers wave to the firemen through the tiny aircraft windows.

The battered speakers of the aircraft vibrate with the deep West African accent of the captain.

Welcome to Liberia, West Africa.

The American-built runway at Liberia's main airport, Roberts Field, is one of the longest in Africa. It was part of a series of military bases and listening stations that served the US through the Second World War and the Cold War. But its usefulness has faded and most of the Americans have long since gone. The airport terminal is small and chaotic. There are no queues; people just squeeze in and out of small offices clutching their passports. There's shouting and pushing as if the planeload of passengers has landed here by complete accident. It's a swirling, noisy procession as money is passed to officials in badly disguised crunchy handshakes. I've been in Africa for five years but I still haven't mastered small-time bribery: the note usually falls on the floor or the person receiving it thinks I've got a twitch when I give them a dodgy nod. A young security guard eventually helps me after I press a folded ten-dollar note into his hand. It's the only way to get through. A colleague and I once said we should set up our own website called www.why-your-airport-is-buggered.com to catalogue some of Africa's most feral fly-zones. Roberts Field would rate a mention but would struggle to match some of the continent's best-worst airports – especially Lagos, in Nigeria, which is a world leader in luggage disappearances, delays and jugular throbbing check-in counter arguments.

The ceiling of the terminal is stained and paint has been scuffed from the walls. The whole scene looks like a second-hand, hand-me-down version of America – the guards are wearing American caps and uniforms that are either too big or too small and their worn-out shoes peek from under the cuffs of their pants. The local accent is still coated with a faint American drawl, more than 150 years after the first freed black slaves came to settle here.

Liberia was a grand experiment. The freed slaves sailed from America to establish a new nation in their homeland, drawing up a constitution based on that of the United States. Liberia was declared independent in 1847. The descendants of the former slaves, known as Americo-Liberians, became an elite; they made up less than 5 per cent of the population but held most of the power and wealth. Freedom was reserved for a privileged few. Local people were denied voting rights and were submerged into forced labour on rubber plantations. Racial discrimination wasn't outlawed until 1958. The deprivation, political opportunism and economic mismanagement fermented into violence. The past 25 years have been scarred by war, coups and relentless poverty. Liberia is the child that the United States has almost forgotten; it's one of the poorest countries in one of the most unstable parts of the world. It sits between Sierra Leone and Ivory Coast and suffers the tides of West Africa's troubles.

At the intersection outside the airport, there's a big billboard with a cartoon of people beating each other. The slogan warns: 'Stop mob violence. Respect rule of law'. It's not the usual welcome. As we drive into the capital, Monrovia, there are military checkpoints along the road with soldiers staring out from behind the sandbags and wire. Liberia has the largest United Nations peacekeeping force in the world, and the presence of the foreign troops has been the only thing stopping the country from tearing itself apart again. Some of the peacekeepers decorate their checkpoints with signs that say 'Peace lovers' and 'Sweet peace', but they are cautious. One soldier was set on fire by gunmen who poured fuel on him and stole his weapon; as a precaution, his colleagues now chain their rifles to their wrists.

Liberia is painfully beautiful. The ragged townships encroach on the edges of the jungle, and beaches with palm trees separate the lush land from the Atlantic Ocean. Monrovia has one of the highest rainfalls in the world: heavy, dark clouds wash the city almost every afternoon during the wet season. The rain doesn't fall gently. It starts in big, clumsy drops and then roars in wild sheets that sting your face and hands. Each storm only gives a few minutes' warning, and if you can see it coming it's already too late. The locals run for cover to get out of its way. The rain turns the red dirt tracks into sticky mud as the water rushes through the markets and the townships.

Katumu sets up her stall each morning at a muddy market on the outskirts of Monrovia. She sits under a rickety shelter with a roof made from woven mats. She laughs and gossips with the other market women as the smoke from cooking fires spills into the path of passers-by. Katumu's stall is right at the entrance to the little market on the side of the busy main road. She was tough enough and clever enough to make sure she got one of the best spots to sell her hotdogs and snacks.

Her body is short, muscly and stocky; she wears tight jeans and a red sleeveless top and her hair is combed up in a mini-beehive. She's only the size of a ten-year-old child but has a hard look in her eye. She seems to sense I'm nervous, so when I sit and talk with her she crosses her arms and looks off in the distance. Katumu's ten years younger and almost a foot shorter than me, but I'm completely intimidated by her. I think if we'd gone to school together she would have made my life hell. The more she ignores me, the harder I try, and my spoken sentences are twice as long as they need to be. I try to build up the conversation but Katumu swings her legs impatiently and rations her attention in small glances and nods.

It takes almost an hour to establish some warmth between us. I show Katumu some pictures of the other women I have interviewed and explain what the book is all about. She tries to hide it, but she seems to be excited that her story will be in print. The corners of her mouth give the hint of a smile and even when she tries to look away, there is a softness in her face. She starts telling her story in a gentle voice.

'They named me after my great-grandmother. My mother died in childbirth when she was having me. So I never knew my mother.'

Katumu was born as her mother died in 1983. Her father married another woman. Katumu knew that her stepmother wasn't her real mother, even though no-one had ever told her.

'The way she treated me made me to question whether she was my mother. The treatment was so awful that I was sure this woman was not my mother. My stepmother would prepare more for her children than for me and my brothers and sisters. She would only take her kids' clothes and start washing them. So I had to start washing for myself at an early age.'

Katumu's father would try to intervene, but he was afraid of confrontation and his work at a local sawmill kept him away from the daily running of the house. Katumu's stepmother didn't bother to send her to school, so she sat outside the gates of the school and played all day.

'My father would even send the company bus to pick me up and take me to his working place. I would stay there the whole day. The two of us would come home. Because of that, I was very irregular in school. My father didn't want confrontation. He would take me away.'

Katumu speaks in a mixture of slang and broken English. Her Liberian accent slides the syllables into a rhythm I struggle to decipher and, in turn, my flat Australian accent leaves her wondering what I'm saying. I feel a bit embarrassed. I always feel a little uncomfortable in West Africa because I don't know it as well as other parts of the continent. It's a bit rougher, more streetwise – it makes me feel awkward. Katumu looks at me blankly, then she stops the interview and watches the progress of a small boy who is walking home from school. The boy waves and grins at her.

'That's Tony. My son.'

She waves back at him, trying to keep her lips tight and tough, but her white teeth reveal a smile. Katumu's movements quicken as she fidgets and pretends to check her manicured fingernails. But every part of her is focused on this boy. She's almost clumsy with her own joy. Tony is five years old. He carries a school bag that's too big for him and scuffs pebbles with his shoes as he gets closer to us. He turns his head to the side and smiles when he looks at Katumu.

Mother and son meet. But they don't kiss or hug. Tony leans on Katumu, his schoolboy legs bend and sway as he gently presses his body against her chair. She notices a couple of small spots on his legs as he climbs up and sits next to her, so she uses my business card to scratch and inspect them. Her eyes check over her son and I watch her looking at him. She rubs her fingers over his hair, brushes down his collar with her hand and straightens his shirt.

Katumu and Tony don't see each other every day. He lives with a foster family at the missionary compound, which is only a ten-minute walk down the dirt track from Katumu's hotdog stall. 'It's a better life for him,' says Katumu.

Tony is the president of his class at school. His foster family pays his fees and buys his uniform. He and his three foster sisters all play under a tree at the back of the house. The eldest girl leads a chant and they jump and clap. Katumu says that if Tony lived with her, he would be an only child spending late nights sitting with her at the market.

'The neighbourhood, it's better. He will grow up with them. He is a very smart kid. I feel big inside that he has come this far.'

Tony wriggles out of the chair and looks briefly into Katumu's eyes. She smoothes his shorts before he runs back down the track.

Katumu wasn't much older than Tony when the war arrived in Liberia. On Christmas Eve, 1989, rebel commander Charles Taylor led his troops into the country, crossing the border from the neighbouring Ivory Coast. Taylor was a fierce opponent of President Samuel Doe. He was educated in the United States and had escaped from jail after being accused of embezzling Liberian Government funds. Charles Taylor was articulate, calculating and charismatic, rallying supporters under the banner of the National Patriotic Front of Liberia – the NPFL. His troops wore red headbands and tied red cloth around their wrists. Charles Taylor's forces pushed their way inland and surrounded Tubmanburg, Katumu's home town. The villagers knew they were getting closer. Katumu remembers families were hiding in their houses.

'On a Sunday morning in 1990 I was at home. Me with some other women and children who were afraid were in my father's house. The freedom fighters surrounded the house and started beating the doors and shooting. Me, being afraid, ran and opened the door and tried to run out. Somebody pushed me back.'

Katumu saw the red headbands and wristbands and she knew that rebels had arrived. The town had been full of rumours that Charles Taylor's troops would kill civilians. The rebels kicked their way inside following the instructions of their commander, Oliver Varney.

'They tied us first and put us in the latrines outside. During the night they took some people out and killed them. In the morning when they opened up and let us out I saw dead bodies.

'When Oliver Varney saw me, he said, "Aren't you Mr Macculay's daughter?" I said yes. He said, "Leave her." So they loosened me and sat me in a chair.'

Oliver knew Katumu's father from the sawmill and he respected him.

'That is what saved me, because he had known my father.'

Oliver Varney and his soldiers worked their way through the neighbourhood, house by house, interrogating the civilians and shooting anyone they suspected of sympathising with the government. Katumu was relieved to be untied, but she feared that the rebels would take her away and kill her.

'People were saying that these commanders were looking for little girls to sacrifice. When he said he was going to take me, I started to be afraid.'

Shots echoed between the houses as the soldiers moved along the street.

'That was my first time hearing shooting.'

Oliver Varney took Katumu with him to the NPFL base, known as Stewart Camp, on the edge of town. He told Katumu she would be his bodyguard but she didn't really know what that meant. She was seven years old and very small for her age: she looked like she was barely out of kindergarten. But many of the commanders kept children as companions and good-luck charms. Katumu didn't have a choice. Oliver gave her a pistol and a holster that was too big for her.

'He had a pistol that he assigned to me. He put these trouser suspenders on me. With the rounds for the pistol.'

Katumu was afraid. Stewart Camp was busy and crowded with soldiers and she didn't feel safe. But she slowly realised that she had been given a special position. Oliver Varney reassured her, he took her to meetings, asked her opinion and placed his absolute trust in her. Her size and his power gave her privileges.

'I was the smallest soldier among them, so everyone would

spoil me. If they brought food they would bring it to me. Anything they would loot and they would bring and give it to me.'

Katumu sits forward and her face is animated when she talks about life at the camp, and she nods enthusiastically when I ask questions about Oliver Varney. It's very different from the way she sits when she talks about her family. Any mention of her stepmother is usually delivered with slouched shoulders and hand gestures as if she is trying to flick something away; or she just folds her arms, brooding.

It's not what I was expecting. Many of the child soldiers I have interviewed in other parts of Africa have been so fragile, and some almost unable to communicate. I remember one boy who escaped the Lord's Resistance Army in northern Uganda after being forced to kill an old woman with an axe. He was a skinny, deeply religious kid who spoke with great shame about what he had done. His head was bowed and his mumbled words fell in soft breaths. He was so anxious he was unable to eat and, when he thought no one was watching, he would push the food off his plate.

But for Katumu it was different. In an obscene way, becoming a child soldier was an opportunity. She was a seven-year-old girl who happened to be good at soldiering and her role as a bodyguard gave her responsibility and respect. Bright, energetic and eager to please, she was receiving the attention and acceptance she had been craving from her family. Her reaction says more about how neglected she was than anything else. Oliver Varney and his wife became her surrogate parents. While many other girl soldiers were raped and abused, Katumu continued to enjoy special treatment. Oliver spent a lot of time trying to build up her confidence.

'He and his wife encouraged me and taught me a lot of things. I felt much better with them. I was accepted. I was appreciated. From that time I preferred to be with other people rather [than] my parents. Even now.'

Katumu's father knew she was with the soldiers, but he didn't try to reclaim her. She was one less mouth to feed during the turmoil of the war and he was satisfied that she was being looked after. Many other women and children were also living at Stewart Camp as cooks and companions for the soldiers. The camp was only a short walk from home, but Katumu wasn't going back; she felt happy and secure for the first time in her life. Almost by accident, she realised she had a talent for her new job – she was a fast learner and her small hands made it easy for her to strip and reassemble pistols. She got the weapons ready for the other soldiers when they came under attack and her skill won her even more praise from Oliver Varney.

'One day they had gone out of the compound. I heard launching, heavy artillery sound. So I got the guns where they had them in the sun and re-assembled these pistols. When he came, he asked who had done it. I said it was me. He lifted me up and said I was very smart.'

Oliver Varney was an energetic commander and Katumu had to skip and run to keep up with him, wearing her pistol and holster and old men's suspenders. Soon she was given her own nickname.

'They called me "Over Plus Active", because I was small and always moving.'

Katumu, now a treasured mascot for the group, was one of the smallest child soldiers in the unit. She was assigned an AK-47, but she was so short the weapon dragged along the ground. One of the fighters took the butt off the rifle so she could carry it.

'Because I was short I couldn't really jump in the vehicle. So they just used to take me and throw me in because I was small. Most of the bodyguards were boys, I was the only little girl.'

There was a young bodyguard called Sweet Sweet in a neighbouring unit; he was eight years old.

'Sweet Sweet, he was the driver. He didn't want to hold arms or go on the front and shoot. His interest was driving, so his commander, One Man One, would take him on days they weren't fighting, take him on the football field and teach him to drive. He became so good at driving, he would carry them to the front. Even when they were shooting they couldn't see the driver, the car was just going because he was so small.'

Sweet Sweet would sit on a big stack of cushions while he was driving so he could see over the dashboard. His driving skills spared him from having to fight; he delivered his colleagues to battle and didn't have to pull the trigger himself. But one of the other child bodyguards was fascinated by weapons. His name was Fire Damage, and he was also eight years old.

'Fire Damage, he was another little boy. He liked shooting the guns any time. So they called him Fire Damage. He would just pick the guns up and start shooting all around. Fire Damage even shot Sweet Sweet in his palm. He took Sweet Sweet's gun and while they were fighting he just pulled the trigger and fired Sweet Sweet in the hand. Fire Damage was crazy.'

One small boy who was a bodyguard for another commander was called Stripped Naked.

'He would be the one to take people's clothes off, you know. It was a name he liked, Stripped Naked. Most of the time the names are given to you according to your function.'

Katumu laughs as she talks about Sweet Sweet, Fire Damage and Stripped Naked. It's easy to be swept along, as she jokes about their exploits. But at the same time it's shocking. I try to imagine these small kids armed, often drugged and under the spell of their commanders. Up to 15,000 children were recruited, abducted and thrown into the war across Liberia. The freedom fighters had entire units made up of child soldiers, known as SBU, Small Boys Units. The boys would be forced to go into battle with the other soldiers and they were also used for reconnaissance. The children who were sent to play near enemy lines were expected to return with detailed information.

'The reason they used children is that children are seen as insignificant. You would have children just here playing, but they were observing and watching.'

Katumu was sent to infiltrate a group of enemy soldiers. She spent almost a day with them. They saw her only as a small girl asking for food; she was tiny and shy. But she was gathering intelligence on their weapons and position.

'They didn't know I was a soldier. I ate with them and

everything. I told them I needed to use the restroom. They told me to go in the bush. That is how I escaped. We would go back, tell how many arms, how many men. The small soldiers were used to do that. They would just think that a child was lost from his parents. They would welcome us, not knowing we were on a mission.'

'People are always afraid of children when they hold arms. If a child kills you he will go free, no judging. Because a child is a child. If it's an older person they will ask you, "Why did you do it?" If a child did it, nothing happens.'

It's chilling to listen to Katumu's matter-of-fact descriptions of the war. She speaks as if it is completely logical and normal for children to be carrying out reconnaissance missions. I keep thinking of my nieces in Australia, who are about the same age as Katumu was when she went to war. It's almost impossible to imagine what it must be like for a child to be thrown into that kind of environment, but Katumu flourished and was rewarded with extra power and responsibility. She was not just Oliver Varney's bodyguard, she was his adviser and enforcer. If adult officers or soldiers wanted to speak with Oliver, they had to go through Katumu first. She was seven years old, armed and often arrogant, and she would make other commanders wait if she felt like it.

'Yes, I enjoyed it. Sometimes I would waste people's time. Even if I had time to talk I would say I was busy, wait for me. Or I would just walk off and leave you. So I enjoyed it.'

There was also responsibility. Katumu was expected to contribute to decision-making. When she sat in on important meetings, Oliver asked her advice. She also carried large amounts of money that she used to compensate business owners if the child soldiers from the small boys units stole or vandalised goods at the market.

'It made me proud of myself and it gave me self-esteem. Because if I would say something it had weight. People would tend to listen. It showed me how to be responsible because my commander had trust in me. He trusted me and I kept that trust. Some of these small soldiers would misbehave in the community. People would be selling and they would just take their goods. They would take and not pay. If I had some of his cash I would just pay for it, when he comes or wakes up I would say so and so caused trouble and I paid for it.'

Katumu went into battle for the first time before her eighth birthday.

'When we started going to the front, I was at the back. I would have a loaded gun and three magazines. He would shoot; when his was empty he would send it back to me. That is what I was doing. Later I got brave and I could go and start fighting.'

The fighting was fast and chaotic; most of the soldiers from both sides weren't trained properly. Wounded and lost child soldiers were often left behind during battle and they had to find their way to the nearest village and retrace their unit. The jungle was deep and disorientating, a frightening battleground, the vegetation so thick it was almost impossible to see the enemy. Katumu was terrified.

'I was afraid. I was in shock. But I had to be brave. We call it "do or die". We had to make ourselves brave to be able to withstand it. If you are not brave and start slacking back, the enemy will capture you. When they capture you, they will really treat you bad. Our unit, we call ourselves Jungle Fire, Men Dropping, Men Moving. Even if people drop, you have to keep on. We had to live up to that name.'

Katumu had some protection because she was crouched behind Oliver during the fighting. But she was scared of being hit by stray bullets, nicknamed AWOLs by the child soldiers. They cracked through the jungle as fighters from both sides fired wildly. Many of the soldiers wore good-luck charms to protect themselves. Oliver had a jacket that he always wore into battle; it had been blessed and doused with traditional potions. The process was known as cooking – if a jacket was 'cooked', soldiers believed it was bulletproof. Oliver took off his cooked jacket and gave it to Katumu during a battle.

'When a lot of our men were getting killed or wounded on the front, he started taking precautions with me. This jacket, he put it on me. It was woven. They dyed it black, brown, white, cream colour. They put buttons and other little fetishes on it. They already cooked the jacket for bullet protection. When I put it on, I could hear bullets whizzing by me. I would hear, phoom, phoom, bullets passing. After we stopped fighting, when I took it off, you could see holes all in it. But nothing hit me.'

Katumu was small and the jacket was big and heavy, but she wore it every time she went to fight. The other child soldiers would also clutch their own good-luck charms and wear their own 'cooked' clothing. Their commanders assured them they wouldn't die if they were shot, anyway. Oliver told Katumu his jacket would not only make her bulletproof, it would also make her invisible – and she believed him.

'It could make me disappear. I could be walking around here and you would not see me. I would see you and hear you, but you would not see me when I was among you here. One time I got missing in action. They left me behind. So, wearing the jacket, I came in the enemy camp. None of them saw me. They were all loading their weapons, filling their magazines. Nobody saw me.'

I look over at Katumu. 'That's impossible,' I tell her. 'The jacket can't make you invisible.'

She shrugs her shoulders and looks me in the eye. Her expression is neutral rather than defiant, as if to tell me she believes in the jacket and couldn't care less whether I do or not.

'It's true.'

The next morning the interpreter and I drive to the junction and pick up Katumu from the market. She's waiting for us by the roadside. We've hired an old taxi to take us to Tubmanburg, where Katumu grew up. It's the first time she's gone back since she was a child. She hasn't seen her family in more than nine years. Tubmanburg is only a few hours' drive away and Katumu could afford the journey but she's put it off.

She seems excited and a bit nervous. She's dressed in a new outfit: tight jeans and a matching denim jacket with criss-crossed leather laces. We both sit on the back seat, and she fidgets and ties the laces on her pants in neat bows.

The taxi stammers through the traffic. The roads on the outskirts of Monrovia are narrow, potholed and crowded, with cars and minibuses competing for space. Police attempt to control the chaos, but most drivers ignore them when they try to pull them over, because they want to avoid paying a fine or a bribe. Market stalls and sellers with goods balanced on their heads spill into the traffic. We drive through an area known as Red Light; the lone traffic light doesn't work anymore, but the name has stuck. Katumu starts pointing out of the window as we drive past a petrol station near a supermarket.

'This is where we used to leave our vehicles and walk to the fighting.'

Katumu smiles and her eyes sparkle with delight when she talks about the anarchy and excitement of the warfare. It was not a conventional conflict with trained armies; instead, there were thousands of children and teenagers armed with automatic weapons and grenade launchers fighting for the city. Katumu describes the battles at a fast pace, almost like a cartoon, even making sound effects when she points out where grenades and shells landed. But she only tells half a story. She gives away few intimate details of what it was really like for her as a child in the middle of it all, for whom the war was tantalising and repulsive all at once.

We pass a corner known as Chocolate City Junction, where one of the generals had his headquarters; there are still some bullet holes in the buildings. Then we drive over the Stockton Creek Bridge, which was the site of some of the heaviest fighting. Katumu laughs and points at the bushes next to the bridge where she had to jump to avoid a rocket-propelled grenade. 'To cross this bridge was not a small thing,' she says.

During the war this bridge was the no-man's land between the two sides, and the roads leading up to it were slippery with thousands of spent bullet shells. The lightpoles are still riddled with jagged holes from the bullets and grenades, giving the metal the appearance of a cheese grater. It's an indicator of just how heavy the fighting was. The lightpoles are narrow, but they were hit hundreds of times because so many rounds were being fired.

We've been driving through the traffic for more than an hour and we still haven't got out of the city. A large sign on the entrance to Monrovia's port proclaims, 'Gateway to Liberia's Economy'. But the port is surrounded by high fences and razor-wire and jobless young men walk past carrying boxes of nail polish and fake fingernails. They work in teams, giving pedicures and manicures to any middle-class women who can afford their services. It's the only business they have. The economy is literally dead.

It feels eerie as we drive out into the countryside: there are almost no farms, no crops, no livestock. The war has gutted the rural areas; we only see five cows and four goats during a whole day on the road. People fled their farms during the fighting and their animals fed hungry soldiers. Agriculture is virtually non-existent and most of the rural areas are now just overgrown jungle. It's quiet and unnerving. There's little traffic on the road and many towns that were damaged during the fighting have almost been swallowed by the bush. We cross an old railway line that cuts across our path and we can see that it disappears into the jungle within a metre of each side of the road.

During the war, Katumu would rarely travel along this road. The soldiers kept to the bush tracks because they feared being ambushed if they dared to take the main highway. She also knew she was a target. The child bodyguards were sought-after trophies for enemy soldiers. They believed that if they could catch Katumu, they could undermine Oliver Varney.

'I was a target for many of them. Many people believe I was his medicine, his charm, his good luck. So if they get me they would get him. So I had to be very careful and not put myself in harm's way. They targeted me to get to him.'

Oliver decided to take Katumu away from the frontline and send her to a training camp with other NPFL recruits. The fighters were taken from schools, villages, marketplaces and homes, and dragged into the ranks of Charles Taylor's army. Katumu was one of the smallest girls on the six-month training course and she struggled to keep up with the adult recruits.

'At first, the first two days I had a very hard time. But I just said to myself, this is where I am now. I overcame that. I endured that. They taught us to be a commander one day. How to address your men. How to put your soldiers in order and things like that. I did well in that. I was seven. It made me to be able to stand up and talk. My shyness went away. I had the guts to be able to stand up and tell him how I felt. I could tell anybody. It did something good for me in that way.'

Katumu wasn't afraid to speak out. While she was willing to kill on the battlefield, she refused to take part in paybacks and punishments of fellow child soldiers.

'A young boy had stolen some liquor from a general called Next to God. The general told me to kill this boy. I said, "You can jail me for 72 hours. I would rather stay in a jail. If someone attacks us I can kill him before he kills me. But not because somebody stole liquor." So I didn't do it and he ordered someone else to kill the boy and the boy was killed.'

When I ask Katumu about whether she killed anyone on the battlefield, she doesn't give me a direct answer. She tells me that when she shot in the jungle it was hard to know where the bullets went. She stares back at me defiantly in order to push my questions away. I get the same reaction when I ask her about whether she was offered drugs and alcohol.

She seems relieved when we finally drive into Tubmanburg. Her eyes scan back and forth as we go slowly along the main street. She tells the driver to turn left, and the car revs and tilts as we try to get through the potholes. Katumu's smile is getting bigger.

'Stop. It's this one.'

We pull up outside a broken-down house with an empty hammock swinging on the front veranda. Katumu grew up here and this is the house from where Oliver Varney abducted her. She takes us down an alley to the back where several old women and an old man are gutting fish and peeling vegetables. They look up and stare at Katumu, but there is no recognition. They look at her as though she's a stranger – then her uncle hurries to his feet and takes both of her hands.

'Katumu?'

He hasn't seen her for nine years. The family thought she had died in the war because they have had no news of her. The old women stand up and look at her with disbelief. She seems to enjoy their reaction as they touch her and look at her. She is well dressed, plump and carrying a cellphone, but they are wiry, dirty and barefoot. There is embarrassment for them, pride for Katumu. I'm trying to make sense of the gestures and the silences. Katumu seems caught somewhere between wanting to embrace her old relatives and wanting to punish them for not taking care of her when she was a child. She talks with them for a few minutes, then she wants to go.

We drive to Stewart Camp, where Katumu lived as Oliver Varney's bodyguard. Initially Katumu seems a bit disorientated because it's changed since she lived here. Most of the buildings are crumbling and some have been overgrown. Squatter families have moved in and smoke from their cooking fires wafts from doorless doorways and windowless window holes. Hungry children squat quietly next to their mothers, waiting for something to eat.

A teenage boy guides us to the back of the camp where Oliver Varney's headquarters used to be. Katumu poses for some photographs. She is solemn. This is where she spent a lot of her time as a child soldier and by the age of nine she was an accomplished fighter. But the war was changing. Charles Taylor was becoming suspicious of some of his commanders; he didn't know whom he could trust. He took brutal action against anyone suspected of disloyalty. In this dangerous climate, rumours started circulating that Oliver Varney was sympathetic to his opponents. Taylor ordered his execution and suddenly Oliver – Katumu's protector and surrogate father – was dead.

'Charles Taylor had him killed because of rumours he was conniving with enemies. Selling arms to other factions. They caught him and killed him.

'I was closer to Oliver than I was to my own father. I hardly ate. It had a real effect on me. When you have somebody who is your main support, your backup who is taken from you, you just feel dejected. You are left alone. That is how I felt. The loss of Oliver dampened the whole spirit and zeal I had to fight.'

Katumu still speaks of him with a lot of loyalty and longing. He gave her the love, self-esteem and sense of belonging she didn't get from her relatives. She was prepared to follow him into battle, just to be with him and to fulfil his expectations. She would rather have gone to the frontline than return to her family. Her role as Oliver's bodyguard gave her the self-confidence she had been lacking. But when he died, she quickly saw it wasn't soldiering itself that fulfilled her; without Oliver, it meant nothing.

When Oliver was killed, she left the fighting and went north to Gbanga where she met with friends and started working in the market. As a nine-year-old she was travelling across the border to Guinea, buying clothes and reselling them in Liberia. She had never been to school but she had a natural talent for business and she quickly made a profit

'I was doing small business. I was selling fish and foodstuffs in the market in Gbanga. I went on to Lofa, which is in the northern part. I would go across the border to Guinea and buy clothing, materials and bring it and sell it. I was staying with friends.'

Katumu decided to stay in the north rather than return to Tubmanburg. She had no interest in going back and, anyway, she wasn't sure whether her family had been displaced by the war. While Katumu was criss-crossing the border for business, the war was worsening. The NPFL attacked West African peacekeepers in Monrovia, who responded by launching a series of bombing raids. The heavy fighting was followed by a ceasefire and an unsuccessful attempt in 1993 to establish a transitional government. The conflict continued.

By the time Katumu reached the age of fourteen, her friends started to notice that she was putting on weight. She was pregnant.

'People used to make fun of me. Even when I went to the clinic the doctors and nurses would ask me why I was so small and pregnant. I would say it was not my fault, I didn't know anything. It just happened to me.'

The boy who had slept with her quickly abandoned her. Her friends gave her traditional medicines to try to abort the pregnancy, but Katumu was determined to go ahead with it. She wanted to start her own family. She bought a bath set and baby clothes, and prayed every night that she would give birth to a daughter.

'I was excited, thinking of names. I thought, if it is a girl, when I deliver I will name it Musu. That was my mother's name.'

But Katumu started to feel pain in her belly just before the baby was due. Her body was sore for almost a week as the contractions stopped and started. Some of the old women in the market said it was just false labour, but Katumu went to the hospital. She knew something was wrong. The doctor examined her and told her the baby had already died inside her. She was taken into the operating room, where they performed a Caesarean to remove the dead baby.

'They didn't show me the baby's body. It was hard for me. They didn't give it to me to bury. They just took it. They said it was a boy. But they never showed me, nothing.'

She woke up in the ward where other women were nursing newborn babies. Katumu was alone; she didn't have a baby to show for all the months of pregnancy.

'I used to be crying in the morning because it was an open ward. The other women had their babies. I would be crying and the nurses would talk to me.'

Katumu clasps the sides of her chair with her hands as she talks. She tells the story of the death of her baby in stiff sentences. She looks down and impatiently slides her sandals back and forth.

A year after she lost the baby, she met a boy called Tony. He was long-legged and thin, and his friends called him Skinny; he was also a soldier with Charles Taylor's forces. He'd been watching Katumu from a distance and gradually got the courage to start talking to her. Initially she pushed him away because she didn't want another boyfriend who might abandon her. She was afraid of losing him.

'I said I hope this one doesn't leave me. That fear didn't stay with me for long.'

Tony was gentle and persistent, and he nurtured Katumu. They made a promise to each other that they would stay together for life. Almost two years after she lost her first baby, Katumu was pregnant to Tony. He fussed over her as her belly grew bigger and on 1 November 1999, she had a baby boy. Tony and his friends crowded into the hospital ward and celebrated the arrival. The baby was called Tony, to honour his young father.

'I wanted a boy because Tony's father wanted a boy. He brought his friends. He brought a tape with music playing. They were all dancing. Happy.'

In September 2000, Charles Taylor launched a large offensive against rebels in the north. Tony and Katumu were called back to the frontline to fight. Baby Tony was cared for by a relative in Monrovia.

Tony Senior joined Taylor's troops who were based along the border with neighbouring Ivory Coast. The soldiers stopped to change a flat tyre on their vehicle, when suddenly a shot rang out. One of the small boys had accidentally shot Tony while he was changing the wheel. The child soldier's rifle shot Tony through the leg. The bullet damaged his femoral artery and he started bleeding heavily. He died on the way to hospital. Katumu was based nearby and she tried to reach him before he died, but it was too late. She confronted the boy who shot him.

'I almost killed him, the little boy. I was very, very angry. But, Tony had liked the little boy. Before he passed out and died he said they shouldn't do anything to him, it was a mistake. His last wish was they shouldn't do anything to the boy. He was a French boy, they just called him Small Soldier. He was eight years old.'

The shooting happened close to the frontline. Katumu tried to see Tony's body but the fighting started again. The hurried funeral procession was broken up by enemy gunfire.

'They were burying him when people attacked them. They just halfway buried him and everyone ran away. They took a few pictures. I have two. One when they were bathing the body and one when he was in the casket. Even now I miss him. When I think about him I am just sad.'

As Katumu talks, I can see the sadness is still there. There's also anger at her loss. It's her most vulnerable moment so far in the interview. I try to ask about Tony as gently as possible; Katumu's words of reply are interspersed with long breaths.

After Tony's death, Katumu went back to Monrovia and started selling clothes and slippers to make a living. One of Charles Taylor's generals came looking for her and other fighters to return to the front. He was driving a pickup truck through Monrovia searching for the former child soldiers when he saw Katumu walking along the street.

'General Musa saw me. I tried to dodge them in between the drugstore. He took a gun and gave it to me. He said, "You were fighting before. You better come and help us to fight now. They are advancing." I said no. I sent the gun back and he sent it back again. He brought the pickup truck and told me to get inside.'

Katumu was taken back to the frontline. The loss of Oliver Varney and Tony had destroyed her desire to fight and she had no interest in the war.

'The whole thing had turned sour for me now. When they would bring fuel for everybody to clean their guns, I wouldn't do mine. I would say it was okay. But when we would go to the frontline I would say mine was not working, just to make excuses not to fight. Some of them would say to me, "Are you afraid to go and die? Don't you want to go on the front?" and I would say, "Yes, scared people live longer and the brave will die. So you can go ahead."'

By March 2003, Charles Taylor's opponents had advanced to within 10 kilometres of Monrovia. One of the most brutal and intense campaigns of the war was about to begin. Katumu and thousands of other fighters were trying to defend the capital. They were cut off in pockets of the city and civilians were stranded in the middle of the gunfire. It was chaotic as drug-fuelled child soldiers from both sides fought from street to street.

'Monrovia was very crazy at that time. No food, no water, no gas. People were cut off. Families on that side, some on this side. People died from running stomach. It was just crazy.'

It was a bizarre battlefield. Fighters from both sides were pumped with drugs, in a haze of violence and superstition. Many of the teenage soldiers wore wigs and charms, designed to trick the bullets into another direction. Some of the boys were dressed in women's clothing and others wore small pieces of mirror in the desperate belief it would confuse the shots heading their way. The cross-dressing rebels were fighting a mad war that had long since lost its political foundations. They strutted through the streets cradling their weapons, wearing combat T-shirts, brightly coloured miniskirts and make-up.

Pressure was intensifying on Charles Taylor to step down as president after he was indicted on war crimes charges for his role in the gruesome war in neighbouring Sierra Leone. His opponents were closing in. By July 2003, Monrovia was surrounded and both sides were fighting for control of the port and the main entrances to the city. The bridges were killing zones. Katumu was a commander leading a group of Taylor's female fighters near the Stockton Creek Bridge.

'People are more afraid of women fighters than men. Because women are more hard to deal with than the men. An enemy, they could easily bribe a man or get by him. But a woman, she will stand her ground. She will not let go. Even in battle, women are more fierce.'

Hundreds of civilians died: some were killed in the fighting, others fell from hunger and disease. Liberians begged the outside world for help and in a desperate plea they dragged the bodies of dozens of victims to the US embassy and dumped them outside. The US was reluctant to get involved. Nigerian peacekeepers finally arrived in August and thousands of people poured onto the streets to greet them. Fighters from both sides were exhausted and were looking for a way to end the senseless warfare.

'We were happy because you could even be brothers and sisters looking at each other fighting for different factions, shooting each other. A lot of lives were lost senselessly. We were happy for peace to come. Most of us were tired of fighting, anyway.'

Charles Taylor's reign was over. He went on national television dressed in his trademark white safari suit and announced he was stepping down. Katumu and other Taylor supporters drove in a procession to the airport. The war had ended.

'We escorted him to Roberts Field. We just took him as far as the fence of the airport. There was just a crowd of people. The generals, everyone was in there crying. It was a sad time. We just turned around and came back.'

Katumu had been fighting for Charles Taylor since the age of seven; she was taken into his ranks long before she knew what he stood for. He was a warlord who led his people deeper into poverty and combat. It wasn't a conflict of ideology – many people found themselves on one side or the other by chance, plucked from their villages and forced to fight. Power changed hands and when the fighting ended, Katumu was on the losing side. Charles Taylor was forced into exile in Nigeria and his supporters were ridiculed.

'In the neighbourhood, people would make fun of us. They said Charles Taylor, he is no longer here. We will see how you will live. We would just go inside and close the door.'

Katumu felt relieved but vulnerable as she handed in her weapon. She found a place to sleep in the compound of one of her former generals. Many of the former fighters gathered together to block out the hostility of outsiders. There were dozens of young ex-combatants living in the compound, and many slid into a numbing routine of drugs and alcohol. Others tried to find work, but there was little for them. Most had never been to school, the economy was in pieces and people were afraid of them. There was a mood of hopelessness.

One morning there was a knock at the gate of the general's compound. Three middle-aged churchgoing ladies in neat dresses said they wanted to speak with the former female soldiers. Katumu had been asleep and she got up and walked to the gate to see what was going on. The church ladies said they were opening a home for the ex-combatants, and they were offering job training and accommodation. Katumu was suspicious. She thought the women were going to try to make money out of the former soldiers. Some of the girls reluctantly decided to check it out and eventually Katumu cooled down and agreed to go and have a look at the centre. She had nothing to lose.

'I took just a few of my clothes put in a plastic bag just to try. I said even if the people will be eating money off my back, I will learn a skill, then at least my skill will stay with me.'

The early days at the girls' home were pure anarchy. The former fighters were used to a life of drugs, alcohol, fighting and looting. Some of them broke out of the home using the ladders from their bunk beds to climb over the walls; others smuggled in booze and boys.

'Yes, we were wild. We would fight with knives, take sticks. We would curse the counsellors, attempt to fight them. [Girls] would run away, jump over the fence. Yes, many would escape, even [though] there was broken glass on the top.'

Katumu wasn't really interested in the chaos or in drugs and alcohol. She was bitter and tired after so many years on the front-line. She was irritated when other girls tried to disrupt the classes, and she decided to ignore them and concentrate.

'I said, "I know why I came here. I came to learn something. So I will stay here until I get what I came for." I was very excited about the tailoring classes. I paid close attention to my teacher. Anything he would do I would go and do it exactly right. I paid keen attention and I learned.'

The home was set up by the three Liberian ladies: Rosie, a nurse; Doris, a teacher; and Gladys, a social worker. They were terrified as they went around Monrovia looking for former female soldiers to join their program. They had few resources, but lots of determination. They feared that if nothing was done, the former child soldiers would become an extremely destructive force in an already fragile nation. Rosie laughs when she tells the story, and admits she and the other women were afraid.

'Yes, we were a bit apprehensive. I looked at Gladys, she looked at me. I looked at Doris. We didn't say anything. The former combatants tend to live together in groups and bands. They say, nobody wants us so we will be with each other. They are very suspicious of people. Living that way too they are a threat to the security of the community. When they are shunned so much they are going to come in and commit these crimes. They just stand in that street at the market and they dare anyone to move them. There is no place for even people to walk. They have blocked the whole sidewalk. You can't tell them anything. They are so abusive. They will hit your car and throw things at people. Something has to be done so that we can live together. If we shun them away we are going to have this big gap and their little ones are going to be even more violent than they are. The danger is Liberia will not have any educated, sociable people. It is going to be total anarchy and chaos.'

Rosie has been my interpreter for the past week's interviews with Katumu. She is immaculately dressed in a bright African kaftan and her hair is smoothed into a neat ponytail. She is in her fifties, but her shiny brown skin barely has any lines. She has a kind face, and she shakes her head and laughs when I ask her about meeting Katumu for the first time.

'She was the one that gave us the most trouble. She was very mean looking, very serious. Her whole face was just tied in a knot. You could tell from her walk, her demeanour, that she is a military woman. People fear them still, they feel these girls are a threat to them. People have marked them. Nobody really wants to come around them. People are afraid, most of the time they ask, "How did you get them?" As if they are untouchable. That is how people act.'

The girls' home became a sanctuary for the former fighters. Their wild escape missions eventually subsided and they immersed themselves in their training, learning how to sew, bake, read and write. Their graduation was big news and officials from the United Nations mission in Liberia were among the VIP guests. Rosie saw it as a chance to break down the stereotypes of the girls as fearsome and rough. Some of the girls were invited to speak on the local UN radio station, and Rosie accompanied them. They apologised for their behaviour during the war. Katumu spoke live on air.

'She said, "I am a beautiful woman. I know I can be somebody good for Liberia tomorrow. So I want you all to forgive me for all the bad I did. It was war and it was the situation that caused me to do that. From today I have promised myself and the Liberian people that I will do my best."'

It's a promise Katumu struggles to keep every day – the end of the war has delivered peace, but also boredom and the temptation to fall into crime and drugs. While some of her former colleagues dropped out of the course, Katumu graduated first in her class with enough skills to start making a living.

'I can buy flour and make bread. When people are having parties they come to me and I make cakes and they pay for it. It makes me feel good about myself. I go to the market in the morning. I buy plantain, hotdogs, fish, meat, and I make roasted meat on coals. I fry plantain. I make little doughnuts at the junction here. Also, I buy crushed rocks from people who pound them. I sell them to people who are doing construction.'

Katumu explains her business operations as if every young woman knows how to buy and sell crushed rocks for the construction industry. I really admire her self-sufficiency. There is no social security in Liberia and few jobs, so people get by any way they can. Katumu and some of the other women at the market have set up a cooperative. They put money aside each month and take turns in receiving the lump sum; this is the money Katumu uses to buy the crushed rocks.

She's still very young and I wonder how difficult it will be for her to continue the daily slog of earning a living when many of her former comrades are making much more money from selling sex or drugs. It must be very hard for Katumu to spend twelve to fifteen hours a day working at a market stall just to get enough money to eat. It's a steady but boring life compared with the anarchy of the war. Then, if she wanted something, she could just take it. Now she has to earn it and there's not much opportunity to move forward. For the rest of her life she could be sitting at the same market stall selling food and buying rocks, watching another family raise her son. I wouldn't really blame her if she went off the rails. She has less status and responsibility now than she did as a seven-year-old child soldier and bodyguard.

Katumu makes enough money to rent a single room next to the market, but she's embarrassed to take me inside. She pretends she can't find the key and looks at me with eyes that urge me to back off. I nod. The building is dirty and run-down. There's no running water, so buckets line the corridor. Some of the people in the market don't know she was a fighter; she prefers to be known as a businesswoman. Katumu sits at her market stall until late in the evening. The hours are long and the profits are small. On quiet afternoons, she sometimes packs up her stall and walks down the track to see Tony.

'He is very important in my life. I am the father, I am the mother for him. I am the everything.'

I ask her if Tony will come to live with her when her business starts to grow and she has more money to look after him. She shakes her head and looks firmly into my eyes. Tony will grow up with his foster family, she's already made the decision; she wants him to be in a safe, steady home. Katumu fears that if war ever starts again, a new generation of generals will go looking on the streets for a new generation of child soldiers.

'I know what I passed through. I wouldn't allow them to do that to Tony. I lost my childhood. I am totally against people using children as soldiers or even training them. They would not take their own children but other people's children, and take them on the front. Look at me. It was just a big waste for me. That was thirteen years out of my life. I could have been doing something positive. Even up until now they have my name on the roster of the Armed Forces of Liberia, but I am not going there. I don't want to hear about army or any soldiers.'

Katumu doesn't seem ashamed of what she did during the war, rather that she took part in it at all. She can now see how pointless it was and how destructive for the country. While the war introduced her to some of the people she's treasured most, it also took them away, one by one.

We walk down onto the beach to take some photographs. It's

windy, and Katumu and Tony hold hands and squint to keep the grit out of their eyes. As they sit on the edge of the grass with their feet resting on the warm sand, Tony chatters about news from school and snippets of games with his foster sisters. Katumu breathes in every word, listening with her head tilted.

'Sometimes I have a feeling to want [to] be with my mother. That mother feeling comes. Other mothers come around their daughters. If their daughters have babies, their mothers take care of them. But I don't have anyone like that. When I see them with their children I feel that longing.'

Katumu brushes the sand off Tony's feet before he walks carefully across the prickly grass and the muddy road to his foster home. He doesn't kiss her goodbye, just gently lets go of her hand and smiles. His foster sisters are playing under a tree at the back of the house: one is pretending to be a preacher, the others sit on a log listening to the sermon. Katumu watches Tony as he takes his place in the game. She has these moments and the chatter rolling in her mind as she goes back to her hotdog stand at the junction. People walk through the smoke of her cooking fire as they do every evening. Most of her customers don't know about her life as a mother and a soldier.

'I am a strong woman. Very strong. I would never fight again.'

On 16 January 2006, Ellen Johnson-Sirleaf was sworn in as Liberia's president and became Africa's first elected female leader.

In March 2006, Charles Taylor was taken into custody by the Special Court for Sierra Leone to face a range of charges, including having committed crimes against humanity.

CHAPTER 6

EUGENIE MUHAYIMANA

Genocide survivor

RWANDA

Eugenie Muhayimana survived the Rwandan genocide, one of the most horrific events of the twentieth century. Her entire family was killed. She was held hostage and gang-raped by Hutu gunmen for almost three months. Her captors then took her to the jungles of the Congo for more than three years. She endured hunger, disease and brutality.

Eugenie gave birth to two children fathered by the rapists. She was eventually freed but was diagnosed with HIV.

Eugenie refuses to give up. Her story is one of determination, faith and survival.

DEMOCRATIC
REPUBLIC
OF CONGO
UGANDA
N
W
E
S
Goma
Gisenyi
RWANDA
Lake
Kivu
KIGALI
Kibuye
TANZANIA
BURUNDI
0
SCALE
75
Kilometres

Waiting to meet a new interpreter is a bit like going on a date. Feeling nervous, I walk into the hotel café and see a young man sitting at one of the tables. He's handsome enough to make me feel shy when I shake his hand. His name is Gabriel, and he's a local journalist who has agreed to help me for the next two weeks. He was recommended by a colleague and we've already been in email contact for several months. I asked him to find me a woman who is willing to be interviewed about surviving the Rwandan genocide. He sent a reply with one-paragraph summaries of half a dozen women he'd interviewed. At the top of the list was Eugenie.

'That's the one I would choose,' he says. 'She is very strong.'

Gabriel is dressed in trendy jeans and sneakers, but he's not flashy. The cuffs of his jeans carry the pale mud of Kigali's back-streets. He speaks gently and I trust him. We go outside the hotel and look for a taxi. Kigali is an unadorned, hardworking city that spreads across the long, narrow valleys and the rounded hills.

Eugenie Muhayimana lives on a hill on the outskirts, where the rain crosses from the green valleys to the city and the clucking of chickens mixes with the hum of the suburbs. Her house is along a narrow, muddy path between two hedges; the mud is sticky like peanut butter. Children run up the alley to tell her we are on the way.

When we arrive, Eugenie is mopping the floor of her house, as heavy rain has left big puddles in the hallway. She is lean, tall and beautiful: her features are almost feline and she has the understated beauty of someone who doesn't really know they are beautiful. She giggles shyly and fusses with the curtains to draw attention away from herself as Gabriel introduces her. When she sits down, her hands flop back and forth in her lap more than she seems conscious of.

The walls of Eugenie's living room are painted tropical blue and the floor is grey cement. Old chairs with torn red vinyl cushions are lined up against one wall and we sit opposite on a wooden lounge suite with embroidered yellow headrests. An AIDS calendar decorates the wall between the windows. It's a simple, clean room. A neat Bible sits on the table in the corner.

Eugenie's two children come inside and shake hands. Claude is ten years old and his sister, Claudine, is seven. They are dressed for the weather in jeans, jackets and sneakers; it's wet, cold and muddy outside. The children whisper questions into Eugenie's ear and she answers them gently before they go to play on the veranda.

Eugenie was born on Christmas Day 1973 in Kibuye, one of the most beautiful parts of Rwanda. It's a place of lush valleys and peaks, a kind land that nurtured bananas, cattle and vegetables.

'We were quite wealthy. We had a big banana plantation. I grew up happy. Really very happy. We still had many relatives. We would visit them and meet them. It was a happy childhood.'

There were six children, of whom Eugenie was the second. Her father, Joseph, ran the farm and worked as a manager at a nearby mine. He was famous for his parties: neighbours would come together to help with planting or harvesting and when the work was over, Joseph would let the beer flow. His brown eyes were sparkling and full of fun, and he had a long beard.

'I don't think he ever cut his beard. I don't know, there were not many men with such long beards. We had relatives in Congo and Burundi, he often went there. Maybe he learned it from them. We liked it a lot as kids, we liked to see our father with a long beard. Sometimes we played around with it.

'My father was a very social person, he would invite neighbours and other people to share beer with him. This would happen very often at our place, he also prayed a lot. You know, Catholics can mix a bit of drinking and prayers.

'When my father drank, he started singing. He even had his own songs about his cows. People who have a lot of cows in Rwanda always have songs for their cows, so he always sang a lot, very loudly. Everyone from the neighbourhood would be there, when everyone [was] partying we couldn't tell that there was a difference between Hutus and Tutsis.'

Eugenie and her family were Tutsis and most of their neighbours were Hutus, but they co-existed without much trouble. The majority of the Tutsis and Hutus were living, praying and working together. Eugenie didn't even know she was a Tutsi until she was a teenager.

'The first time we came across the Hutu–Tutsi ethnic divide was when I was in my fifth year of primary school. They sent us to get identity cards. They checked your dad's file and checked what ethnic group he was and that's what they put on your identity card. I didn't know before then that I was Tutsi. I didn't know at all. Between the Hutus and the Tutsis, I didn't see anything. I just saw that we were the same people. I had not even noticed their badness at the time.'

Hutus and Tutsis shared a common language, religion and culture, but their differences were exacerbated by jealousy and injustice. European colonialists regarded the fine features, height and lighter skin of the Tutsis as signs of superiority, while the shorter, darker Hutus were stereotyped as less capable. Some Hutus resented the fact that Tutsis were receiving preferential treatment from the colonial administrators.

It began a cycle of attacks and reprisals. In 1959, Hutu activists staged their own revolution to remove Tutsis from power and carry out a campaign of violence across the country. Rwanda became a republic in 1961 and, for the next three decades, thousands of civilians were killed or displaced as Hutu and Tutsi activists answered each other's attacks with more violence. By the 1990s, the seeds of the genocide were already being sown. Bloodletting, distrust and division were all part of a deadly mixture. Discrimination became a component of everyday life.

Tutsi families noticed that their children were receiving poor results in their exams, no matter how hard they studied; pupils who had topped their class throughout primary school were denied the chance to go on to high school and university. The exams were marked nationally and students were forced to write their ethnicity next to their name on the front page.

Eugenie was a clever student who worked hard and did well, but when the exam results for her final year of primary school came through, she had failed. She was ordered to repeat the year, so she studied hard and did well during the school terms, but when the final results came back, she had failed again.

'Of course, it wasn't a surprise, but I was still angry. I can't tell you how discouraged I was. When my parents saw my results, they just said, "Well, there is not anything we can do about it." I was comforted by the fact that there were others who were like me. Neighbours who had also performed well in school but failed their exams. So when I failed, I just thought of all these others.

'I thought maybe I have a chance that they may forget I was a Tutsi. They might mistake me for a Hutu or something might happen that would make me go through. Or even if they don't take me, at least I might pass. Maybe they might give out my place to someone else, but I am still going to pass. But I didn't.'

Life was slowly changing for Eugenie's family. The discrimination began as something official and far away but it soon became local. The banana beer parties held by Eugenie's father stopped and people began to keep to themselves. Hutus and Tutsis didn't mix as they used to. The Tutsis started to fear for their safety.

In October 1990 the Tutsi-led Rwandan Patriotic Front

invaded Rwanda and, in response, Tutsis were massacred in several regions, including Eugenie's home of Kibuye. Eugenie was sent to school across the border in Zaire, and when she and other schoolgirls were crossing back to Rwanda at the end of each term they were subjected to increasing threats from Rwandan security forces. The Tutsi girls were called *inyenzi*, or cockroaches, by the border guards who taunted them.

Thousands of young Hutu men were joining the Interahamwe, a militia group made up of those who pledged to 'stand together and fight together'. Many of the recruits were unemployed youths or street boys who were easily swept up in the anti-Tutsi frenzy. The Interahamwe were responsible for much of the killing during the genocide – they had the muscle power needed to carry it out.

As the situation worsened, in 1993 a new radio station, Radio Télévision Libre des Mille Collines, started broadcasting anti-Tutsi messages. It was a streetwise station that became popular among the young men who would later take part in the genocide. Many Tutsis felt frightened, but didn't fully understand what was to come. The government was importing massive stocks of arms: everything from grenades to thousands of machetes. Hutu militias were being trained and organised. The preparations for the genocide were already under way.

On the night of 6 April 1994, a plane carrying the Rwandan President, Juvenal Habyarimana, was shot down. It was the spark the Hutu extremists had been waiting for; they blamed Tutsis for the assassination. The killing was about to begin.

That night, Eugenie was in the capital, Kigali, far away from her family in Kibuye. She was spending her school holidays teaching French to the daughter of a middle-class family. She was twenty years old. It had taken her several extra years to finish her schooling, because she was failed so many times for being a Tutsi. She was full of fear as she sat listening to the radio. Unconfirmed reports of the President's death were starting to spread.

'That is what I remember about that night. I immediately felt afraid. When I heard it was the President who had been assassinated, I knew we were going to die. That was the only thing that I thought about. I knew this was now death.'

The killing started within hours and went on through the night. Hutu gangs set up roadblocks and set about slaughtering Tutsis. Eugenie couldn't leave the house and she didn't know if she could trust the family she was staying with. The husband was European, but his wife, Beatrice, was a Hutu, and Hutu gunmen were already gathering in the compound of the house.

'[Beatrice] said, "There are a lot of men out there who want to rape you. The other girls from the neighbourhood have been killed. Some have been buried alive. If they are only going to rape you and not to kill you, I think it is better than what the other women in the neighbourhood have experienced."'

Beatrice spoke to Eugenie in a kind voice, but her motives were unclear. If she had really wanted to protect Eugenie she could have hidden her in the roof or elsewhere in the compound, but if she wanted to abandon her completely she could have left her to the gunmen. Beatrice could have put herself in danger if she protected Eugenie fully, so she allowed the Hutu gangs to come inside.

'It took about 30 minutes before the first gang came in. I think it was about ten o'clock or eleven in the morning, the day after the President was shot down. When they came, I was sitting in the living room. Beatrice said, "Eugenie, you have been visited." I remember those are the words that she used. "You have been visited." They were walking behind her. She was leading them in. They looked at me and said, "Hey, we just got ourselves a vegetable." They said, "We've killed all the other Tutsi girls you know around. We just killed them. You are lucky we are going to keep you alive. We want to see what the vagina of a Tutsi woman looks like."'

The gang members were carrying rifles, machetes and sticks, and it was obvious that they were still high from a night of killing. They took Eugenie from the living room and pushed her into her bedroom. She was so afraid, she could hardly walk.

'When they got me into the room, there was this very fat guy who said, "Undress very fast. We want see what you have. Don't waste our time. We want to go and continue killing the others. We don't want any of them to escape." He pulled down my pants. Then he started raping me. When he finished, others also came. They were queuing up outside the door. One would finish and then the other one would get in.

'By the time they started raping me I think I had lost my mind. I don't think I even knew what was going on. I wasn't thinking anymore. In my mind I was dead. I thought they were definitely going to kill me.

'I sort of regained my consciousness when they left. I started feeling pains all over. I just felt as if they had poured pepper in my private parts and I was almost going crazy. I stayed on my bed until the woman came and said, "So they didn't kill you." I said, "But I think they have killed me. They've killed me. They must have killed me." It was as if I couldn't wake up, as if they had cut me up and dropped pepper everywhere.'

Eugenie was numb and physically exhausted. Her muscles were taut and her limbs shaky after so many hours of rape; her mind was shutting down.

'To tell you the truth, from that time, I was dead. Every moment after that time. Every moment after they raped me I knew they could kill me anytime. I was under their mercy. So I thought death was definitely coming. I felt like it had already come. I had seen them kill many other people and I knew there was nothing special about me. I knew that they didn't like me, they didn't love me. I thought my death was coming like everyone else. That stayed in my mind all the time.'

Eugenie was raped by at least ten men on the first morning. It was the first time she had had sex and she lost her virginity in a terrifying blur. When the rapes were over she stayed in the bedroom and peeked outside through a small gap in the curtains. The compound had become a base for the local Hutu gangs, who were coming back with treasures they had looted from the homes of Tutsis they had killed. Electrical goods, kitchen cupboards and even cars were piled up outside. Then a second group of gunmen arrived and Beatrice took them to Eugenie's bedroom.

'There was nothing I could do. It was in the morning. I remember this because the house boy had just finished mopping the house when they came in. They asked me if I was Hutu or Tutsi. I lied. I said actually my father was Hutu but my mother is Tutsi. I had the misfortune of taking on the appearance of my mother. I said, "Are you going to kill me just because of that ? My father is Hutu."'

On the third day an older man came into the house who said he didn't sleep with Tutsis, he just killed them. He was armed and angry as he pushed the other men out of the way and started shouting orders at Eugenie.

'He told me to stand against the wall and raise my arms. He had a Kalashnikov. He was pointing it at me. Inside I actually felt peaceful because I thought killing me was better than continuing to go through what I was going through. I thought, if he kills me, it just ends here. All of this ends. It's fine. Immediately, he shot. But he only shot the wall next to me. As if he was trying to vent the anger to get the anger out through the wall.'

Killing had became a full-time job for the Hutu militiamen; they nicknamed it 'work' as they went from house to house butchering entire Tutsi families. Roadblocks were set up to trap any Tutsis who tried to escape. Eugenie could hear the shouting and the terror from outside, and she could smell the stale blood on the clothes of the men who raped her. There was a roadblock on the street less than 100 metres from her bedroom. The bodies of those who were killed there were thrown under a bush on the side of the road and the stench of the remains came through the bedroom window.

'I could never get out beyond the gate of the compound. When the gangs came in, they came singing about what they had done, how many people they had killed. Each of them was proudly telling who they had killed, how they had killed, their highlights of the day. That is how I learned what was taking place outside.

'They were clearing up all the Tutsis, they asked people to bury themselves. They dug holes; when they got into the holes they said, "Start burying yourself. Let's see how much you can do." Then they were told, "Leave one hand up and wave to your family, wave to the corpses of your family." Sometimes they didn't kill them completely, they buried most of the body leaving the head, then hit the head. There were times that crows came and started eating at people who were almost dying but were still alive.'

Eugenie had no way to contact her family in Kibuye, but she was sure they had already been killed.

'At that time I knew that they were dead. I knew that they would definitely have been killed because I knew that all Tutsis in the country were being killed. I thought I was the only Tutsi alive left in this world, the only Tutsi alive. It wasn't any question of my family being alive. I thought it is only me left in the world.

'The only thoughts that came into my mind were death. Nothing else. I knew that they had besieged the whole country. There were roadblocks everywhere. The idea of escaping never crossed my mind, given the picture I was getting of what was going on outside. I did not even have a Hutu identity card that may have helped me. There were no other thoughts I had. I only thought about death. Nothing else.'

Eugenie slices the air with her hand as she says there was 'nothing else'. She turns her palms upward as she mentions death, to emphasise there was little she could do.

We have been talking for almost two hours. When we stop, Eugenie sits back on the couch, stretches her long neck upwards and rolls her chin as if she's just settled into a warm bath. She looks relieved, but tired. I ask her if the interview is stirring up bad memories and she shakes her head.

'I haven't remembered for a long time, but it is good to make sure I don't forget. Nobody has really asked me about these things. We don't talk about it because everybody in Rwanda has their story. Who would listen if we all talked? Who would we cry for? There are so many sad things.'

The next afternoon we go to the neighbourhood where Eugenie was held captive. She sits behind the driver, giving him directions as the taxi bounces along the dirt road.

'Stop, this is the place,' she says.

We get out of the car and Eugenie points at a building site – the house where she was raped has been demolished and a church is being built in its place. Eugenie walks calmly and Gabriel listens carefully as she talks before relaying her answers to me in English. He treats her so respectfully and I'm grateful for the way he handles it all. His Tutsi family had to flee the genocide too, so he nods his head knowingly when Eugenie speaks.

The dirt road runs along a long, narrow valley, where large houses with tall walls overlook the lowlands. Some of the Hutu men who raped her came from the surrounding neighbourhood. Two of them lived in a big white house across the road; they were the sons of a local official. The striking thing about the place is how ordinary it is, it doesn't look any different from any other neighbourhood in Kigali. There are no clues that this was a place of killing, because there was killing almost everywhere. Imagine the brutal logistics of murdering almost 1 million people in 100 days. There was so much killing to be done, the militiamen would murder all day, go home at sunset and come back in the morning to continue: it was like a nine-to-five job. Thousands of Tutsis who sheltered in churches and schools across the country spent the day in terror as the Interahamwe hacked their way through the crowds, then called it a day and returned the next.

Eugenie walks ahead and points to a place on the corner of the compound. This was the site of the roadblock and the bush where the bodies were thrown was just next to the fence. Further up the road is where people were forced to bury themselves; their self-dug graves pockmarked the open ground. Eugenie then points across the valley and starts listing where all the other roadblocks were.

'Across the valley near the garage, there was a big pile of bodies. There was a roadblock there. There was another one up the street only a short distance away.'

All the escape routes were sealed. She points again, to a road on the other side.

'That is the way they took me to Zaire.'

What happened here was so profound and all-encompassing I can barely understand it; the terrible memories are carried quietly person by person, out of my view. Sometimes I watch people in the streets and wonder which parts they played: were they victims or perpetrators who have blended back in to daily life? My eyes can barely tell the difference between Hutu and Tutsi. The divisions that cost people their lives in 1994 are blurry to me.

On the surface there are few signs of what happened. Kigali is a polite place, the car horns of the minibus taxis don't seem to toot as loudly or as often as in Nairobi or other cities. But the peacefulness is deceptive. Almost every street corner, marketplace and neighbourhood was stained with the blood of the genocide. Remains, bloodied clothes and bones are often found when people dig gardens and clear land for new houses. There was no formal battlefield – people lost their lives in the most random and mundane of places.

Children are walking along the road carrying plastic jerry cans of water back to their families. Some stop and try to listen in as Eugenie talks, but Gabriel tells them to keep moving. Eugenie talks softly, stalling while the children put the jerry cans back on their heads and move on. During the genocide the Hutu militiamen would walk along this road every afternoon, returning to the house after another day of 'work' and then taking turns to rape Eugenie.

'All I can say is, all those days I was there, for all those months, there is no single day that they didn't rape me. At some times they started fighting between the four of them, saying, "She is mine, she's mine." Towards the end they asked me, "Should we kill you or are you coming with us?"'

The militiamen knew they had to leave Kigali because the Tutsi-led Rwandan Patriotic Front was closing in on the capital. The RPF was fighting its way across the country to stop the genocide and thousands of members of the Interahamwe were trying to escape on foot to neighbouring Zaire.

'You know, life is something quite interesting. Even under such conditions, the first thing that came into my mind was just

[to] hang on to life. Maybe I could escape along the route. So I said, "Don't kill me. I'm going with you." So that is how we went.'

Eugenie was caught in the middle: ironically, the men who raped her became her only protection against other Hutus who wanted to kill her. They kept her alive so that they could keep raping her. One of the Hutu men had worked as a house boy at the compound in Kigali. His name was Janvier and he was aged in his mid-twenties, a short man with a short temper. Eugenie hoped that when they reached Zaire, she might have a chance to escape.

For the first time in more than two months, she left the compound, setting off with the men who had been raping her because she thought if she refused, she would be killed. As she walked, she saw the gruesome wreckage of the genocide. Bodies were rotting alongside the road; the killers had long since given up burying their victims.

'When I saw all these people dead, all this destruction, I kept thinking, when is my time coming? When am I going to die? Most of the bodies that I saw had been mutilated. They were naked. I thought all Tutsis had been killed, everybody that I knew had been killed. It was still shocking for me. I sort of became traumatised. They continued to kill along the route, I don't know if these were Tutsis they were killing or if it was just Hutus who look like Tutsis. If anyone pointed a finger at you and you didn't get anyone defending you, you got killed there and then.

'There was a group that was shot while I was looking, just on the side of the road. At the next roadblock they stopped us again. They looked at me and said, "Where is this cockroach going?" I told them, "I am not a cockroach. I am Hutu." Somehow I think God protected me. They were killing people. Some were being hit with gun butts. Others were being chopped with machetes. They were just killing.'

Eugenie and her captors crossed the border with hundreds of thousands of others, leaving the genocide behind and stepping into a new hell. People swarmed in filthy camps, there was no clean water and not enough food. Cholera and other diseases started taking lives. It was a festering, putrid catastrophe – some people died where they fell because they were too weak to go any further.

Eugenie's middle-class childhood of prayers, study and parties didn't arm her with many skills for the grubby business of life in the camps. She had to compete with thousands of others for any food or water she could find.

'I don't know how I survived. There was all sorts of diseases. People died in big numbers. Burying was no longer even considered. When someone died in a tent they just got the bodies out and piled them by the road like tree logs.

'People started drinking stagnant water, collecting it in holes and other places whenever it rained. The water that people used to wash their clothes, they used that same water for cooking food and other things. Some people went to fetch water and died on the way. Some went into the forest to look for food and they just died there and didn't even make it back.'

Eugenie collected rotten tree bark and chewed it, and when the bark ran out she collected leaves and boiled them. Aid agencies eventually arrived, bringing food and setting up clinics, but thousands of people had already died.

While Eugenie was gathering bark in the forest, her thoughts were centred on escape, but amid the chaos of the camps, the leaders of the genocide were still enforcing a makeshift system of terror. No-one was allowed to leave without their permission and anyone suspected of betraying the Interahamwe was murdered. The killings happened with few repercussions – people were hacked to death between the rows of tents.

Eugenie was afraid to run or to tell aid workers that she was a Tutsi who had been brought to Zaire against her will. Freedom was just out of reach; she couldn't get an opportunity to speak with the aid workers without the risk of being overheard.

'There was always something that stopped me from doing it. There were a lot of Hutu men and women who worked with these people. People who were sort of educated and they were assisting there. So I always looked at them and thought, if I went and told those white people my problem, these Hutus will hear and then

I will be in danger. I will be dead. Even if they didn't hear they might ask them, then they would know what I was saying and that would be worse than everything else.

'It was very frustrating. Very frustrating. I did not just see these foreigners at their offices, they even came into the camp. They came into places where we lived, looking for people who were very ill and couldn't make it out of the tents. So these white people came, I could see them pass by, even next door. I kept imagining that if I find a way of secretly telling them, I would be out of this place. But there was no opportunity. It was very frustrating.'

Buses also arrived at the camps to take people back to Rwanda. They parked at the entrance, but few people were able to reach them. The Interahamwe set up roadblocks in the camp and anyone who tried to make a run for the buses was killed on the spot.

'They would just kill you at the roadblocks. Some people used to hide and lie that they were not going to the buses. But I always thought, me being Tutsi, with my physical appearance, there was no way I was going to make it past even the first roadblock. They would just kill me before I got to the bus.'

Janvier was assaulting Eugenie and threatening to kill her. She found food and water for him and he raped her whenever he wanted to. Eugenie was at his mercy, her survival never guaranteed.

'He always told me, "I don't know why I saved you, why you survived. We killed a lot more beautiful women than you. You are such a disgrace to me. Can you look around, can you see anyone else who looks like you? You are a snake. You shouldn't be alive. There is no other person in this camp who has a Tutsi woman. It is just a shame to me that I am with you." He pushed me around and beat me up. I didn't feel like a human being anymore.

'If he wanted to kill me, he could have killed me. He had the right to do it without any problem. Nobody would have even questioned him at all. If he wanted to beat me up in public, or even to kill me in public, that still would have been no problem to him. He could have just said, "I have discovered I have a snake for a woman." Nothing would have been said of him. Maybe even people would have supported him. I don't know.'

In September 1994, Eugenie noticed her body was changing. At first she thought she was sick – maybe it was the lack of food, maybe the dirty water.

'It took me time before I realised I was pregnant. I felt changes inside my belly. That is when I knew I was pregnant. I just felt like I just wanted to die. I didn't want to live.'

When she was seven months' pregnant, Janvier ordered Eugenie to kill the baby and dump it in the forest. He accused Eugenie of sleeping with other men and said the baby was a Tutsi cockroach.

Eugenie kept quiet. She gave birth to a boy and called him Claude.

'Claude looked like me a lot. Even much more when he was younger. You could really see he looked Tutsi completely. I think it was only God's mercy that worked here. [Janvier] never tried to attack Claude or do anything bad to him. He only abused me but did nothing to Claude at all. He never touched Claude at all. I think it was God's plan.

'When Claude became two years old I now started feeling that I had a companion, that I had a friend. There was no-one else in the entire camp whom I could talk to. I felt like it was only the two of us. It was Claude and me in the world. I had a relative, someone close to. When he started speaking, that was a wonderful, great experience. At least finally there was someone I could talk to.'

Claude was a reason to live. He was the only human being Eugenie had spoken to freely for more than two years. She was surrounded by Hutus, so she survived by keeping quiet and becoming almost invisible. If she was asked, she used her well-worn lie that her father was a Hutu and only her mother was a Tutsi. She endured the beatings and abuse from Janvier because without him she was dead; he was her greatest tormentor and also her greatest protector.

But time was running out for the Interahamwe. The Tutsi-led Rwandan Patriotic Front was sweeping through the jungle in large numbers, hunting members of the Interahamwe and forcing them back to Rwanda. It didn't want the ringleaders of the genocide to have a chance to regroup and re-enter the country on their own terms.

Janvier and other members of the Interahamwe decided to flee. They were on the run, living like fugitives in the jungle, often walking for several days without rest, trying to escape the RPF. Eugenie carried Claude on her back and a few possessions wrapped in a blanket on her head. She was hoping the RPF would find her.

'The Interahamwe wanted to move around Zaire until they had enough power to attack Rwanda and take control again. They did not want anyone to return to Rwanda, they wanted to keep everyone with them so they could mass enough troops to fight back. So they kept us in the jungles.'

The RPF launched an attack at dawn, sealing off the escape routes and starting to herd the Interahamwe fighters back towards Rwanda. Eugenie was gaunt, dirty and exhausted after months of being on the battlefield in the jungle.

'When we got to Goma, there were Congolese Tutsi women, they saw me and they knew I was a Tutsi too. They said, "Hey, you are one of us." It's funny because I felt scared. I had turned into some form of animal. I was actually afraid of them. I was used to life on the run. I was used to dirty clothes. When I saw clean people for the very first time in a long time, I was actually afraid of them.

'I knew that something had changed in me. I was no longer a human being. I was very dirty. I thought about what I could have been doing if my life had continued. I thought I might have been a very presentable person. Maybe I would have even been the one helping such needy people. But I realised that wasn't where I was. I was in a totally different place. Something big had changed in my life.'

Eugenie had been in the jungle for almost three years. Janvier had gone missing during one of the RPF attacks and she never saw him again. After he disappeared, the situation became more dangerous because Eugenie and Claude didn't have his unintended protection. However, they survived. The years of misery in Zaire were almost over.

'When I realised we were moving towards Rwanda, I instantly became happy. I felt that whatever is there, going back to Rwanda must surely be better than this. By far. My morale raised a lot. I also saw that the Hutus were now also suffering. They were now also on the run. But for me, I had so much energy. I thought, finally, I am heading back to Rwanda. Throughout that period, I was walking in front of the group because I just wanted to reach Rwanda as fast as I could get. So that is how I came back. I arrived in Rwanda in 1997, December.'

When she crossed the border, Eugenie and hundreds of thousands of others were put into transit camps where most of the returnees were Hutus – many were the perpetrators of the genocide. Eugenie was still in danger from those who didn't want to see any Tutsis alive.

'A woman who I knew from Kibuye, who I went to school with, primary school. She came and told me, "They are going to kill you. They say they know you very well. You are a Tutsi rebel. So they are going to kill you. They are going to kill you when you come to collect the saucepans and blankets." Everyone in that camp was Hutu.'

The Tutsi soldiers at the camp were kind to her, giving her milk and gentle conversation, but the camp was too big for them to guarantee her safety. Eugenie had to fend for herself; she held little hope of finding any relatives alive. Eventually, the fate of her family was confirmed, piece by piece: former neighbours from Kibuye passed on the numbing details of the slaughter of her family. Her parents, grandparents and all of her brothers and sisters had been murdered.

'My mum was the first one to be killed, with my little four-year-old brother. They cut her with the machete, then they hit her with clubs. But she did not die. They just left my brother, they didn't kill him the first time. The Interahamwe came back and killed her and killed my brother too. They said, "These people are real snakes, they don't die." So they killed her that time. They were killed at my grandfather's place, where they had gone to take refuge.

'You see, in my area, people fought back. They fought against the Interahamwe and put up some resistance using stones and spears and anything they could come across. My grandfather lived on a very tall hill. That is where they gathered with all the other families and started from there. During the day it was running battles, at night they would come back to the high ground in the hills. And that is where they would spend the night protecting themselves.

'As for my grandfather, my brothers and sisters were killed first and then my grandfather was chopped for the first time. My grandfather was attacked three times. Every time they thought he had died, but he didn't. By the time he died, there were even worms coming from his skin because he had been injured several times. All the time my father stayed with my grandfather because my mother had been killed, all the children had been killed, all the relatives had been killed. He stayed close to where my grandfather was. After my grandfather died, my father sort of went crazy and walked out of hiding, shouting, and that's when they killed him. They shot him. My father was one of the last to be killed. He died the day before the French soldiers arrived.'

Eugenie's family members were killed by their neighbours: some were the Hutus who used to come to parties at her parents' house, sharing the banana beer and listening to Eugenie's father laughing and singing songs about his cows. Some were filled with the hatred that had been inflamed by the government; others killed purely because of fear. If they didn't join in, their own families could be next.

'When this all started happening in our area, the Hutus all banded together. They held meetings and they would attack as one group. The Tutsis were also in one group, trying to defend themselves. This group also included those who came for parties at home. Some of them worked for us on a part-time basis. I know that they all participated in the killings of my family. But I don't know who specifically killed who, because they were always in groups. I know who killed my grandfather. That man is still in Kibuye. He is still there, where we lived.

'I decided one day to go back to Kibuye and go back to my area. When I got there I realised that all the people I knew were not there. There were only Hutu people. There were no Tutsis. I couldn't see any Tutsis. That's when I knew they had all been finished.'

Eugenie decided there was nothing for her in Kibuye. Her family was gone and their house had been destroyed. Only the killers were left behind.

' I thought, going back to this area, if I saw these people who had killed my family, I could not live with them.'

She went to Kigali in search of a place to stay. Within the first few days she saw a young woman she knew. They traded their stories of survival and the woman said she'd heard one of Eugenie's relatives had also come back to Kigali. It was the first whisper of family in almost four years. Eugenie's aunt, Bernadette, was alive. She was a businesswoman who had escaped to Uganda and now decided it was safe to return to Rwanda.

'I was extremely happy and kind of shocked. I just started crying, crying. Wailing, shouting out very loud. I just didn't believe there was anybody in my family who was still alive. All along I thought my entire family had been eliminated. There was nobody I could find. I just cried loudly a lot for a long time. I just couldn't believe what I was seeing. It was like seeing someone who was resurrected.'

Bernadette took Eugenie by the hands and promised to look after her, welcoming her into her home.

'When I got there, she found some nice clothes for me. Nice clean clothes, shoes. She did a lot of things for me. I started taking a shower, smearing myself with body oil. I just felt fresh. I felt like a new human being. She was someone who liked treating her hair. So she also gave me some hair products to do my hair. I now felt like I was starting a completely new life. She told me I now had to start planning to go back to school. She was someone who was really educated. She said, "Look. No problem. Forget about everything that has happened." So everything felt completely new. For me, I knew this was a new beginning. I was putting aside all the burdens, all the difficult life. I was now starting afresh.'

Eugenie felt an overwhelming sense of relief: the years of suffering in the bush were over. She took delight in sniffing the sweet fragrances of the soaps in the bathroom, she polished her new shoes, and stroked the clean fabric of her dresses. She felt human again. There was joy and anticipation in the house: Bernadette was pregnant and Eugenie was helping her prepare for the arrival of the new baby.

But further tragedy was to strike. Bernadette died during childbirth. Eugenie lost her aunt, only eight weeks after finding her.

'When she died, I just didn't know what was happening. It was a haemorrhage. She continued to bleed and spent about four days in hospital. After four days it sort of went down a bit. The bleeding ceased a little. We brought her home. But it started all over again. We brought her back to the hospital. And she died. I started crying out very loudly. They couldn't even stop me. They tried but nobody could stop me.'

Eugenie was in a rage that came from grief. She was full of shock, sadness and anger; her hopes of a new life had crumbled.

'Shortly before she died we had been talking. She was showing me a plan of how I was going to rebuild my life. She was telling me, "Don't concern yourself with any of the troubles at home. Just try to relax and settle back into life." She was a businesswoman, so she was happy that I was at home when she was away and I could take care of the kids and that sort of thing.'

Eugenie's tone is measured and deliberate, there are no tears. But I find it hard to look at her, I want to cry. I feel ill. Gabriel looks at the floor too.

'I'm sorry. I'm sorry to ask you about this.'

'I'm okay,' she says.

In the evening, when I try to transcribe the interview, I find myself pacing around my room. I read her words again and again and I feel hollow. I can't find any justification for the kind of suffering Eugenie has endured, it's beyond even the most extreme lessons hardship could teach. It's suffering for the sake of suffering. In my five years in Africa this is one of the few times I have felt utterly overwhelmed. The continent has already stretched my boundaries of what is fair and what is life, but I just don't know why God or fate, or whatever it is, would put one person through so much. I feel physically heavy, angry, as well as deeply sad. Eugenie is not an old woman telling of another time. She's a young woman like me.

The next morning I follow Eugenie to church. Mothers and children walk up the steep road to the top of the hill. The steps to the door are made from sandbags, to stop the heavy rain washing away the soil. The church is in a poor neighbourhood; some of the windows have glass, others are just holes with frames. The dirt floor is paved with red bricks.

The choirs are rehearsing when I arrive, one each side of the preacher. A band with drums, a bass and keyboard accompanies the singers through a rattling speaker system. Most of the women in the congregation also shake home-made tins full of seeds and pebbles. The mix of sound is lively and African, the hymns set to local beats.

I like going to church with the gogo mamas to see them in the congregation: the pews where they sit, the Bibles they hold in their hands and the way they mark and fold their pages. But it also makes me feel very homesick for my own family. I've still got another four months of travelling alone.

I am the only foreigner in the church and Eugenie is a bit embarrassed, so I sit up the back. A small child in front of me spends the whole service sitting backwards so he can stare at me. When the service starts, the preacher welcomes me in the local language, Kinyarwanda, and the congregation says, 'Hallelujah!' I stand up and give a quick wave. I'm not quite sure what to do. A man with terribly bad breath sits next to me and decides it will be his job to translate the highlights of the entire sermon. He whispers in my ear in a huff of halitosis.

'Abraham is number one,' he says.

'Jeeeeeeeeeeesus.' He power-whispers. 'Jesus . . . is informed.'

He nods at me with a Mr Bean-like expression of self-satisfaction, but apparently no sense of the ridiculous.

'God . . .' he announces. 'God, has a plan.'

'Right, thank you,' I reply.

I watch the congregation. At first I can't quite pick what is wrong, but then I realise that people are missing. There is almost no-one over 30 years old: the middle-aged and the elderly are missing. Many of those who were old enough to be adults during the genocide were killed. Eugenie is one of the oldest people in the church. Normally, churches are havens for old women in Africa and ironically that is where many of them went for shelter in 1994 but lost their lives in ones like this. In some places their bodies have been left where they fell, as a vivid and terrible memorial.

There are also very few complete families. There are mothers and children, groups of young men, groups of young women, older children fussing over their younger siblings. Families are pieced together depending on who survived. Eugenie's aunt's death left her to rebuild her life alone. She didn't have anywhere to live, so she took Claude and went in search of a distant uncle. But as the uncle was only on the fringes of the family, he had no real connection with her. He was trying to look after his own children and didn't trust Eugenie because she had been with the Interahamwe for so long.

'I lived at his place for a short while, then he told me, "Look, I have children here. I work. I have a lot of trouble with family issues to take care of. I think the best thing for you would be to go back to your family ruins in Kibuye and try to dig and grow some plants there and live off that. I can't have you stay here."'

Eugenie went back to Kigali. She stayed with friends and eventually managed to get shelter at a housing refuge run by a non-government organisation called Rwanda Women's Network. She started noticing her belly changing again, but this time things weren't right. She was becoming weak and thin.

'After I gave birth to Claudine in '98, I started getting sick. I started coughing a lot and had all these illnesses. In 1999 I took a test and I was found to be HIV-positive. I became so angry, so sad. I just tore the results, the piece of paper they gave me. I just tore it into small pieces and threw it away. I felt angry at all these men, I started remembering what had happened to me in 1994.'

Her condition quickly worsened. Eugenie spoke to a friend at the women's network and gave her instructions on what to do with Claude and Claudine if she died.

'I told her, "If I die, take my kids to an orphanage." Because I knew I didn't have any relatives. There was nobody else to take care of them. I told her, "Take my kids to an orphanage and they can just try life there."'

Eugenie was finding it hard merely to do the daily domestic chores. She didn't have the strength to walk to the market, and couldn't lift pots and pans when she was cooking. Her appetite was fading and she was losing weight.

'It was very, very difficult. When I tried to carry something I would feel very weak and cough many times. I just couldn't do any physical work. I didn't even eat a lot at the time. I didn't get any medication. There was just nothing. I just wanted to die quietly by myself.

'When I came here to Rwanda Women's Network, you could read it all over my face that I was dying of AIDS. I looked really bad. I was just like a grandmother. I looked like 80 years old. When you saw me, my face was just skeleton. My hair had all become weak. You could just see I was dying. I was just bones and nothing else.'

Eugenie was scared to get help; there was still a stigma associated with HIV and she didn't want to be rejected by those around her. She feared losing her house or her place at the market, but the genocide had left many women infected with HIV.

'I talked to people and I realised there were others who also had HIV like me but were trying to live positive lives and they were doing very well. I didn't die and here I am. I started a new life here. I've improved a great deal since then. Now, you see, I look like a young girl. I am very healthy.'

Claude and Claudine tested negative for HIV. Eugenie is now receiving vital anti-retroviral medication from a charity group. It is keeping her alive, but it won't cure her. Eugenie is one of more than 250,000 Rwandan women who were raped during the genocide – of those who survived, 70 per cent were HIV-positive. Some found it hard to love their babies who had come from rape and terror. But Eugenie never had any feelings of rejection towards Claude and Claudine. She felt almost as if they were fatherless because they looked so much like her, and she was raped so many times she is still not sure exactly who the father was, anyway.

'People who died have now been forgotten. Their lives are gone. But my life today, I have my kids. I have a boy and a girl. I have both. They give me a lot of strength. They are very close to me. Sometimes we sit and Claudine says, "Let me pretend I am the mother, Claude is the father." Then we sit and chat and talk a lot. They sing a lot. Neighbours start wondering what is going on at Eugenie's place. What is going on? All these are things that many people have not had the chance of experiencing. They have a lot of dreams. I hope that God can help them to achieve all their dreams.'

Claude and Claudine get changed into their best clothes so I can take some photographs. They're excited, and Eugenie smiles as she watches them. Her mothering is gentle, but it draws respect from her children: she asks them to do things rather than tells them. She's almost like a responsible older sister, who seems to share their joy and sense of fun.

Claude and Claudine follow us outside, and ask if they can ride in our taxi to the end of the street. It's only a 200-metre journey, but the children rarely get the chance to ride in a car. It's a big deal for them and a great way to impress their friends. It's lovely to watch Claude and Claudine getting so much happiness from such a simple thing. They sit up straight on the back seat, swinging their legs back and forth and looking out the window.

'Whenever I get some clothes for my kids, that is the happiest thing that happens to me. They don't feel like they are missing out on anything, that makes me very happy. In fact, when they go to other places and they see people who are having problems, people whose kids do not have good clothes or don't take a bath as often as they do, then they tell them, "Why don't you talk to our mum about it? She has a lot of money. She will take care of you. She cooks French fries for us and everything. You should talk to her. She can help you." So they think that I am a very wealthy woman. It makes me happy to see that they are contented with what I can give them. In their eyes, they think I am one of the wealthiest people in this country.'

Eugenie makes a living selling tomatoes at a nearby market, and in the afternoon she walks home to sweep the house and start making supper for the children. It's a simple life, very different from the dreams Eugenie had as a bright schoolgirl in Kibuye. This is not where she hoped sitting exams would take her, but she's proud and quietly contented. There's little sense of regret when she talks; she never cries during the interviews, and she never raises her voice or speaks with much bitterness.

As the afternoons of interviews progress, some of her shyness disappears. One day we have a break and go under the back veranda to watch the rain. The water soaks into the soil where Eugenie has planted maize. She smiles politely at my jokes and answers with her own little pieces of information, but not too much. She doesn't try to impress me and she doesn't mind the moments of silence. She has an appearance of peace.

'I have learned a lot of lessons about not giving up. I have learned that God will always help you, regardless of what man wants to do to you. The fact that I stayed alive was not because people liked me, it was not because I was special, there was nothing extraordinary about me. I have learned many, many lessons through some of the things I have been through.

'I think I have gone beyond the hard life, the difficult life that I experienced. I have mostly forgotten about it, it is no longer part of me. To me, it is just a spot in a long life. The life I'm living today is a happy life; I think if I looked at it from today, I have lived a fantastic life. I am ready for anything. Many people have died, but I am still alive, I think that is very important. Many people have not been as lucky as I am.'

Eugenie explains her outlook with such simplicity. She believes she was kept alive for one reason only: to be a witness to God's miracles. She looks at me without blinking. I'm not religious, so I don't know what it's like to have that kind of faith. Part of me wants to tell Eugenie that she has been deceived. How could a caring God let one person endure such suffering? How can she thank God for saving her, but not condemn him for what he put her through?

But the alternative doesn't seem to offer much more comfort or logic. If she doesn't believe in God, and the suffering she endured was simply due to the acts of other human beings, there doesn't seem to be any justification for it anyway. It doesn't explain why she was put through all of that and why she survived when she could have been killed in any one of hundreds of moments. I'm in awe of her faith, even though I don't understand it.

Up to 1 million people were killed in 100 days during the genocide: most were Tutsis, but many Hutus also lost their lives. Eugenie is the only one left from her family in Kibuye. The speckle of intimate memories, the nicknames, the routines, the softness of her mother, her father's songs, the whispers between siblings rest only with her now. Their bodies, their clothes, their photos and their house have gone as if they never existed. Many families can't even be remembered; there was no-one left to mourn them.

'I think the world should take lessons from what happened here. See, what happened here is dumbfounding, it's horrible. It affected everyone. Many Tutsis were killed, but they also died, the Hutus. They were dying in thousands in Congo, from diseases, from hunger, from everything. All of this should teach a lesson to the world, you can't just do it and get away with it. There are still some of them in Congo, running around in the forest, still wanting to return to Rwanda by force, still interested in killing people. I don't know whether the world has taken any lesson from that. The effects are still there up until today.

'There will come a time when I will have to tell my children what happened. When they grow up I have to tell them.'

CHAPTER 7

Agnes Pareyio

Maasai activist
KENYA

Agnes Pareyio is a member of Kenya's Maasai tribe. When she was fourteen she underwent the brutality of female genital mutilation. As a young woman she started walking from village to village, carrying a wooden model to show the damage caused by FGM. She has now convinced hundreds of Maasai communities to stop the practice and has set up a rescue centre for girls trying to escape it. She has become an international activist and has travelled the world, including New York and Europe, to gather support for the campaign.

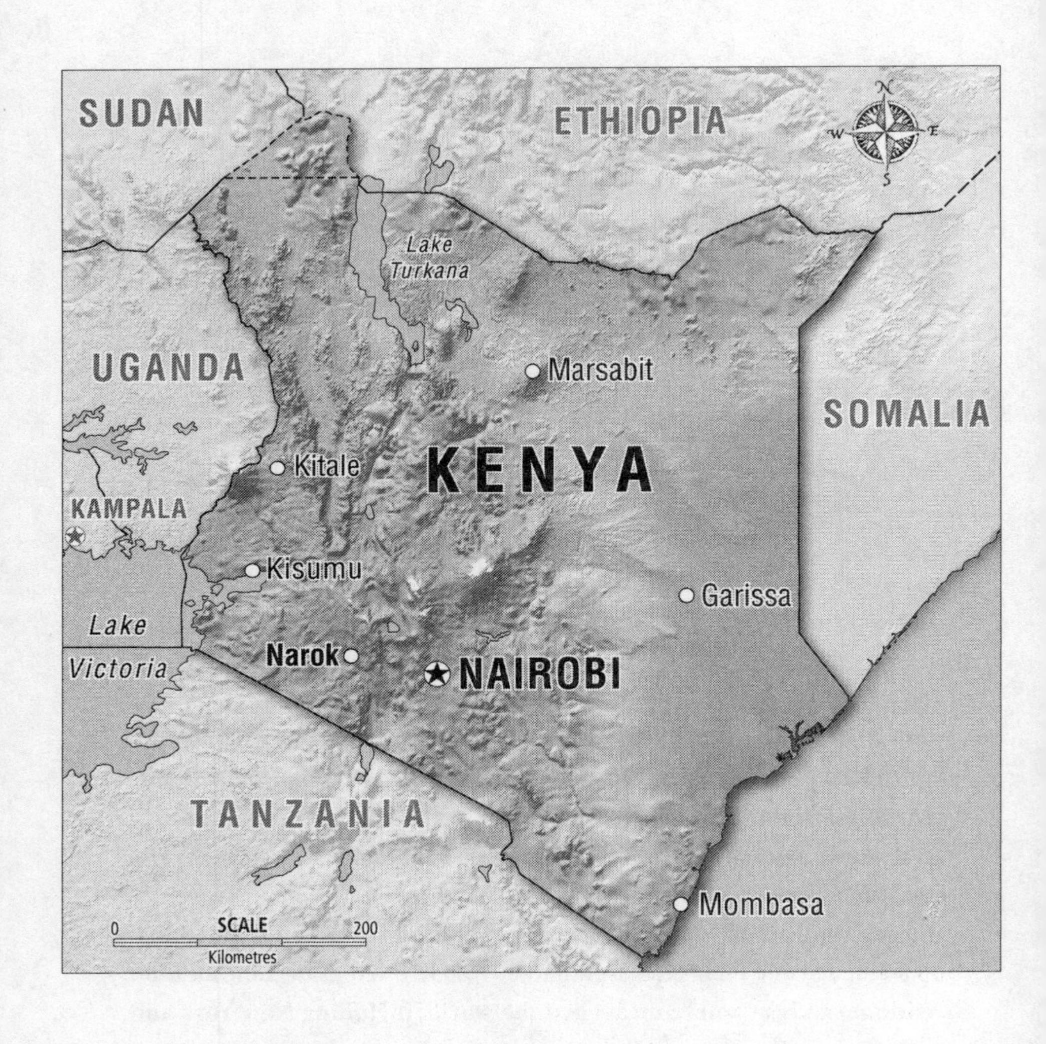

SUDAN
ETHIOPIA
N
W
E
S
Lake
Turkana
UGANDA
Marsabit
SOMALIA
Kitale
KENYA
KAMPALA
Kisumu
Garissa
Lake
Narok
NAIROBI
Victoria
TANZANIA
Mombasa
0
SCALE
200
Kilometres

I've never been to a Maasai beauty parlour before. I've never even seen inside because the salon windows are blurred with dirty lace curtains. I'm trying to act cool, as if I've seen it all before, but there's a woman in the corner with white smoke billowing from her head as a stylist armed with a brush and a hairdryer tries to straighten her locks. It's a muscly, no-nonsense kind of hairdressing: there's no running water, so the stylists fill yellow buckets from outside every time they want to wash someone's hair.

When I look outside through the curtains, I can see Maasai men dressed in red robes and sandals herding their cattle through the dusty streets. Narok is a Maasai town and the tourist buses stop here on their way from Nairobi to the Maasai Mara; it's a spectacular drive winding down the lip of the Rift Valley. The valley is so big and hazy, it looks as if you are seeing it from the air. Enterprising Maasai men have set up stalls on the most spectacular part of the road – their home-made wooden decks provide a vantage point for tourists wanting to take photographs. But the decks are so dodgy they look like Acme contraptions from a Road Runner cartoon, balancing delicately on the side of the cliff.

I've come to Narok to meet Agnes Pareyio, one of the most outspoken Maasai women in Kenya. I've been waiting for her for six days: each morning she calls promising she'll pick me up from the guesthouse, but she never arrives. Her phone is out of range all day and when I finally get through in the evening she apologises.

'I'm sorry, I got called away to a funeral in one of the villages. I'll pick you up at 8.30 tomorrow.'

The next day she doesn't arrive again, so, after six days of waiting, I've decided to leave. It's frustrating enough to wait a few hours for someone, but after doing it every day for almost a week, I've had enough. I'm packing my backpack when Agnes arrives early on Saturday morning; she apologises and promises she will give me all the time I need. I'm not sure she'll be true to her word, but the alternative is going back to Nairobi and starting from scratch, so I agree to give it a go. That's the deal: for the next few days, wherever Agnes goes, I go. That's how I end up in the Maasai beauty salon. I tag along while Agnes has straight artificial hair woven into her short Afro.

'Do you want to get anything done?' she asks.

I imagine myself with black weaves amongst my blonde hair.

'No thanks.'

Agnes is a big, sturdy woman, her belly is well fed and her arms bulky and she carries herself with her shoulders back and a trace of a swagger in her hips. When she walks along the street in Narok, people greet her with genuine respect, bowing their heads slightly and shaking her hand. Others watch her from a distance; her presence is noted. When we stop for a drink at a local café, all eyes are on her. The manager insists on taking our order and he fusses to make sure Agnes is comfortable. When he brings out a glass of cold water, she looks annoyed.

'I can't drink that, it's too cold.'

Even when she's travelling overseas, Agnes doesn't drink refrigerated water. She doesn't like it because she grew up in a village where the water was warm from the sun. I remember an interpreter I worked with in the desert in Sudan was the same: if I gave him an icy-cold Coke, he'd frown at me and put it on the hot dashboard of the car to warm it up.

If I had to describe Agnes in only one word, it would be 'tough'. She makes eye contact with me, but her concentration flickers on and off. She's not at all rude, just a busy woman who is almost constantly distracted by a big workload. I'm grateful for her time. There seems to be nothing about me that impresses or interests her, but when we get talking I can start to understand why. Agnes explains to me that it's all about courage – without courage, a Maasai is nothing; the worst thing in the world is to be a coward.

'I was naughty, I enjoyed fighting other girls. I enjoyed also looking at other girls fighting. We were trained to be courageous, we would go to the bush, get sticks, and then start fighting and nobody would cry. If you cry you will be called a coward. I could even fight boys. I remember one day I fought a boy and he cried. I was strong. My body now is just the same body that I had. I grew up with a strong body. I didn't cry, even when I was about to I pretended not to. It is really important. A Maasai woman, she can fight you to hell. You must fight back and you must be strong. You don't want to be called a coward.

'My mother didn't like a joke. She used to beat us a lot using a whip. She was a hard, no-nonsense woman. For us to be late in the evening, you have to say where you were. If you have not done your job, your duty, you have to say why. We were afraid of her because we knew we were going to be caned. But she was fair. If you are good, you have no problem.

'It is a mother who is close to the girls, fathers are not close. We feared our father. We still fear our father. A father is far from a girl. You don't even see your father eating. You have never shared a meal with him. He talks to you once when there is something to be done. When your father is eating inside, you go out, you sit outside until he finishes eating. The food of the father is put separately. The father cannot eat in the presence of the girls. You don't really know your father very well.'

It's a completely different way of seeing the world. Even as a grandmother, Agnes believes courage is vital. If she sees two children arguing, she won't tell them to shake hands and apologise; she'll give them sticks and tell them to fight. She'll pick up a stick and fight too, if she has to defend herself. As Agnes explains it, even if you're a small child or an old woman, you're expected to fight if you have to.

Agnes says the stick fight is the best way to deal with children, because if they don't fight they will keep undermining each other anyway. She leans forward with her strong arms flexing inside the tight sleeves of her dress and explains to me that stick fights only finish when one of the fighters is beaten so badly they give up. She becomes more animated and engaged when explaining Maasai culture. But there's something in her voice that tells me she's had to explain this to foreigners many times before.

'I have to hit you and you hit me until one says, "I surrender." If you don't surrender, you fight until somebody pulls you apart. It is difficult to be courageous all the time because you have to pretend so that people will not say you are a coward.'

It's strange to hear a grandmother in a floral dress explaining the value of a knock-'em-down stick fight. But she doesn't flinch when she talks: for Agnes, it all makes perfect sense. It certainly goes against all the reasoning, conflict resolution and tolerance preached in western playgrounds. I don't need any convincing that Agnes could just about knock my head off my shoulders.

She shakes her head in disgust when she describes Americans who cry on television chat shows; she has absolute contempt in her eyes when she talks about them. The first time she went to the United States she couldn't understand why wealthy people who had everything could claim to be so miserable. Even now, when she sees Americans interviewed on television after a hurricane or a tornado, her sympathy is overshadowed by anger.

'They are just human being like anybody else, but they think they are exceptional. They say, "Why should it happen to me, being an American? Why should wind blow down my house?" They think they are more human beings than anybody else, they

Hellen Lanyom digging in her cassava field. Gulu, Uganda.

Hellen with her nieces and grandchildren.

Masinda Mafiano feeding rice to her daughter, Juditte. Mudja, Democratic Republic of Congo.

Masinda and Juditte sitting on volcanic rocks at the base of Mount Nyiragongo.

Martha Yar Gak with her family. Labone, South Sudan.

Saying farewell to Martha at the airstrip.

Bi Kidude outside her childhood home. Zanzibar, Tanzania.

Courtesy of Busara Promotions

Bi Kidude performing in Durban, South Africa.

Katumu Macculay at Stewart Camp. Tubmanburg, Liberia.

Katumu and her son, Little Tony. Monrovia, Liberia.

Eugenie Muhayimana. Kigali, Rwanda.

Eugenie with her children, Claude and Claudine.

Agnes Pareyio checking her cattle. Narok, Kenya.

Agnes with the girls at Tasaru Rescue Centre.

Tenagnework Mekete on her way to the Patriots' Day march. Addis Ababa, Ethiopia.

Tenagnework Mekete at the Patriots' Day march.

Lucia Mazibuko outside her house. Alexandra, South Africa.

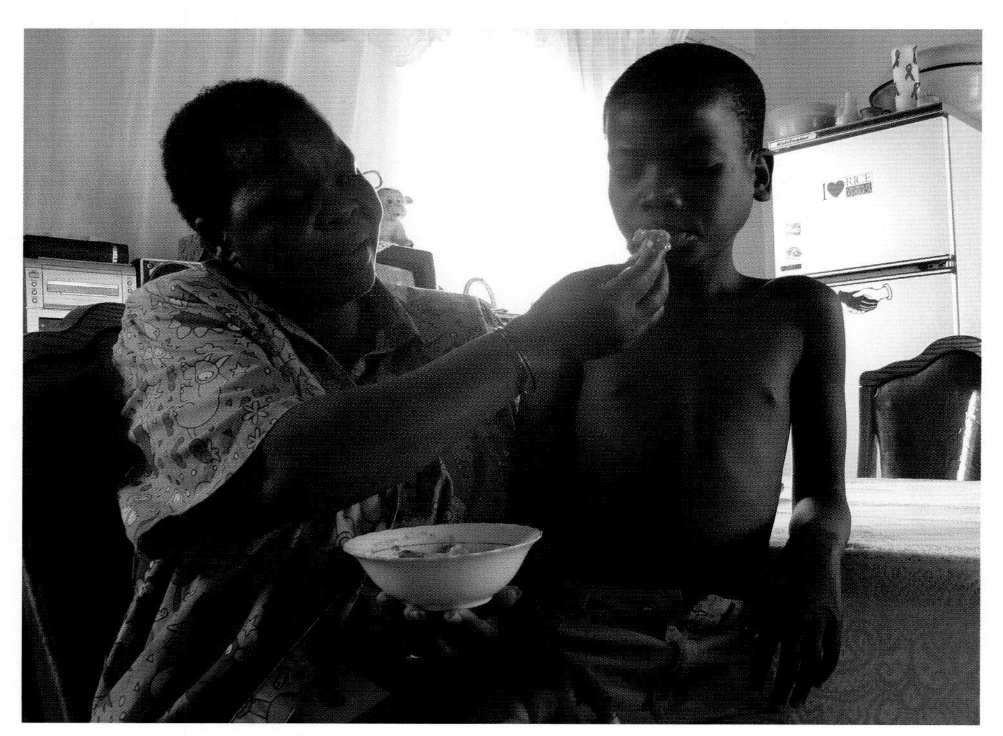

Lucia trying to handfeed Bobo.

Nagwa Fouad at home. Cairo, Egypt.

Juliana Dogbadzi with her daughter, Blessing, at their street stall. Adidome, Ghana.

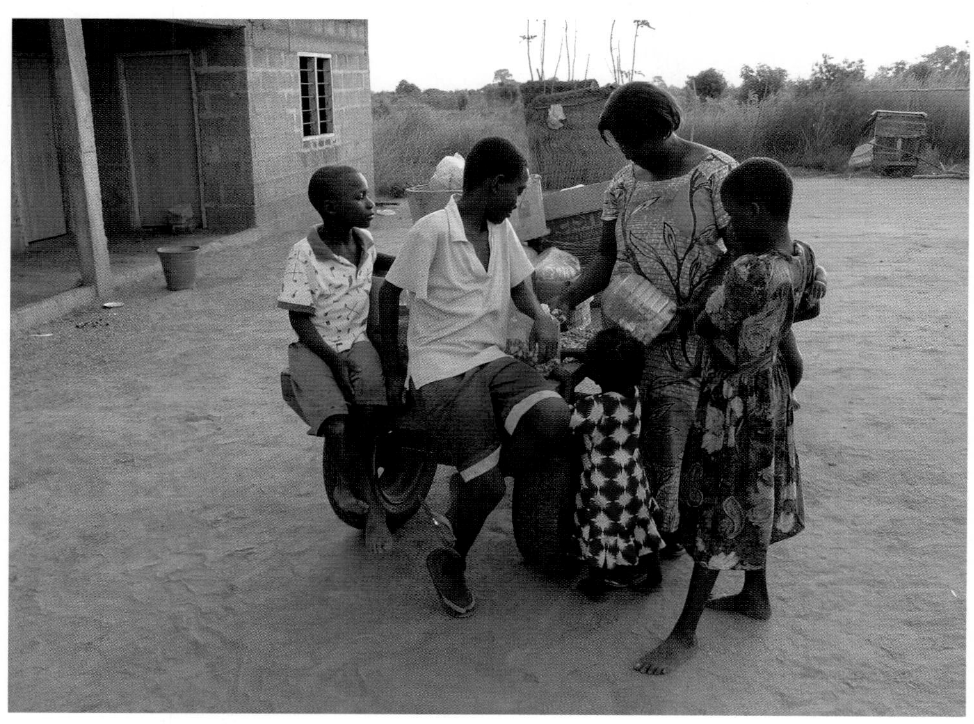

Juliana counting the day's takings from her stall.

Madame Traoré Fatoumata Touré. Bamako, Mali.

Exploring Dogon clifftop village with Abdoulay in Mali.

think they are super. Super power. If a Maasai lose his house, he cries but he calms down. You don't complain because you have nobody to complain to. But when you look at the Americans, they complain.

'Everybody these days cries [in] America, I don't know why. They cry for nothing. When I went to America, I thought maybe they put some chemicals in their eyes so that the tears can roll. I didn't see anything important that was making them cry. I am a Christian, I go to church. These people at the end of the day will be punished by God; they think they are knowledgeable, but they should know that knowledge and riches is not enough. You must also have courage.

'I can't cry now, even if you try to make me. I'll only cry if I see something happen to somebody, then I feel my tears falling. Or if I hear that somebody has died, or I feel pain. When I'm moved by emotions, I cry. But I just can't cry for fun.'

I feel a bit taken aback by what Agnes says. It's so blunt, but it's also a refreshingly plain-spoken African view. A lot of what she says resonates with my experiences in Africa. When I think of the women I have interviewed so far for this book, only one of them has cried. In fact, during my five years in Africa, it's been very rare for someone to cry on camera while I was interviewing them, even though they had been through horrific events or lost absolutely everything. I wonder if people learn there's usually not much point in crying because it won't do any good and there's no-one to hear you anyway.

Agnes spent her childhood in a village near Narok. It was a simple, traditional upbringing. The children belonged to the whole village; they ate, slept on cow hides and played in the houses of their neighbours. Most of the children were naked and rarely washed, and education wasn't paid much attention either. The important things in the village were men and cattle – women and children came last. The Maasai drank the blood and the milk of the cattle, believing these gave them strength. They didn't have much food. Sometimes there was porridge in the house, but rarely any tea or sugar.

'Life was lovely, we enjoyed our childhood. Our house was mud, we didn't have expensive things. We slept on cow skins, we didn't wash because nobody cared about it. Some young children had no clothing, they just walked naked and it was not a problem.

'We went to school, but the school was not given the seriousness it deserved because nobody knew the benefit of going to school.'

Agnes knew her place from an early age. As a girl, she was only a temporary member of the family; her purpose was to be married off. Her father's house was not her house – she would have to go to her husband's family when she was old enough.

'Girls in the village were treated like people who are going, they are not given the priority that is enjoyed by boys. Parents value boys more than girls. My mother kept saying to me, "You are soon going to somebody's home, behave like a woman." So Maasai girls always are prepared, knowing their home is not their real home.

'I never had any dreams because there was nobody else who had done anything. The dream I had was just to be a wife. I dropped out from school. I didn't finish, my parents didn't care.'

When Agnes and her sister returned home for the school holidays, they could smell traditional beer being brewed and saw relatives arriving on foot from neighbouring villages. They knew something was going on.

'My mother said, "My daughters, you are going to undergo circumcision. You are not supposed to cry." I told her I didn't want it. My father supported me, he said, "Leave my daughter alone." But my mother said, "How can I live in a house with a lady who is not cut? What will I call her? Shall I call her a woman or what do I call her? She has to be cut." In the village, everyone started saying I was a coward who doesn't want to be cut. My grandmother joined in and said, "You should be cut, because there is no way you can stay uncut." They cut me. I was severely done.

'What happens is, a day prior to being cut they shave you at around three in the afternoon. You are left naked with a small piece of cloth. There is normally water that is left outside to be cold in a pot. You sleep and then very early in the morning, around five, they use it just to make your blood a little bit cold, so that you don't bleed before they finish the operation. It happens in a room in the house. Your father is on the other side. He cannot exactly see you but he can hear if you cry. They had already said I was a coward, so I had to make sure I don't cry.

'When a woman is cut, everybody is drinking. Sometimes the circumciser herself is drunk. I had to look at my sister being operated and then I had to sit in the same place. They just removed the blood and I had to sit down there. There is a traditional circumciser who does it. You don't lie down. You are called. You come in, you sit down, just the way I'm seated now. There is a woman behind you, then they put your legs apart. Then they start working on you. It takes about five minutes. There is normally a woman who checks if everywhere is cut. The problem I had was bleeding, because I bled too much. They had to bring the cow and I was given some blood. You want to put your mind to be brave, not to cry in front of your father. That is the only thing you keep reminding yourself, not to cry.'

There's not much emotion in Agnes's voice as she tells the story. She talks at a steady pace, in plain words. She keeps checking that I understand the detail of what she's saying, but has no interest in extracting any sympathy from me. She explains it was the women who were insisting the circumcision go ahead. They were enforcing the mutilation of their own daughters, while the men didn't really care whether it happened or not. The women believed it was necessary to remove the clitoris and the labia to reduce the sex drive and promote the chastity of young women. They also believed the practice brought prestige to a girl's family by making her eligible for marriage.

Agnes knew circumcision was dangerous and pointless but, to her mind, being labelled a coward by her community was far worse than any pain she would endure, so she gave in.

'It is something you cannot imagine. For the first weeks I couldn't wake up. I was anaemic, but they fed me lots of blood. We had no medication, so what we used to wash the wound was your urine, you know how painful because urine is salty. You have to put your legs together, there is an old woman who makes you put your legs together so that the urine is used to wash your wound. Day by day, the urine passes through there. You put your legs together and the wound will not be septic. One loses the mind. You even don't know where you are. The pain is just too much that you cannot bear. You feel like you can burst. You shout, you scream.'

The women who carried out the circumcision were also the midwives for the village. So, after cutting a young girl, several years later they would be battling to help her give birth through all the scar tissue. They created the damage and then had to deal with its consequences, but kept doing it even though they knew it made childbirth excruciating.

'They believed it was an entry to adulthood. So when you are not cut, you are still a child. They call you a child and you cannot be accepted in the community. So you had to be cut to be accepted. These days I know it is meaningless, it is just harming the girls and making them feel pain for nothing.

'I had prolonged labour pains as result of the cutting. What is left there is a scar . . . when you are giving birth, you know, a scar is very hard. It is tough. It cannot expand the way the normal body is supposed to . . . it cannot stretch. So when you are giving birth, you are bleeding at the same time. You feel like all the bottom of you is all gone, because of the scars.'

Agnes doesn't lower her voice when she talks about it; it's almost as if she wants the people sitting at the other tables in the café to hear her. She looks at her watch.

'We should go, the sun is going soon.'

We drive out to Agnes's farm to take some photographs before dark. The orange glare of the sunset catches the dust in the air and turns the spindly African trees to silhouette. A narrow white hook of moon hangs above the horizon and I can feel the coolness of the night before the light really starts changing. A small Maasai woman with a red blanket around her shoulders comes out to greet us: she's the shepherd's wife, so short and wiry she looks more like a boy than a woman. She answers politely and nods as Agnes asks her about the cattle. The two women stand peering through the fence into the cattle yards; Agnes's big frame and the petite shape of the shepherd's wife are stretched into long shadows on the ground. Agnes tells her the cattle are not fat enough, but the shepherd's wife says she and the cattle are hungry. The start of the rainy season has brought some fine shoots of green grass, but not enough to fill the bellies of hungry stock or grow crops for hungry shepherds. By the time the long conversation is finished, the sun has almost gone.

There's a glow from the doorway of the shepherd family's simple wooden hut near the cattle yards. A small boy leans against the door, warming the backs of his legs from the campfire inside. The shepherd's wife invites us in to where it's smoky and warm. A tiny black puppy and a newborn goat are lying side by side next to the fire on the dirt floor; their front legs are tucked in neatly and they nuzzle each other for extra warmth. The smoke stings my eyes as the shepherd's wife shows me her home – it's smaller than a caravan inside. Her wooden bed is at one end of the hut, her husband's is at the other. When he wants sex he calls her; the rest of the time they sleep apart. The children sleep in her bed or on the dirt next to the fire. There are no lights inside, just the flickering of the flames that throw orange light onto Agnes's face as she talks. Outside, there is darkness and cold.

I ask Agnes about the shepherd's house and sleeping arrangements as we drive back into town. She says it's very common for the husband and wife to sleep separately. She laughs and shakes her head when I ask about love. Love has nothing to do with it, she tells me.

Agnes was married when she was eighteen: her parents chose her husband, she didn't have any say in it. The marriage of a daughter is a source of wealth for the family; the more beautiful, capable and respectable she is, the larger the dowry. Her husband-to-be started bringing gifts to the family, giving sugar to her father and blankets and tobacco to her uncles. The night before the wedding, the older women of the village came to Agnes's hut.

'The women told me I am now somebody's property. You

see, a Maasai husband doesn't request for sex, he just gets hold of the leg and he starts off. After he has satisfied himself, then he goes off. You have no choice, you cannot say no, you cannot say yes. It has to be. If he wants it, even if it is during the day and you are working, you have to do it. You have to attend to him. So that is how it is. There is a lot of pushing and bumps, you cannot talk. He can use you the whole night depending on his strength.'

The morning before her wedding she woke up before dawn and her mother and friends started decorating her with elaborate Maasai ornaments. They put milk in a small calabash, which she wore on her back, and they splashed her legs with milk and alcohol to bless her for the long walk to her husband's village. She walked most of the day. Some people cheered and others teased her as she passed through other villages on the way; the locals saw the calabash on her back and knew she was a bride. When she arrived at her husband's village, she gave the calabash of milk to her new family and in return they gave her a new name for her married life.

'You are given that name in the evening, then, very early in the morning, your husband takes you out to show you the cows to look after. Your husband will give you five cows, maybe your mother-in-law will give you another cow, you are supposed to know all those cows. You have some ink or something to put a mark. They are the cows you are supposed to milk. You have to take care of them and identify them, even from far.

'The following day you are shaved. You cannot sleep with your husband until they shave your head, to remove the hair you came with. It is like making you a new day.

'You don't even know if you are supposed to be afraid, you don't even know where you are. You don't like the whole thing. You are just used like an object. An object. There is nobody who loves you there, they are all new people. Your mother-in-law is very harsh, she keeps saying, "What kind of woman did we get?"'

I see young Maasai women walking along the rocky streets

in Narok. They wear traditional dress and tiny black canvas tennis shoes on their feet and they rarely make eye contact with me: their gaze is fixed ahead while they balance heavy loads on their heads. They still have the thin arms and small hips of girlhood, but they already carry babies on their backs. Some of them cross to the other side of the road as Agnes and I walk past because they are too shy to say hello.

I'm following Agnes to church, a round redbrick building on top of the hill, overlooking the muddy bus station. Members of the congregation greet each other with warm handshakes but the children are not allowed to shake hands. They have to bow their heads to adults, who touch them on the scalp, almost as if they are blessing them.

The sound of the church bells competes with the Muslim call to prayer that crackles from the speakers of a nearby mosque. As we walk inside, Agnes hands me her English Bible and reads from her Maasai version. Two young preachers take to the pulpit – one is wearing a badly fitting suit and the other is in a bright pink shirt and tie. They preach in tandem – one speaks Swahili, the other Maasai in a rapid-fire double act, each translating the other's sermon line by line. They zigzag their way amongst the pews, in an energetic performance that goes down well with the crowd. Most of them don't have television so this is their weekly entertainment. Sometimes the young preachers get the giggles when the translations go wrong. Even Agnes, who doesn't give away her laughter easily, smiles at their jokes.

After church we catch a taxi to a pub on the outskirts of town, a Sunday meeting place for Agnes's family. Her son and grandchildren are already sitting around a table and her youngest granddaughter, Nellie, runs toward her with her brightly coloured plaits flopping from side to side. Her son, Paul, stands up to greet her. Agnes is very clearly the head of the family, which is extremely unusual for a Maasai woman. Even as a young bride, Agnes was slowly starting to question the traditions that were smothering women's potential.

'I hated the whole thing. From the beginning I was not happy.

I started mingling with the women, we started forming groups with women. I was elected as a treasurer.'

The women began with a simple question. They wanted to find out why so many Maasai girls weren't finishing school. As an untrained village teacher, Agnes saw talented girls dropping out of school and being married off and in late 1992, the women decided to carry out a survey, village to village, hut to hut. In every house they visited, female genital mutilation was put forward as the number one reason why girls were uneducated. As soon as the girls were cut, they became women in the eyes of the villagers. They pulled out of school and started their lives as wives and mothers. The results of the survey were almost unanimous.

Agnes and the other women knew that if they wanted girls to further their education, they would need to stop female genital mutilation. It was a staggering task, like trying to convince a western society to stop celebrating Christmas, FGM had become such a part of the culture. The 'cutting season' during the December school holidays was deeply entrenched and families looked forward with great pride to the time when their daughter was about to be circumcised.

But Agnes and the other members of the women's group were slowly starting to see through the ritual. They had all experienced horrific labours and deliveries when birthing because their vaginas were so scarred from circumcision. And the more they researched, the more they found out: they had lost a great deal of sexual function.

'We thought, this contributes to a lot of love missing from our families, because a woman is just used like an object. If she could have her clitoris, it would stimulate her, she could enjoy sex as well. When one is having sex, it is the labia that develops the wetness. Because of the cut you will always be having dry sex. We got the information from the doctor, we did research. Then we talked to different people. We looked at it deeply and we decided it was something that should not be happening.'

The women knew they couldn't attack the practice of FGM head on; that would get them nowhere. Instead they decided to talk about it in terms of education, declaring that they were trying to find ways to stop girls from leaving school.

'When we started the project in 1995, we couldn't mention FGM directly. We used education as an entry point because [the issue] was sensitive. We would talk about education until they would say, "Why are you asking us the reasons why? We know it is circumcision, that is why our girls drop out from school."'

It was a very clever strategy and the women had the credentials to carry it off: they weren't outsiders, they were local women who had been through it themselves. It made all the difference and was far more effective than bringing in foreigners or large non-government organisations.

'The problem with most NGOs, they come and they bring outsiders. But when you use people from the community you will get what you want, because the people are not suspicious. Me, they know that I am cut. If I was not cut they would say, "Ah, this one is not cut, what is she telling us?" Because I'm cut they listen to me.'

Agnes set off on foot armed with a wooden model of a vagina to show women the damage caused by FGM. She travelled from village to village, meeting with women under trees, in huts and in the grazing fields.

'We wanted to show them what it is. We thought if we could get a model, it could speak louder than the words. The model shows all the types of female genital mutilation. It was made in America. When it was brought here, we used that sample to take it to the people who carve. They just looked at it and they carved it.

'For the first two years, people thought I was mad. Crazy. But now they have seen, we have more people talking about it and more people are coming to our centre to borrow it to use it.'

I get the giggles when I imagine the local carpenter being asked to make wooden vaginas but Agnes shakes her head and says the man wasn't embarrassed – it was just business. I picture him carefully measuring the dimensions and carving replicas. The extra models meant Agnes and the other women could visit even more villages. They walked, caught minibuses and rode donkeys to reach as many women as possible. At night they slept on the floor of huts in the villages.

'When I come to your house, I don't need your bed. Even if you give me your bed, I don't need your blankets. It was enjoyable because I was working with my community. I came to understand them more.'

News of Agnes's work started to spread as she hiked from one village to the next. Aid groups in Nairobi were hearing stories about the Maasai woman and the wooden vagina, and soon word reached an international activist who wanted to help.

'I started in 1995. In the year 2000, I met Eve Ensler from New York, who is the writer of the play *The Vagina Monologues*. She found me in the field when I was doing my work with my model, walking. She said, "We will buy you a jeep so you will not be walking."'

The arrival of the jeep was a big step forward. Agnes could now reach many more villages, but the more she travelled, the more she realised she was only dealing with part of the problem. It wasn't enough merely to raise awareness and move on to the next village; girls who were facing FGM had nowhere to go if they wanted to escape. Agnes decided to set up a rescue centre in Narok, a haven for girls who ran away. Eve Ensler's organisation, V-Day, agreed to provide substantial funding.

Agnes found some land on the outskirts of town and started to build the centre, which she decided to call Tasaru, meaning 'rescue' in the local language. In the beginning it was only a few simple buildings with a big fence and a tall gate. There was deep suspicion when word got out that a woman was building a place for girls who didn't want to be cut, but Agnes persisted. She continued to travel to the villages, educating women and girls, and giving them directions on how to reach her centre if they ever needed to get there in an emergency. Even small girls were told how to get to Narok if they needed to escape FGM. Some of those who are now in the centre found their way with the directions they received when they were very young.

I travel with Agnes in her jeep to visit the centre along a rippled, rocky track several kilometres out of town. A tall, old Maasai man wrapped in red robes and carrying a stick stands at the gate. He squints until he can see the jeep properly, then he waves at Agnes and opens the gate. Agnes explains that the man is Ole Kunkuru, the night watchman: his job is to protect the girls and stop angry relatives from trying to harm them. He greets her with military-style respect and seriousness. She has an obvious affection for him and smiles as he fumbles to open the gate. Ole Kunkuru is old and poor, and Agnes describes him as 'shaggy', because she regards him as a man too ragged to try his luck with the girls.

'Ole Kunkuru takes care of the girls day and night. It's good to have one you can trust, one who is very shaggy and cannot have any relationship with those girls. Ole Kunkuru plays a very big role at the centre. Whenever these girls need anything or they have a problem, Ole Kunkuru rushes here to call me. He locks the gate, he rushes to me. It's up to Ole Kunkuru to know who is coming in and who is going out. He has to be very strict.'

As we drive inside, dozens of girls meet us. Some are sitting in circles on the grass, reading books and talking, some are washing clothes by hand and others are wiping the windows with pieces of newspaper. The girls form a long line as soon as Agnes steps out of the jeep and one by one they bow their heads in greeting. Agnes touches them on the crown and addresses each one by name. They treat her with absolute respect, but not fear. Agnes walks from one girl to the next, checking and greeting them, asking if they are getting enough food and if their studies are going well. I watch her looking into their eyes carefully as she asks them if there are any problems. Many of the girls are genuinely religious: one raises her hand and says that they want to go to church, but Ole Kunkuru won't let them out of the gate. Agnes smiles and promises she'll tell him to let them go. The girls applaud, but one hangs back shyly; she's a newcomer, thinner and quieter than the others. Agnes speaks with her gently and the girl lifts her skirt to show welts on her legs where she was beaten by her father. She arrived last night, after running away to escape a forced marriage to an old man in her village.

All the girls at Tasaru have run away from their villages, risking their lives and leaving their families to escape FGM. For some, it's the first time they've travelled alone; many found their way using directions from sisters or friends who attended one of Agnes's seminars. Agnes speaks of the girls with great admiration.

'They need a lot of courage and they must have made their own decision.'

The girls are in their teens and most of them are tall and strong, the combination of Maasai genes and good food giving them an athletic appearance. They dress simply in skirts, sandals and T-shirts, their hair is plain and short and on first greeting they're often shy. They call me madam until I tell them it's okay to use my name. I watch them studying, cleaning and washing, all of which they do with great joy and enthusiasm – if they're asked to carry out a task they do it straight away and without complaint. It's a daily routine that may appear sparse and strict to western teenagers. But it is still a novelty to many of the girls, who have come from the villages where they spent their days carrying heavy loads of water, looking after cattle and enduring the strict discipline of traditional life.

'They behave so well, I have never had any incident. You are seeing that some of them are cleaning the windows, that is their duty. Some of them are preparing lunch, some are working in the classroom. I love them. They are amazing.'

The girls know that if they had remained in their villages, they would have been circumcised, married off and pregnant. They live at Tasaru in the school holidays and during the term they are in nearby boarding schools where their fees are paid by donors. Their security is carefully monitored to make sure they're not snatched or harmed by relatives who come in search of them.

Agnes and the workers at Tasaru try to reconcile the girls and their families and often the parents reluctantly accept what has happened when they realise the future benefits of having an educated daughter. In the August school holidays, they hold ceremonies to take the place of circumcision.

'What we usually do is bring these girls into a five-day seclusion. There is feasting, dancing, we slaughter a cow. We bring women that we call godmothers who come and teach these girls their culture. So we are not really saying the whole culture is bad. What we are trying to say is the bit of it called cutting, we do away with it. The marrying-off of a young girl who is fourteen, we do away with it. But if your daughter is 22 and agrees to be married off, then marry her off. Because she is a grown-up, she can decide for herself.

'The topics we teach these girls are the normal topics that a woman teaches her daughter after the cutting. Preparing a girl to be a woman, teach her about her body and just to build self-esteem, understanding her body well and the relationship between her and boys.'

I stand at the back of one of the classrooms at Tasaru while Agnes talks with the girls. She sits on the edge of a desk, next to one of her wooden model vaginas and the girls start giggling as soon as she brings it out. It has detachable parts showing the effects of various stages of FGM. It's pretty gruesome. I try to imagine her carting this thing from one village to the next. Once the nervous laughter stops, the girls are captivated as Agnes shows them the most severe form of FGM.

'This is me,' she tells them. 'This is how I'm cut.'

The model shows the grotesque mess left behind. There's silence. Some of the girls look at the floor. I do too.

Agnes invites me to go into town and meet some of the former female circumcisers. We find them in a dusty alleyway, gathered outside an old building. A few of the Maasai women are squatting down shaving each other's heads with razor blades and I can see drops of blood marking the small cuts on their scalps.

'They don't have enough water in the bush, so it's better to shave the hair; it's cleaner,' Agnes explains.

When the women get up to shake hands, their palms are dusted with white from an old milling machine coughing flour into buckets. A mixture of flour and dust splutters from the doorway of the building and I can hear the noisy clatter of the machine. This old contraption provides a living for eighteen former circumcisers. Instead of carrying out FGM, they now run the mill. The women are dressed in full Maasai costume as they tinker with the machinery. A procession of customers brings in buckets of maize to be ground into flour.

Agnes introduces me to an old, wiry woman called Noolamala; she's the leader of the former circumcisers at the mill. She's a traditional woman: her earlobes are stretched into large holes, her neck is covered in layers of intricate necklaces and her wrists are heavy with Maasai bracelets. Noolamala cut hundreds of girls when she was a circumciser.

'Noolamala inherited the practice from her grandmother. It was a way of living. She was married to an old man, he was not responsible, she thought the easiest way of earning a living is doing the cutting. When you cut, you are paid a lot of money, it happens over the month of December, that is when they do female genital mutilation. You cut twenty girls, that is 20-thousand shillings. This is something she has done over twenty years. So you imagine that in a year you have cut twenty girls, then in twenty years you cut 400 girls.'

Noolamala was one of the first circumcisers in the district to stop cutting after Agnes sat down with her and explained the dangers. It was a long process. Noolamala was not only defending tradition, it was her way of life; however, she'd also seen the damage caused by FGM.

'Noolamala also happens to be a traditional birth attendant, so she could easily understand the effects. Most of the circumcisers are birth attendants and circumcisers as well. It needs a lot of courage to cut somebody, it's not easy. So it happens that if you are a circumciser, you are also capable of assisting to give birth. So it was easy to convince Noolamala to stop the cutting, and assist her to earn a living.'

The United Nations Population Fund provided funding for the old milling machine: a simple, local solution. Now, eighteen circumcisers have found a new way to make a living, sharing the workload and the profits.

Agnes shakes hands with the women and shouts greetings over the clatter of the mill as we leave. We walk up the street to a café and all the way Agnes's mobile phone keeps ringing, as it does almost all day. Sometimes she doesn't even bother to put it back in her handbag, because she knows it will ring again. In the street, too, she is approached by dozens of people, some simply wanting to greet her, others wanting help for problems. Agnes is treated the same way I've seen male chiefs treated in other places, but it's unusual to see a woman given so much attention and status. When we reach the café, too, people are watching her. The manager greets her again and makes sure the waiter gives her water at room temperature, the way she likes it.

I notice a man sitting in the corner with his teenage daughters. They watch Agnes and start whispering questions. The man laughs and waves to Agnes. She smiles.

'They are asking me if [I am] the vagina lady. I told them yes.'

Agnes smiles, enjoying the joke and her apparent fame. She's known not only for her work at Tasaru, but also as the first woman elected to the district council.

'It was controversial. Men were crazy, even those who didn't come from the area, came to interfere. Saying, "Oh, it is a woman. How can they elect a woman?" It was 2002. Everybody who was in politics didn't want to be associated with the campaign against FGM: they thought by doing it they would lose the votes. I wanted to prove to everybody that our community should not live the way it was because you fear losing votes. In the beginning, the people felt guilty for voting for me. Everybody was telling them, "Shame on you. How do you go and elect a woman?" But they voted me in and when I came to the council, the group of 47 councillors elected me a vice chairperson. So it means they have trust in me. It was exciting.'

I admire Agnes but she hasn't been the easiest woman to get to know during the interviews for this book. In the beginning I wondered what I was doing here, spending six days waiting for the lady with the wooden model vagina. But having spent some time with her, I can begin to understand the way she operates. Her day doesn't always start with a strict plan and her mobile phone and conversations in the street can drag her from one issue to the next. In the week I waited for her, she did two trips in as many days to Nairobi, while juggling dozens of meetings and commitments.

I like her toughness, even though I find it a bit intimidating. On the first day we were scheduled to meet, I was ill with a severe stomach bug. I spent the day between bed and the bathroom, vomiting. I went downstairs when Agnes arrived and apologised for cancelling our interview. Even though she was very understanding, I wondered whether she thought I was a bit soft.

Now she has softened, or maybe I'm not quite so intimidated by her. She looks tired after a long week. Her phone keeps ringing as we sit in the café.

'Let's go to my house and I'll turn this thing off for a while,' she says, slipping her plump feet in and out of her sandals.

We take a taxi to the edge of town, walk into a yard and down a narrow corridor between two houses; it's barely a metre wide. Agnes's front door is locked with a big padlock. She opens it and we go inside. Her house is very small and looks like a mini chalet – there are wooden panels on the wall and a steep ceiling. We sit in lounge chairs covered with pink embroidered cloth and we're surrounded by neatly arranged ornaments: it's neat, clean, and grandmotherly. The furniture is almost too big for the room. The dining table and chairs are pushed to the side and a green curtain covers the doorway to Agnes's bedroom. She lets out a sigh as she slumps into the chair, her soft folds filling the gaps between the cushions.

'Woo, I'm tired. Everybody is chasing me with things they need done.'

She turns off her mobile phone. The quiet, cosy room is a relief after a chaotic morning. I tell Agnes I'm grateful for her time. She nods, but I'm not sure if coming home is merely a break for her or a bit of a peace offering to me after so many delays. Her voice is gentler when she settles into her favourite chair, and I take my shoes off as we talk. Some of the friction and her resistance has gone now.

'We can have some quiet time.'

Agnes lives alone, but close to her son's house. She left her husband when he announced he wanted to marry a second wife.

'In our culture your husband still goes back and gets married again. Men are not serious in bringing up their families. After having my kids, my husband started saying he wants to marry again. When the era of HIV came I told him, "You can now leave." I live alone, because how do we trust three people? It is even hard to trust with just two. So now I live by myself with my kids.

'I wanted freedom to do what is right for me. It was difficult, it was controversial. Our culture does not allow women to have property. Our culture does not allow women to move around doing her own things. So you can have a lot of knowledge but be oppressed by someone who is not knowledgeable.'

Agnes's situation is extremely unusual; few Maasai women have economic and personal freedom. Many of the transactions which affect the rest of their lives are made when they are only teenagers. They are uneducated, married and bear many children before they even reach their twenties. Their husbands are often older and it's very common for a teenage girl to be married to a man in his thirties, forties or even fifties. It's an uneven relationship from the beginning – her bargaining power is minimal, then, by the time she reaches full adulthood, the workload of motherhood has already enveloped her. That's the cycle Agnes is trying to break.

'If I had nine kids, do you think I could have time with you? Do you think I could be a leader? The way to tame a woman is to make her give birth so that she is always breastfeeding or carrying a baby or thinking of what her baby will eat. That woman will be tied, she will never know what is happening beyond her house.

Neither will she ever have any time to join other women for discussion or go to a meeting. She will always be by herself. You know when you don't have food for your child, there is nobody you can listen to. Most of the women are poor. They can't afford a cup of tea to share some discussion with somebody. You can't have your mind straight because you will always need to kneel down for somebody or bend down for somebody because of poverty.

'If I could speak to the President of Kenya I would tell him to put more resources on family planning, that would stop our young girls from bringing up children without a plan, giving them time to organise themselves. Reproductive health has to be addressed if the government is serious. We have so many unplanned families.'

Ironically, in a similar way to FGM, often it's the women who perpetuate and enforce much of the oppression. They maintain the status quo and because of their lack of education they are easy targets for manipulation by others. When Agnes ran for the district council, some of the fiercest opponents of a woman being elected were themselves women. They were outraged that a woman would try to break into an all-male domain.

'That is it. It is them who carry the law. The women are so oppressed mentally that when they look at another woman doing something they think, how can a woman do that? Women were used to attack. I want to address this issue of women fighting women.'

In many traditional villages, the number of women who are educated, choose their own husbands and have control over their reproductive health is minimal. It's in dramatic contrast with life at home in Australia, where women often feel the pressure of having so many choices.

The lack of choice and freedom for many traditional Maasai women means their talents remain untapped.

'They are wasted. There is a lot of it. You look at the young lady who was talking to me in the street this morning, that was the husband standing next to her. Look at how beautiful the young girl was. Look at how ugly the old man was, he stands there as the young girl talks to me. That is a girl who should be in the university, but now she has four kids. She was married forcefully, the husband was picked by her parents. You look at that young girl and you know there is a lot of knowledge. But it is wasted here. She could be a doctor. She could be a lawyer. But she has no chance. She is looking after a very old man.

'Tasaru has rescued many girls but there is still a big number that are being wasted, because nobody is addressing the issue. When these girls come to the centre they are shy, but after three months they know what life means to them.'

Agnes shows me some photographs from a visit to the United States, where she was a special guest for V-Day celebrations run by Eve Ensler. Her picture features in a book of women activists from around the world and she displays it proudly, rubbing the pages gently with her finger.

'I could never imagine. I never thought I would travel. It has given me a lot of knowledge. It has really shaped me. I can support myself and I can lead my own life.

'When I saw New York for the first time, it was just like a dream. I remember talking to eighteen hundred people, addressing them. I was terrified. Kofi Annan was there. The wife of Clinton was there. I went to the stage. I said, "Here I am. I was cut at fourteen."'

Agnes pauses and looks at her watch.

'Woo, we've been talking for almost an hour. My people will wonder where I am.'

She reluctantly turns her phone on: it squawks with messages and rings within a few minutes.

'I better get back into town, I've got some work to finish.'

A taxi takes us in to the main junction. I shake hands and say goodbye to Agnes, and start walking up the hill to the guesthouse. Donkeys bellow in protest as they haul heavy loads along the street, and several young Maasai women carry buckets on their heads and babies on their backs. They look down shyly as I pass them. When I look back I can still see Agnes on the corner; she's standing with her shoulder shrugged up into her neck as she takes another call. She waves goodbye.

'One has to have a vision and a goal that you want to achieve. You have to come through all the difficulties that are there. I had to go and sleep in people's houses. I did a lot of work, I went through many things. It takes time and you have to be consistent, what you say today is what you say tomorrow. You have to be genuine in whatever you do. The moment you look like you have something funny in you, people will not have trust in you. Whatever you do, do it with all your mind.

'Women have a lot of power and a woman is somebody who can lead. Men do most things to satisfy themselves alone, but women care about the other people. I think a woman can really do it. The community is changing. It is not only me.'

The old, dishevelled hall is full of military uniforms and hundreds of pairs of army boots piled into a mound several metres tall, as if they have been dumped from the back of a tip truck. Battle pictures in heavy gold frames and old rifles are mounted on the wall. There's even a life-sized statue of a warrior riding a horse blocking part of the doorway, complete with home-made armour, a shield and a sword. It's so big and life-like, I say 'Excuse me' as I squeeze past it. The room reminds me of an old-fashioned country town hall that has overgrown itself. It's a museum gone feral, but it's fascinating; the kind of room I would have pored over as a child.

This is the headquarters of Ethiopia's oldest war veterans, those who fought against the Italians when they invaded in 1935. The invasion was supposed to be Mussolini's grand campaign in Africa, but it backfired and the Ethiopians won. They are known as the Patriots: most of them are aged in their eighties; some were only children when the war started. As I walk around, one of the leaders apologises for the mess in the hall.

'The boots and uniforms are for our parade on Patriot's Day. But we don't have anywhere to keep them properly.'

Outside the hall, dozens of Patriots sit in the morning sun, chatting and drinking coffee. Some of them wear old army tunics or hats with their civilian clothes. The hall has become a daily meeting place for many Patriots, who, more than 60 years after the war, still feel a very strong sense of belonging.

This is my first day in Ethiopia. It feels very different from other places I've visited in Africa; in fact, some Ethiopians speak of Africa as if it is a separate place. Ethiopia is the continent's oldest independent country. It has never been colonised, apart from the brief Italian occupation. Its independence is a great source of pride. Ethiopia has its own distinctive food, dress, language, religion and history.

I spend much of the morning with a group of women Patriots. They ask me if Australians know much about Ethiopian history.

'Did you learn about our victories at school?'

They look surprised when I shake my head.

'Your people learn about British history, but you do not know about Ethiopia. You only see us on the television news when we have famine in this country.'

It's true. Ethiopia's history has been overshadowed by images of hunger and suffering. As I speak with the Patriot women, it's easy to see there is a large gap between the way they view their country and the way it's seen by outsiders. As the conversation goes on, a tiny old woman hovers around outside. I can see by the way the men treat her that she's regarded with a great deal of respect. Space is made for her on crowded benches, and the Patriot commanders greet her at length and with extra politeness.

The old woman is dressed in a droopy navy blue skirt and layers of cardigans in order to keep warm. A white Ethiopian shawl is draped across her shoulders and she leans on a darkly varnished walking stick. When I go outside, she is almost always in my peripheral vision; she flashes me a smile when I make eye contact with her. Eventually, she starts talking with my interpreter. The old woman's name is Tenagnework. It takes me a few attempts to pronounce it: Te-nan-ya-work. It's a bit like Tania-work with an extra syllable thrown in. Tenagnework asks if we can give her a lift back to her house.

On the way home, she sits in the back seat chatting and laughing. She was a child during the Italian invasion in 1935, but she and all her siblings volunteered to fight. She is captivating and lively. She beams and nods her head enthusiastically when I ask if I can interview her. She kisses me on the cheek and hand, and we agree to meet tomorrow.

The next morning arrives in a misty haze; the smoke of cooking fires is mixed with the moisture that hangs over the city. Addis Ababa is one of the highest cities in the world, and mornings there are cool and damp. We drive to the old neighbourhood, where Tenagnework lives. Her small house is near the top of a busy commercial road.

Knock. Knock. Knock. I spy through the hole in the iron gate and wait. I can hear the scuff of muddy footsteps, and then a groan and thud as a big wooden stump is rolled out of the way. Brown fingers open the lopsided gate. One of Tenagnework's granddaughters holds it open, bowing and smiling shyly.

The front yard is slippery and uneven and there's no garden, just rocks and muddy ground. A clothesline hangs above it and there are plastic bowls and buckets near the door. The yard is small; it's less than ten footsteps from the gate to Tenagnework's front steps.

It's cold and rainy, but the front door is almost always open. This is Tenagnework's bedroom and it's also the lounge room. Tattered lino covers the floor and old sacks are spread on the step to collect the mud from damp shoes. Her bed is just inside the door and it is always neatly made; she smoothes it with her hands as she talks. Pictures of saints and an old poster of the Emperor Haile Selassie sit on the sideboard – these are Tenagnework's treasures: God and the Emperor.

She sits on her bed, straightening a shawl around her shoulders to keep out the cold, but her feet are bare. Tenagnework is almost 80 years old, and her skin is so paper thin and wrinkly, it scrunches around the edges of her face when she smiles. Her eyes are kind and sparkly; they sparkle even more when she talks about the past. The memories seem to give her bursts of dignity and energy and she giggles with a sweet granny laugh.

She holds and rubs my hands as we sit on her bed and talk. There's something about my white palms that fascinates her. She says they remind her of St Mary, so she calls me Mariam, St Mariam. My hands are smooth and fair, and she is convinced that I have never done any hard work in my life. She dots kisses all the way from my wrists to the ends of my fingers. Her mad giggle is pure delight.

She shows me several old tattoos on her hands and feet. The patterns of circles and long crosses have become blurred with time and sunk into the creases in her skin.

'This is a cross, the priests did this one for me. They had ink and they put it in a small cup. Then they draw the cross with a stick and then they put the needle. It hurt a bit and it bled as well.'

Her left hand is tattooed with words written in the local language, Amharic; she says it is her name, Tenagnework. The tattoo was done just before she went off to the war, so that she could be identified if she was killed or injured.

'My skin was smooth then, so anyone could have read it from a distance. Now I am getting older and it's not smooth.'

Outside her front yard, the neighbourhood goes about its business. The houses in the street have rouge-coloured mud walls and rusting iron roofs. Women sell tomatoes and onions spread on sacks right in front of her gate, and young men herd groups of donkeys and goats in the middle of the traffic. Tenagnework has lived here for almost 40 years. Half her life. But she grew up in the countryside: she was a little girl from a wealthy family, who spent her days reciting the Bible and learning to sew. Her father was a bodyguard for Emperor Haile Selassie, dividing his time between the palace and the family home in Debra Libanos. He wasn't a high-ranking official, but rich enough to have twenty slaves, purchased for less than a dollar each, to run the farm and look after the family.

'We had ten women slaves and ten men slaves. They were bought from southern Ethiopia for 6 or 7 Ethiopian birr. We would buy them when they were very small, little boys and girls. After we buy them, they give birth and also have slave children.'

Most of the slave men worked outside, while the women ran the household and helped to look after the children. They were almost like nannies to Tenagnework and her brothers and sisters. The slaves were ordered to make sure the children behaved themselves.

'They used to discipline us, teach us how to act when a guest comes. We were very disciplined. If we were not, the slave was assigned to punish us. My mother would make sure they don't beat us very badly, but they were told to discipline us. So we were very polite.'

Slavery was still common in Ethiopia in the 1920s and 30s, and some wealthy families had more than 100 slaves to labour in their fields and houses. It was just part of growing up for Tenagnework, who was supervised in particular by a strict slave woman with deep black skin and strong arms.

'Her name was Ayesasam Ejuae. She was very big, she was almost the size of this door. My mother gave her orders to teach us how to cook. I respected her and feared her much more than my mother. Every time she gave me an order, I would reply, "Whatever you say." She also taught us how to weave cotton. When we were not doing it right, she would make us swallow a piece of it so we don't repeat the mistake next time. Our mother used to say to her, "It's getting too much, stop it." But she used to say it was for our good.'

Tenagnework and her siblings had a tutor who taught them about the Bible, but they didn't go to school – they stayed in their compound and had little contact with strangers. When she was ten years old, the routine in the compound started changing. The slave men were erecting a large tent and the slave women were making alcoholic brews. There were deliveries, decorations and discussions. Tenagnework was curious and she started asking questions about all the extra activity.

'At that time everybody was running around getting ready to throw a party. They were building a tent, so I was wondering, what is happening? My friends, they told me, "You're getting married." I didn't trust them at first but even the older ladies were making local drinks and cooking. They teased me, they said, "Is this enough for your wedding? We have heard he is a priest. We will see how you end up being married to a priest." So that is how I learned that I was going to get married.'

A respected young deacon, Abayneh Wolde-Michael, asked for Tenagnework's hand in marriage. He was almost 30 years old, but Tenagnework, at ten, was still a child. His superiors in the church decided it was time for him to get married because they were worried that if he didn't find a bride he might be led into temptation by an unsuitable woman. It was the accepted custom that a man would take a young girl as a bride. She would live with his parents until she reached puberty, then she would start sleeping with her husband.

The marriage had been arranged between the two families without Tenagnework's knowledge. She wasn't told until it was time to get dressed for the ceremony.

'I was just a little girl. I was just playing around with my friends. I didn't understand the whole thing. It was very exciting. My friends were dressing me up. I remember telling them, "I wish you will be getting married soon too."'

When Tenagnework's father told his colleagues at the palace that his daughter was getting married, the father confessor to the Emperor, Abba Hanna, was concerned. He thought Tenagnework was too young to be given away to a husband. Abba Hanna was a monk, a stern, frugal man who kept the Emperor's money and best interests at heart. He was also godfather to Tenagnework's brothers, and a respected family friend. Abba Hanna made Tenagnework's father promise that she would not be forced to have sexual relations with her husband until she was fifteen. The family and the groom agreed.

Tenagnework was dressed for the wedding in a white cotton dress with an embroidered cross and she wore a black cloak and a white shawl. Her face was covered with a veil and as she looked out through the woven cloth she saw her husband, who put her on his back and carried her to the ceremony.

She doesn't talk about the wedding with any bitterness or embarrassment. It was just the way things were done, it was completely normal and acceptable for a small girl to be married off to a man aged in his twenties or thirties. Tenagnework remembers being excited when she met her husband.

'That was the first time I saw him was on the wedding day. He carried me on his back. That is the culture here. The groom comes in, carries the bride on his back and takes her to a room. I was prepared for that. He put a ring on my finger. He put a necklace around my neck, a cross.'

The wedding celebrations went on for eight days. Relatives arrived with lambs, goats and gifts, and a special hut was built in the compound for the wedding party. The bride and groom, best men, bridesmaids and their friends all lived and slept in the hut together for the eight days. Tenagnework slept next to her husband, but there was no sex because of the agreement made with Abba Hanna. She studied her husband: he was short, dark-skinned and handsome.

'I sat quietly next to him. I was a little girl, so I didn't have any feeling for him. I was sitting there quietly. The best man was trying to talk with me. I told him, "There is no one for me to play with. You are all boys." So he went out and got some girls, who came and sat next to me.'

When the celebrations eventually finished, Tenagnework packed her clothes and prepared to go to her husband's house, a six-hour journey by mule. She would be escorted to visit her parents once a month. Tenagnework took a slave with her to help with the domestic chores. She was farewelled by her parents and her brothers and sisters. The slaves also said their goodbyes and the feared slave woman, Ayesasam Ejuae, who had disciplined her throughout her childhood, gave her advice before she left.

'She said, "If you misbehave, then everybody will be insulting us that we didn't raise you properly. So respect your husband and behave as you behaved here."'

Tenagnework's face is deeply serious when she talks about discipline. In the middle of the interview she gives orders to the granddaughters who share the house with her. There is extra activity: it's Orthodox Easter. Freshly cut green grass has been scattered on the floor of the house; it is a tradition for special ceremonies, a sign of the prosperity of the land. Tenagnework has been fasting for the past 55 days – she hasn't been eating any animal products. But in the early hours of tomorrow morning, the fast will end and Tenagnework will spend the night at the church with thousands of other worshippers. The prayers will finish at 3 am and families will go home to eat, celebrate and eventually sleep. Easter is the most important religious event of the year.

I say goodbye to Tenagnework to let her get ready for church. The streets are already crowded with men and women dressed in white cotton shawls, and the crackling speaker systems of the neighbourhood churches pour prayer across Addis Ababa. It's difficult to overestimate the importance of the Orthodox church in Ethiopia. Its traditions are at the heart of what it means to be Ethiopian. Christianity began to take hold across the land in the fourth century AD and the Orthodox church has been an important part of life there ever since. It permeates the country's culture, politics and beliefs. The Ethiopian Orthodox brand of Christianity is traditional, formal and often strict. It is one of the religion's oldest strands. For a nation in which so many people are uneducated, the church has particular importance. It sets the rhythms and boundaries of daily life.

Gentle rain leaves the roads glistening in the evening and the roadside is cluttered with people walking to church, their shawls wrapped tightly around their heads and shoulders to keep out the drizzle. Candle-sellers and beggars gather outside the church gates, hoping for a little last-minute business.

There's been a sense of excitement and preparations all day. Herdsmen have brought thousands of goats and sheep into the city to sell to families getting ready for the Easter feast. The animals spill out onto the road; they're marked with brightly coloured spray paint, so the herds don't become mixed together. Men carry the live sheep home around their shoulders, clasping the legs with their hands to prevent a last-minute escape. As I look out my hotel window, I can see almost every house has a goat or sheep tied up in the yard, unknowingly waiting for slaughter. When the dawn of Easter Sunday arrives, men start sharpening knives as cats with tails pointed in the air smooch the legs of their owners, hoping for some scraps from the carcass.

I go back to Tenagnework's house to visit her on Easter Sunday afternoon, when her room is crowded with visiting relatives. There's even more cut grass decorating the floor and a large tray of sheep meat on the table: the family is feasting. People are dressed in their best clothes. Most of the women wear long white Ethiopian dresses. Tenagnework's granddaughters are sitting on small stools roasting raw coffee beans over a small charcoal stove on the floor. A lively niece arrives, chatting and laughing. She bows down and kisses Tenagnework on the knees as a sign of respect.

Tenagnework is the head of the family. When she was a child, her father was unquestionably the leader, but by late 1935 he was spending more and more time at the Emperor's palace in Addis Ababa. Ethiopia was carefully watching its borders as Italian troops prepared to invade from neighbouring Eritrea. Italian dictator Benito Mussolini wanted to add Ethiopia to Italy's fledgling colonial empire.

At dawn on 3 October 1935, 100 000 Italian troops crossed the border and overwhelmed the Ethiopian forces. The Italians set up garrisons in towns and villages. The war started two months after Tenagnework was married.

Tenagnework's father was called back to the palace by the Emperor, who gave him several boxes of official documents and made him swear to look after them. Her father took the boxes and hid them in a cave near the monastery at Debra Libanos. But the Italian invasion brought division and suspicion. The Italians used cash, weapons and propaganda to lure collaborators. Those who collaborated were called *bandas*; they fought side by side with the Italians and were despised by other Ethiopians. The *bandas* were the forward scouts, spies and workforce of the Italian invaders. Some of the local *bandas* told the Italians that Tenagnework's father was hiding boxes for the Emperor.

'When the Italians came, the *bandas* told them that it was hidden there in the cave,' says Tenagnework. There were rumours circulating in the village that the boxes contained gold and treasures. But when the Italians recovered the stash, they only found the documents.

Tension was increasing. Tenagnework's family had already been singled out as part of the establishment and her father's position as one of the Emperor's bodyguards made him a target.

'He told my brothers to be ready. He told us the enemy was coming.'

Tenagnework's parents were arrested and jailed by the Italians, and the family's twenty slaves were also imprisoned for two months before being freed. The Italian soldiers interrogated Tenagnework's mother, examining her soft, flawless hands and accusing her of never doing a day's work in her life. The Italians condemned her for practising slavery.

Tenagnework's eldest brother, Seyum, gathered the siblings together and a decision was made to go to the bush before they too were jailed by the Italians. Their father had given them several rifles before he was arrested.

'They put all the eight rifles on the floor. They made a promise to each other and swore on the Bible that they would not give their hands to the Italians. They would rather commit suicide. I was by the side looking at them. I was the little one. I was ten years old. I remember standing there.'

Abba Hanna heard about the arrest of Tenagnework's parents and realised that the children had no choice but to go into hiding in the bush. He sent uniforms and supplies from Addis Ababa as the older brothers started planning their departure.

'They were telling me and my sister, "Get ready, wear your belt." Everybody at that time felt that heroism. We were telling each other, "We are not going to give our country to the Italians." There were around twelve people. Five of my brothers, some of our relatives including my husband and the husband of my sister. There wasn't fear. We were all ready to go and fight. I didn't feel bad about it because nobody was left at home. We all were together. That togetherness gave me the strength. We didn't know at that time the days that were waiting for us. We didn't feel at that time that we were going out to die. At the beginning, the excitement was from the outfits we had. I had a coat and trousers made of khaki. Abba Hanna brought that to me.'

The brothers and sisters had limited experience of life outside their compound and little experience of hardship. Having come from a wealthy family, the years before the war had been plentiful: there was always meat in the house and the children had never felt the emptiness of hunger. Tenagnework was a child bride with few responsibilities who had been exposed to little beyond her own and her husband's families. The group gathered as much dried food as they could carry and set off into the dark together.

'We left during the night. I remember walking through the forest. Twelve of us left together. That night, I remember there was a moonlight. It wasn't very dark but it was very rocky. So we were all holding a stick to lean on. I walked next to my sister. The people from the village promised that they would give all the provisions and the supplies. They blessed us before we left. We set up camp. We made a small tent with leaves.'

Tenagnework and the others set up camp in the forest near Debra Libanos, constructing small shelters from branches covered with leaves. Across Ethiopia, thousands of other families were doing the same: they were known as the Patriots, bands of fighters who were getting ready to take on the Italians. They were amateurs armed with old muskets, swords, shields and rifles. Husbands, wives and children went to the bush together, entire families arrived on the frontline. The war was still in its early stages, but the Patriots were preparing for battle.

'We used to practise shooting. We had the head of an ox on a tree. We used to practise to shoot that target. They were really good, they used to shoot it right in the forehead. The ladies also used to come and try. They gave me a prize for shooting that head.'

Tenagnework was the youngest in the group and she slept next to her older sister, under the shelter made from leaves. Her husband would come and wake her up early in the morning and then she would wake the others for prayers.

'Most of them were older than me. I was the little one there, so he used to send me with messages. I would go around waking them, saying it's time for prayer. Everyone would gather around the priest. He would read from the Bible. It was like being in a church.'

Some of the men and boys would spend the day sitting in the treetops watching for the Italians. The Patriots knew that it wouldn't be long before the fighting would start at Debra Libanos. The Italians had easily defeated the Ethiopian troops in the north and they were now moving inland, taking control of towns and setting up garrisons.

'We stayed there in the bush for two months before the Italians started shooting. The villagers in that area came with whatever weapons they had. When they came we made them swear on the Bible. At first there were only twelve of us but later there were around a thousand people.'

The Patriots were a home-made army; most had never seen battle before and they had little idea about tactics and training. They were led by regional commanders but there wasn't much communication or coordination between the different groups; in fact, in some areas there was intense rivalry. The Italians, on the other hand, were well equipped and well trained, outnumbering the Ethiopian troops by four to one in some of the early battles. But the Patriots were full of confidence, Ethiopian forces had defeated the Italians at the historic battle of Adowa in 1896 and they were sure they could do it again. They soon learned how to deceive and agitate their enemy. The spotters in the trees could see the Italians digging in above the valley near Debra Libanos.

'We could clearly see them. We could see their cannon on the mountain. In the beginning, what we did was misguide the Italians. We made fire with gasoline. The smoke would come out in that place and the Italians would shoot in that direction. They were shooting in the wrong place.'

The men were on the frontline, while most of the women looked after the wounded, carried the dead off the battlefield and maintained the camp. But some also fought with great distinction. Tenagnework helped the women and was a runner for the fighters. When the Patriots in the trees whistled for more ammunition, she would take cloth bags full of bullets to the front.

'I don't have these childhood memories of playing. When they ran out of bullets, we used to run with the bullets. That was childhood for me.'

I ask Tenagnework if she could show me the old battlefields near Debra Libanos. She nods and smiles with anticipation. We arrange to go on Tuesday morning and hire a four-wheel drive for the three-hour drive north of Addis Ababa.

When we arrive, Tenagnework is dressed all in white. She's fidgeting with anticipation as she goes into the back room to straighten her outfit and brush the dust off her white shawl. She is carrying a brown handbag that is broken at one end and she has a freshly ironed handkerchief in her other hand. There are small strips of meat drying on strings hanging above her – the leftovers from Easter. The dark pieces of meat look like seaweed.

Neighbours gather on the footpath as we help her into the car. It's a special journey and she has told everyone she knows that she is going back to her birthplace. It's difficult for her to climb into the four-wheel drive and she giggles when she eventually comes to rest on the back seat. I give her a kiss. She smells sweet; her granddaughters have put some perfume on her for the trip. She shrugs her shoulders with excitement and kisses my hands before pressing my palms on her soft, warm cheeks. Her eyes are bright and sharp as she peeks out from her white veil. It is a rare treat to make the journey in a private vehicle – she normally goes by bus.

Tenagnework asks if we can go to church so that she can pray for a safe journey. The church is only a few hundred metres away up the hill. As we drive through the gates I put on a white veil. When we climb out of the car, she introduces me to the priests and anyone else she can stop. She calls me St Mariam and laughs, and the priests wink back at me as she goes to the veranda of the church to pray.

This church is one of the most important places in her life. She is a leader here, and a member of the disciplinary committee. She uses her walking stick to hit beggars who shuffle around the gates. She talks with two young policemen who are assigned to look after the church, telling them to keep everything in order. They bow their heads in response. The other members of the church also greet her with genuine respect and warmth. She belongs here.

We drive out of Addis Ababa and into the gentle green countryside. Tenagnework chatters most of the way. We pass herd boys guiding their cattle along the side of the road and horsemen cantering along the tracks on ponies with brightly coloured traditional saddles. It's open grazing land with clusters of huts and few fences. The straight road gradually changes into tight turns and bends before we wind into a spectacular valley that looks like a small-scale version of the Grand Canyon. It is rocky and rugged with a pebbly river at the bottom; there is mist rolling down from the hills and a curtain of rain is slowly moving towards us.

This is where Tenagnework, her husband and brothers spent most of the war. They were camped in the forest in the valley and the Italians were up on the high ground. It looks different from what I expected; it's spectacular. Tenagnework's stories come to life as we stand on the lip of the valley peering down on the battlefield.

We can see the dome of the monastery shimmering in the distance as we take the narrow road into Debra Libanos. When we arrive, monks dressed in bright yellow robes and beggars in rags crowd the entrance. Tenagnework pushes them away with her walking stick and kisses the front gates. She walks slowly into the compound and carefully circumnavigates the church, stopping to kiss each door, before leaving a donation in the box near the gate. This is a sacred place for her. She was born not far from here and the bones of her loved ones are wrapped in the soil of Debra Libanos. It is a place of faith, family, war and history.

She becomes quiet and stern, and when I ask her if she is tired she replies that a servant of the Emperor never gets tired. The clock below the steeple chimes five times: it's eleven o'clock in the morning, but the clock is set on the local time system. Initially, it's a bit confusing. The day starts at 6 am, so by eleven it's actually five o'clock Ethiopian time. Ethiopia also follows a different calendar, which has a thirteen-month year. As a result, Ethiopia is always at least seven years behind the west. The differences began back in the 1500s, when Ethiopia stayed with the Julian solar calendar and much of the Christian world adopted an updated Gregorian calendar. So, even though my digital watch says it's April 2005, in Ethiopia it's only 1997.

As we walk back to the vehicle, Tenagnework calls over a boy to collect some holy water. He's wearing patched pants and sandals made from car tyres, and he bows his head obediently as she warns him not to cheat and get the water from the tap. When he returns, she gulps it down, spilling droplets that bead on her handbag. She tips the remainder into her cupped hands and rubs it on her face.

Tenagnework rests in the car as the boy offers to take us up to a cave behind the church, to see the resting place of some of the monks who were shot dead by the Italian soldiers at Debra Libanos. Soon we are walking along a steep path that climbs up to the cave. When we look in the cave we see that it is cluttered with boxes of human remains. The powdery soil cradles dozens of bones and skulls. The bones have spilled out of broken wooden crates and there are also some new wooden boxes which are small and covered in names and dates written in Amharic. The boxes contain the remains of dead infants, their bodies brought here by their parents because they believe it is a holy place. One of the boxes is cardboard, bound with string, and the name of the baby is written on the side. The boxes are not buried, they just sit on the floor of the cave and have a haunting and uncared-for look about them. Before too long I climb down and walk back to the monastery.

We drive out of town and stop on the hillside to eat some lunch. There's not much food on sale in Debra Libanos, so we brought some hamburgers with us from Addis Ababa. The burgers are enormous, but Tenagnework eats nearly all of hers as she sits on the back seat. She smiles with delight. We also have some biscuits for her and she eats almost a dozen: she's still hungry after more than a month of fasting.

She talks virtually all the way home, sometimes to the interpreter, sometimes to herself, while I watch her carefully. I feel a big sense of responsibility: she is frail and treasured. I'm sure she wonders why I keep asking if she needs a drink or something else to eat or a toilet stop, but she looks tired and I don't want to push her too hard. When we get to her place, she seems a bit overwhelmed and confused; it's been a long journey and she stands for a moment, unsure of which way to go to her house. I guide her up the lane to her back door, where her granddaughters are waiting. I kiss her goodbye and promise to return the next morning.

Each morning, just after dawn when the sun starts projecting its yellow through the mist, I go running in Addis Ababa. Running in Ethiopia is a bit like wandering into a sumo training camp and asking for an arm wrestle. This nation is home to some of the best distance runners in the world. Natural talent combined with high altitude have produced athletes of extraordinary endurance. I can only run for about twenty minutes when I first arrive in Addis Ababa: the altitude sucks my breath and empties my legs. It takes me almost a week to get accustomed to it.

My driver helps me to find an Ethiopian Olympic running singlet at the market, which I wear over my T-shirt. The locals think it's very funny to see a white woman wearing the national colours, but this makes me go faster because I'm too embarrassed to run slowly when I wear it. It's good fun.

There is very little green space in the city, so I join the other runners on the road. The athletes run to Meskel Square in the centre of the city, where they train along the terraced steps of the amphitheatre. Each morning there are hundreds of runners training in the square; the best wear the distinctive Ethiopian national tracksuit, others wear second-hand clothes and sandals. Some of the world's greatest distance athletes have trained in this square. The national athletes laugh and clap when I run past in my singlet. I've never seen so many runners training on the streets during my travels in Africa, even in Kenya, which is also renowned for athletic talent.

Some mornings I end up in spontaneous races with other runners. At first I didn't know what was going on. I would hear the breath and footsteps of a runner behind me and they would stay less than a metre from my heels, no matter how much I sped up or slowed down. It's the athletic equivalent of saying, 'What are you looking at?' There is laughter from the commuters at the bus stops when I run past with a local runner in hot pursuit. The best I can do is turn off suddenly down a side street towards my guesthouse, calling a spontaneous end to the race.

After breakfast, I go to Tenagnework's house. She's alert and she's been waiting for me. She starts talking about the Italians during the war, spitting on the floor when she mentions them. But her real venom is saved for the *bandas.* The other Ethiopians hated them for giving their local knowledge to the invaders and leading the Italians through the forest. They were often the first to be shot, and the Patriots relished killing them.

'We would climb the tree and say a *banda* is coming from this direction. Everyone hated them at that time. They cheated their people and they abandoned their people. Our major enemy was not the Italians. It's the *bandas* who guided them to where we were. So they were our major enemy. We used to see the *bandas* coming first. The Italians most of the time stayed at the back. We hated them and we wanted to kill them. Our fight was with them, not the Italians. We didn't know the Italians.'

By the end of 1935 the bitterness and the bloodshed had started in many parts of Ethiopia. The Patriots in the forest of Debra Libanos who had practised shooting the ox's head now had *bandas* and Italian soldiers in the sights of their rifles. The horrible reality of war was beginning to take hold. Tenagnework was hearing and seeing death for the first time. Her eldest brother was the first member of the family to be killed.

'The first brother who died was the oldest, Seyum. He was under the tree. He shot four *bandas*. Then the person in the tree told him to run away because someone was coming from the back. He turned to run and then they shot him right on the chest.'

Tenagnework's brothers were some of the youngest fighters in the group. The commanders told them not to go to the frontline, but they refused and took shifts in the most dangerous positions on the hilltops overlooking the Italian lines. One by one, all of the brothers were shot dead, and Tenagnework and her sister undertook the heartbreaking duty of carrying their bodies and burying them in graves that were dug by hand.

'The person in the tree would give the whistles saying that so and so had died. My sister was well built and much older than me. So she would run to the battlefield and carry the dead bodies to the side. She would take a stick to dig the soil there. They would look for a swampy place and dig that place. And put the body there. They had nothing to cover the face with so she would get a big leaf and put some soil on it. That is how we buried all five of my brothers. I feel bad that they were left there in the bush. I blame myself and I regret not reburying them later. We should have reburied them later in the church.

'It was very painful. We brought soil in our dresses. It was like we went crazy at that moment. We hit our chests with stones. We cried. Now I have been crying all my life. Whenever I go to a mourning place, I remember them and I cry. There was a professional weeper who knew about all my brothers. So, whenever I go to a mourning place, she starts naming my brothers who died. When she starts telling their names, I go to the centre and start beating my chest.'

By early 1937, the war was worsening. An assassination attempt on the Italian Viceroy Marshal Graziani on 19 February triggered a brutal response by Italian troops, who carried out three days of massacres in Addis Ababa and in other parts of the country. The bloodshed intensified. On 20 May, 297 monks were shot dead by Italian soldiers at the monastery at Debra Libanos. But the killings didn't dampen the resistance. Instead, thousands of angry Ethiopians joined the fight. Tenagnework and the other Patriots in the bush were determined to carry on.

'When more people were dying, we started comforting each other. We comforted each other by saying, "We came here to die for our country, it's not our wedding day." My older sister used to say that we should cry for ourselves because we are alive and still suffering. But they are dead. Nobody has brought anyone back by crying. We started comforting each other and getting stronger and stronger.'

Tenagnework's childhood had been slowly taken by the war; she and her sister were the only family members left alive on the frontline and their parents were still in jail. She had her fifteenth birthday in the bush. Her husband had kept his promise not to sleep with her for five years, but now it was time for them to consummate their marriage.

'At that time we were in the forest near a village. He took me to the village. He spoke to the farmers there and they gave him a hut. I didn't know what was happening. But once we were inside the hut, he told me, "Now you are fifteen, you should be sleeping with me." He took my virginity on that night. I screamed and the neighbours were saying to my husband, "Are you beating her? What's happening?" I was bleeding and went out and washed out my clothes.'

Eight days later, her husband went to the monastery at Debra Libanos. The villagers told the Patriots that the Italians had damaged the church and one soldier was using the altar as a makeshift bed. Tenagnework's husband walked inside the church to confront the soldier.

'One Italian took all the crosses away from the church and he was sleeping on the holy table. The people were really offended. So he wanted to see and check. He went in. He thought that Italian was the only one in that church. So he walked in, but there were *bandas* there and they shot him. He died just in the church.'

Tenagnework and the other Patriots heard the shots and ran up to the church, where they found his body. They stood in a circle and prayed. His father, who was also a priest, led the prayers. Tenagnework was inconsolable; she had been widowed at the age of fifteen, barely a week after she had lost her virginity.

'I cried. I felt so sad because my husband died before me. My wish was to die with him at that spot. I was crying bitterly. He is still buried there in the church. He was a very holy man. He served God. That is why he died there. That is an honour. His tomb is there. Every year I go there. I greet him and kiss the tomb.'

By 1940, the war was entering a new phase. The Patriots and their supporters used guerrilla tactics to increase pressure on the Italians. But their hopes were also focused on Europe. On 10 June, Mussolini declared war on France and Britain, a much anticipated announcement that opened the way for Britain to take action against Italian forces in Ethiopia. By early 1941, British troops were working their way towards Addis Ababa and their aircraft dropped hundreds of leaflets from the air. Tenagnework and the other Patriots picked them up and gathered in a circle. It was the news they had been waiting for.

'The plane came and they threw the message. When it fell on the trees, everyone was running to get it. We opened it together. We read it together. The message said that the British people are here to rescue us and they are escorting also the Emperor. They told us not to shoot when we saw their flag.'

The Patriots left the forest near Debra Libanos and walked for three days to reach a place called Entoto. Thousands of Patriots from other regions were already gathering, and local farmers also arrived with oxen and shovels to repair the road ready for the arrival of the Emperor, who had been in exile in Europe during the war.

'We were singing the war songs. One song was that the Italians are the road-builders, the British are the leaders but the anointed king is the Emperor. There were around 8000 Patriots escorting him. When we saw him, we were wearing very short shorts. We were not in a good condition, the Emperor took a handkerchief and he cried looking at us. He was very sad to see us like that.'

The Emperor accompanied the Patriots to the prison at Fiche, where hundreds of people had been held during the war. The gates of the prison and the doors of the cells were opened and the prisoners were set free. Tenagnework was in the crowd as the inmates took their first steps of freedom in almost five years. She was looking for her mother and father, who had been locked up since the start of the war.

'That was the first time I saw my parents, I saw them coming out of the prison. My father bowed down and kissed the knees of the Emperor. When the Emperor saw his clothes were torn and they were patched, the Emperor was very sad about that. He asked him what happened. My father told him he didn't change his clothes over five years. He thought he wouldn't change his clothes until the victory.'

It was crowded and chaotic as the prisoners were reunited with their relatives, and some family members barely recognised each other.

'I heard rumours that my mother was pregnant and gave birth. I was waiting to see that baby. When I saw my mother and the baby next to her, I knew that it was her. I was so happy. We were singing and shouting. After we greeted the Emperor, we got closer to our parents. We bowed down and kissed their knee. Everybody was hugging. My parents looked at us and said, "We are glad we have you. We are very grateful. At least we have you."'

Haile Selassie re-entered Addis Ababa on 5 May 1941. He was driven into the city in an open-top car and was met by thousands of supporters lining the streets waving British and Ethiopian flags. The day is now commemorated as Patriots' Day – a day of celebration when the veterans parade through the streets.

Tenagnework invites me to spend Patriots' Day 2005 with her. When I return to her house, she's in the back room, where her granddaughters are combing her grey hair into a fluffy Afro. She is dressed in white but not wearing her veil: instead, she has a military cap with a red band and a gold badge on the front. This is the uniform of the Patriots. Tenagnework keeps the hat carefully wrapped in a plastic bag on top of her cupboard and only brings it down once a year.

She reaches into a drawer and pulls out a tattered red-and-pink quilted purse. This is where she keeps her medals. She opens it and cradles the three medals in her hands. Her granddaughter approaches with a safety pin and carefully attaches the medals to Tenagnework's white shawl.

Roads are closed and hundreds of people are gathering at the Patriots' monument in the city centre. Many of the Patriots are dressed in old khaki uniforms with red, yellow and green sashes; some are carrying spears, shields and swords. Most are aged in their eighties or nineties but there are no chairs for them – they're expected to stand for the memorial service. Some of the old women become distressed and squat down, before trying to stand up again. I feel sad watching them. They look ashamed that their old knees will no longer hold them.

Marching bands and boy scouts in home-made uniforms march around the monument before the Patriots march in a procession. Tenagnework and another woman Patriot are the last to finish: they look tired and distressed.

We follow them to the headquarters of the Patriots Association. There's no morning tea and, again, few chairs. It is mid-morning and many of the Patriots have been up since dawn. Most sit in the car park or stand in the street. There is a café inside, but many can't afford a cool drink. We take Tenagnework in and find a table; she's hungry and we get her a plate of meat and *injera,* a flat pancake made from a local grain called *teff.* Another group of women has ordered some food to share, and when they have almost finished, the women pick up the last scraps and hand-feed others who haven't eaten. A skinny old man who has been sitting next to them gulps down the offering, looking both embarrassed and hungry. Tenagnework gives him her leftovers too.

It was different when Tenagnework and the other Patriots arrived in Addis Ababa in 1941. The Emperor invited them to follow him to the palace. They stayed in a large hall in the palace grounds where they were given food and new clothes. Patriots from all over the country came together.

'We used to tell war stories because we were from different war fronts. One would say, "I killed this Italian there." Whenever the Emperor came to see us, we would sing the war songs.'

Some of the Patriots had spent five years in the bush; they were worn and weathered. Their makeshift uniforms were threadbare and their hair had grown into wild dreadlocks.

'Our hair was very long. All of the Patriots, we let our hair grow over the five years. So we looked very different to the rest of society so whenever we went out, people laughed at us. Abba Hanna told the Emperor that we all should get good outfits. We were each given nice outfits from white material, so we were all dressed up in that.'

In the months following the end of the war there were dozens of weddings amongst the Patriots who had gathered at the palace. The ex-fighters were given houses in a former Italian army base.

Tenagnework and a driver named Tekele were married and she quickly became pregnant. But the relationship slowly started to deteriorate.

'He was a good person. We lived peacefully for four years but after that he started being very jealous whenever my cousins were there. I swore on the name of God, I never cheated on my husband.'

The marriage continued for almost eight years. Tenagnework's mother tried to keep the couple together, but the relationship eventually failed. Tenagnework went back to the countryside to live with an aunt, where she quickly attracted the attention of a wealthy local farmer, Chernet Wakene, who asked for her hand. Her brothers and mother assessed the proposal. Tenagnework was the last to be informed.

'They made the arrangements and told me at the last minute. They were preparing for the feast and making local drinks. Somebody told me this would be my wedding. My permission was not in it. They arranged that wedding. On the wedding day he came well dressed and on a mule. He had another mule for me.'

Tenagnework and Chernet were married for almost seventeen years. But she wanted to move to Addis Ababa to make sure her children received a better education, so she eventually left him and went to the capital. A cousin offered her a small house, which she took. It's the same house she lives in today. She made a living by collecting rent on land that the Emperor had given her in the south of the country. But the political climate started to change. A group of dissident army officers calling themselves the Derg started challenging the Emperor, Haile Selassie.

On 12 September 1974, the Emperor was arrested. His driver, Tenagnework's former husband, was also caught up in the unrest.

'When the Derg came and arrested the Emperor, they took him to prison. He was the one who was driving. He was standing next to the car. The soldiers asked him to bring the key of the car and he told them, "You have already taken the Emperor and you've jailed him. Why do you want the key of the car?" The soldiers beat him. They beat him on the head. They took him to the hospital but he didn't recover. He was badly hurt. He died in the hospital.'

The hierarchy was turned upside down: those who had supported the Emperor were now pushed aside. Tenagnework lost the land that the Emperor had given her, so she started brewing traditional drinks to make a living. Her family's history as part of the elite left her on the outer.

'They used to name me as someone from the Emperor's side. I had a reputation of being a feudal. There is nothing to compare during the Emperor and the Derg time. During the Emperor's time we were given a piece of land. I rented that land. I had a lot of money then. There is nothing to compare. During the Derg time I didn't want to be involved in any activity. I didn't even get an ID card.'

On 27 August 1975, the Derg announced that the Emperor had died. Tenagnework was at a family funeral when she heard the news.

'I don't want to remember that day. We were like insane people. We were right in the middle crying.'

Tenagnework keeps a picture of Emperor Haile Selassie on her mantelpiece. This small house has become home and, despite growing up with wealth and slaves, Tenagnework has become used to living a simple life.

'Even if I had a bigger house, what would I do? All my relatives, brothers and cousins have died. There are no men of my age in my family. They all died. So even if I had a bigger house, there is no use. What would I do with a bigger house? All of them have died.'

Tenagnework believes the sacrifice was worth it; she has no regrets about being a Patriot and fighting against the Italians.

'It is very important. If you abandon your country, if somebody else seizes your country, you don't have a house, you don't have the land, you don't have a life. You lose everything. So it is very important. Young people are very lazy. They don't follow up what is happening to us. They are not interested in our history.'

Even now, the Patriots receive limited recognition. The mayor of Addis Ababa has invited the Patriots to lunch at City Hall on Patriots' Day. The hall is several kilometres away; there is no transport provided, so the Patriots walk or take public buses to get there. They're hungry and many arrive more than an hour early. There's no seating for them outside, so they sit on the black-and-white painted gutters of the car park, talking and waiting. To an outsider like me, it looks sad.

But when the lunch starts, there is unlimited food and drink. The Patriots are waited on and a band plays on a stage to entertain them. Dozens of whole beef carcasses hang on big hooks and the Patriots use large knives to cut off as much meat as they want and eat it raw. It's a tradition; raw meat is the food of celebration at weddings and feasts. The old men and women pile their plates with meat, salad and the staple Ethiopian food, *injera*.

The Patriots drink *Tej*, a traditional drink brewed from honey: there are dozens of bottles on each large table. By the end of the lunch, some of the men are quietly drunk; others are reciting war poems and songs, to the delight of their comrades. They stagger out of City Hall carrying swords and spears. Even though most of them are aged in their nineties, there are no relatives to collect them or help them on the journey home. They stumble to the bus stop and find their own way.

Tenagnework is not alone. She's grateful that she shares the house with her granddaughters, but she is firm and gruff with them. One of the granddaughters, Tsigue, has a baby daughter who is only a month old, a striking-looking child with fair skin. While visiting relatives fuss over her, I never see Tenagnework pay any attention to the baby; she doesn't pick her up or show her off to me. But underneath the displays of stern discipline her gratitude is apparent.

'I am very happy to live with them. I give them order. If they are not doing it, I hit them with my stick. I make sure they obey me. They respect me.

'Being lonely is the worst thing that could happen to you. So it is always good to have people around you. Especially grandchildren. When I come back from somewhere, I know that they are here. That is a very good part of my life.'

Tenagnework savours simple pleasures. She walks up and down the hill to the church several times a day and prays for the family.

'Over the past few years no-one from the family has died. We have not been mourning. We have had a break from that. I am so grateful about that.'

Later, we go to Tenagnework's house to say goodbye, but she's praying at the church. The granddaughters go to collect her. I hear the big wooden stump being rolled out of the way as they open the gate. It's dark and raining outside when they return, and Tenagnework's eyes sparkle and raindrops glisten on her shawl. She's full of energy tonight. She makes jokes with her granddaughters, stops and looks at me. She asks when I will get married. She has a cheeky look in her eye as she offers to find me a nice captain from the military, and she pats my hands and giggles before wishing me a long life and many children.

It's taken almost two weeks of interviews to get her story. We have sat together on her bed each morning, and I've held my microphone in one hand and her hand in the other. Most days, she has been talkative, warm and lively; some days, she has been distracted.

I give her laminated copies of some of the pictures I have taken. She shuffles through them again and again, and says her favourite is the one taken outside the church in Debra Libanos. Then she stops and looks at the close-up of her wearing her white veil.

'They will carry this one on my funeral day,' she says. 'It's beautiful.'

She catches her own seriousness and shakes her head, giving a half-smile. She knows it is time to say goodbye.

We walk outside into the drizzle. The path from the front door to the gate is even more slippery than usual: the mud is wet and shiny. There are pots and bowls on the doorstep to catch the rain. Tenagnework walks solemnly and we hug goodbye several times as she talks quietly in Amharic to me. I kiss her and get into the car. I wave and look out through the droplets of rain running down the car window. Tenagnework tries to look away. When we turn the car around in the street, I see only her brown hand closing the gate behind her.

'I am very strong. I have gone this far. Nothing can happen to me.'

CHAPTER 9

LUCIA MAZIBUKO

AIDS grandmother

SOUTH AFRICA

Lucia Mazibuko lost two of her daughters to AIDS and was left to care for her two HIV-positive grandsons. Ten-year-old Bongani died; his younger brother, Bobo, is trying to outlive the disease.

Lucia is one of thousands of South African grandmothers who are caring for grandchildren who have been orphaned by AIDS. She is trying to cope alone, with limited assistance. She was subjected to discrimination and rejection from her community, but now she is speaking out about HIV/AIDS and is working with other grandmothers to fight the disease.

ZIMBABWE
BOTSWANA
Limpopo
Limpopo
WINDHOEK
NAMIBIA
GABORONE
PRETORIA
MAPUTO
MBABANE
Johannesburg
SWAZILAND
Bloemfontein
MASERU
Orange
LESOTHO
Durban
REPUBLIC
OF
SOUTH AFRICA
N
W
E
S
Cape Town
Port Elizabeth
0
SCALE
300
Kilometres

'He was just a quiet boy. He liked listening. He wasn't so naughty. He knew the meaning of HIV. He knew it. He knew he was going to die. Yes, he did. He used to ask questions, big questions. He would ask about his mother, his father, the people who passed away. He wanted to know, "Where are they? Am I going to follow them?" All those questions that you can't even answer sometimes.

'He was the first grandchild that I had. I spoiled him too much. I was carrying him, he was my briefcase. Bongani, he was my everything.

'Bongani didn't like to play. He used to sit in here and be quiet, watch the TV. He knew almost every advertisement. He learned a lot from the TV, especially gospel music. He liked gospel music.

'We used to sit here. He would say, "Gogo, do you know that song?" I would say no. So, he would just be singing it. Then he would say, "Follow me.

'"There is a race, that I must run.
There are victories to be won.
Give me power."

'I would say, "Who is going to give you power?"
'He said, "God."
'Okay.

'"Give me power, every hour to be strong."

'He was the one who taught me the song. At school they didn't know it. When Bongani passed away, I organised one old lady; I sang it here for her. I knew she was a good singer. She went to the school and she taught it to the kids. It was new at Bongani's funeral, they say it's Bongani's song. It's something nice.'

Bongani's coffin was small, a child's coffin. Lucia sat next to it. There were too many mourners to fit in her house, so they put up a big striped tent outside. Funeral workers erect tents every Saturday morning in Alexandra: if you stand on top of the hill overlooking the township you can see the tents outside the houses where families are grieving. In Alexandra, Saturday is funeral day. Some weekends there are so many that policemen direct traffic near the cemetery and undertakers use sirens fitted to their hearses to push their way through the congestion.

Lucia has lived in Alex for most of her adult life. Her house is basic and only the size of a caravan. The main room barely has enough space for the kitchen table; it's like a perpetual puzzle, people step and shuffle out of each other's way, chairs are pushed in and out, bags are lifted over the heads of others. There's a bench near the door, under the window, where neighbours and friends sit to talk and dispense advice. Sometimes, in the afternoon, children come inside with wide eyes and open hands to ask for money for ice cream or sweets, as they know that if Lucia has anything to spare, she'll give it to them. The iron bars on the doors and windows are set in diagonal patterns to make them look decorative rather than necessary, but Alex can be a violent place. The roads on its outskirts have signs warning 'Car hijack hot spot'. When I drive to Lucia's on my own, she always insists one of her adult sons accompanies me in the car until I reach the main road, in case I get hijacked.

If you can imagine packing more than 200 000 poor and unemployed people into a little valley the size of a small suburb, you may start to understand Alexandra. It's one of the most densely populated townships in Johannesburg. Many families live in shacks, others in clapped-out multi-storey hostels or crumbling old buildings. Thousands of people share portable toilets and communal taps. The shack dwellers cut grooves in the road to run frayed illegal electricity wires from one squatter camp to the next, because there's no proper power either. It's no surprise Alex is nicknamed the 'Dark City'. In a cruel twist, it happens to be situated right next to the richest district in the city; in fact, one of the richest in Africa. The sleek office towers of Sandton peek over the ridge at the broken-down shacks of Alex. Many white residents of Johannesburg speak fearfully of Alexandra, even though most have never been there and most of the security guards who shiver through the night shift looking after palatial suburban homes actually come from Alex.

Lucia is plain, warm and modest. She dresses simply in bright colours, with no earrings and just a single bangle around her wrist. She keeps her hair in a short Afro and her plump frame gives her a slightly laboured gait. She is a no-frills traditional woman.

I know her house well, but there are things I don't see. Although Lucia is excruciatingly honest when she talks about her family and herself, I don't see the day-to-day breaths of this house; people are on their best behaviour. Sometimes there's a large, round ashtray in the middle of the kitchen table when I arrive, but it's quickly taken away. Lucia's family and neighbours smile and welcome me, but I am an outsider. The real conversations are in siSotho, not English. I don't understand everything that happens here and it's not mine to know.

I've been visiting this house for almost three years, but I didn't find Lucia, she found me. I was in Alex filming a story about grandmothers looking after their HIV-positive grandchildren. I'd already interviewed another woman, and I was getting ready to go when Lucia sat down across the table. In a shy voice, she told me she'd lost both her daughters to AIDS and was now caring for her two grandsons. Bongani sat next to her while she talked. He was nine years old, but his body was out of sync with his age, and his skinny neck and big eyes looked out of proportion. AIDS was already inside him. He looked out at the world with a distant, slightly disapproving, expression and he only spoke to me when Lucia prompted him.

I remember that when I first went to Lucia's house, Bongani was lying on his stomach on a blanket on the floor, looking out through the sunray metal bars on the front door. He could see the vacant block across the road, and most afternoons other children would sit on the step and tell him the news from school.

Lucia has painted a small picture of a hat next to the front door: it's a 'Mokorotlo', a traditional hat from Lesotho, Lucia's homeland. She grew up in Lesotho, a mountainous country South Africa surrounds. Her father was a farm labourer and her mother was a domestic worker at a nearby Catholic mission.

'My mother didn't think she would have another child. But, after fourteen years, a fortune teller told her she was pregnant. She said no. But I was there. It was me. I didn't even have a name, they just called me Mampi, a naughty thing. I only have my baptised name, Lucia. I haven't got a Sotho name because I just came from nowhere.

'My parents were happy that I came along. In Lesotho, when it's winter it's very cold, there is snow, my father used to carry me on his back and take me to school. I was big but he used to carry me. I was spoiled, I think.

'I grew up in a Roman Catholic family. They didn't even want us to play with other children who were not Christians, they didn't want us to jive like other kids, they didn't let us wear short dresses. We were told if you touch a boy you will get pregnant and you will never go to God. So we were afraid.

'I wanted to be a nun, because my sister was there at the

mission. I just felt like I would be holy, I would be near God when I pass away. It was a nice thing at that time, but when I came here I just said, no.'

When she turned nineteen, Lucia went to Alexandra to visit some friends. She'd heard about life in the townships and she wanted to see it for herself. Alex was loud and lively compared with the conservative ways of the mission. When she arrived, she was introduced to a young Zulu man called Elliot; one of his relatives was married to one of Lucia's cousins.

'At that time I didn't know how to speak Zulu and he didn't know how to speak siSotho. So we used to write in English and translate. If he just wanted to tell me something and he didn't know how to explain it, he write it down in English and explain it in Zulu. It would take maybe 30 minutes. It was funny but it was nice.

'Elliot, he was a darling. He just liked to sing, jokes. He used to tell the wishes, all the nice things. His wish was to have grandchildren, sit with them, tease them, he used to sing Zulu music and he wished to teach those things to the grandchildren. He used to tease me and say, "Look at you, you are so thin. I want to buy food for you to get fat." We were husband and wife but we were friends too. We were friends with our kids also. It was nice. I got pregnant soon – 1973 I got a baby, the first one, and 1976, the second one.'

Lucia went to live with Elliot's family in rural KwaZulu-Natal, where she assisted with the domestic chores and they helped raise the children. It was one of the happiest times of her life. She was part of a large, strong family, her mother-in-law taught her how to run a household, how to cook and how to brew traditional beer. She caught up on many of the lessons she'd missed out on as a spoilt child in Lesotho.

Elliot got a job with a removal company in Johannesburg: it was good, steady work and he was earning enough for Lucia and the children to come back to the city. But in 1990 he started struggling, he couldn't keep up with the other men at work when they were carrying heavy furniture. At first he thought he had the flu, but the pain in his chest and back didn't go away and the doctor diagnosed an abscess on his lung. Elliot tried to keep his illness a secret at work because he didn't want to lose his job, but the physical labour soon became too much for him. He died two days after Christmas 1991.

'It was two o'clock in the morning. I tried to make first aid. I tried mouth to mouth. I tried to do those things that I know but it was the end. He was cold from the feet upwards and he was closing the eyes. The kids were just sitting on the bed looking at him and the little one was crying, they said, "Mama, is he dead?" I didn't know how to explain where he was going because they were small.

'It was the first time for me to see a dead person. I didn't know he was dying. I just thought he would come back. It was difficult. When I saw his body at the mortuary it was then that I see that he's dead. I just thought everything is gone. I am nobody.'

That was almost fifteen years ago, but there is still a lot of emotion in Lucia's voice and eyes as she talks about it. It wasn't just the loss of Elliot that was so distressing – his death left her vulnerable. She was widowed with six young children and no job. She went on foot from Alexandra into the suburbs in search of work and found a job as a domestic worker at an aged home. It was a time of great uncertainty. Nelson Mandela had been released from prison a year earlier, South Africa was on an untried path to democracy and extremists on both sides were warning of possible civil war. The black-on-black violence had already started in Alexandra. Supporters of the African National Congress clashed with rivals from the Zulu-dominated Inkatha Freedom Party in a contest for political power. The workers' hostels in the township became the focal point for the violence and Lucia was living in a small shack just a few hundred metres from the biggest hostel in the township; she and her children were right in the middle of the shooting. There was so much street-to-street fighting, the neighbourhood was nicknamed 'Beirut'.

'It started 1991 and early 1992. There were people from KwaZulu-Natal staying at the Madala Hostel, they were fighting with the ANC people. In the old days you couldn't drive here. They would shoot through the windows. They just shoot. Just for nothing. We didn't sleep because of shooting. We couldn't walk in the street, we just sit in the houses and wait for the police, then we could go to the shops. We used to sit in our houses day and night. I wasn't a member of any political party, I was just a Christian.'

Hundreds of families were cowering in their houses as the shots ricocheted off the rooftops. At night, the attacks and reprisals played out in the streets: the victims were shot, clubbed to death or 'necklaced' in burning tyres. Lucia and her neighbours were terrified and in early 1992 the situation was becoming more dangerous week by week. Eventually, they abandoned their houses and ran for shelter at the nearby old city council offices, and hundreds of families crowded into the broken-down buildings.

'It was 770 families. It's a small place, we were sharing, in each small office there were about six families, with kids. We used to cook with the paraffin stoves; those who were not working used to cook during the daytime, those who were working used to cook later. That is how we were.'

The families were sharing the few toilets in the building, sleeping on the floor and washing in buckets, squatters in their own neighbourhood. It was too difficult and dangerous to go back to their houses near the hostel and retrieve their possessions. The conditions inside the council offices were filthy and Lucia sent her children away to a church shelter for several months. She was left alone, shunned by many of the other people because she was still in mourning.

'It was just three months after my husband passed away. I was wearing a black dress, the traditional one a woman must wear when her husband passed away. The people don't like to mix with the person who is wearing black. They didn't like me. I was like somebody who is not a part of them. When we were sitting they don't like to sit next to me because I will give them bad luck. I used to sleep alone near the door. It made me feel like a ghost. It made me feel like I am not a person. I was just lost. Losing a husband and suddenly being displaced, staying out there without any family. It was a hard time.'

Lucia leans forward in the back seat of the car as she guides us to the old council offices. It's grim and scary and reminds me of a drug dealer's den in an American movie. It's a filthy, broken place, the red bricks stained with soot and the smudges of accidents and neglect. I look up, and I can see broken window frames with jagged glass and frayed curtains. Some of the windows are half-blocked by cupboards, giving a hint of the crowding inside. I can smell paraffin stoves and alcohol as we walk past several middle-aged women sitting outside; some are drunk and they greet us with bleary smiles. This is where Lucia used to sit.

'I used to drink after my husband passed away. I didn't know how to drink a beer. I took a cold drink and mixed with the beer. I started like that. It made me sick because I think starting to drink when you are old, it's not a nice thing. When I was drunk, I just cry and cry. All those memories came back, just like a big dish full of all those bad memories. Bongani did see that. And when Bongani started getting sick, I thought, this isn't right. I thought one day I will wake up and find Bongani dead next to me, so I stopped drinking.

'Bongani used to have a dream. He said, "When I grow up I want to build a big shop. I will sell everything. Everything. But I'll never sell liquor." I said, "Why?" He said, "I don't like people who are drunk." I thought, woo, this boy is talking about me.'

We walk around the back of the building and open a battered door with graffiti written above it.

'This room is protected by the mafias. You shoot, we shoot back harder.'

This is the room where Lucia lived with more than 30 other people and this is the doorway where she curled up each night in her black widow's clothes. Two young women are sitting in the corridor and Lucia greets them as we step over their outstretched legs; she's walking and talking excitedly and seems almost proud to show me this place, or proud she survived it. She takes me to another room, but it's not really a room: it's an abandoned toilet under the stairs.

'This is the toilet but we used to make it a bedroom. This was the room I used to have. It was my home. I used to sleep here. It was my bedroom, just under the stairs.'

Lucia lived here for eight years – eight Christmases, eight winters, eight birthdays from 1992 to 2000, until she was allocated a government house in Alexandra. She couldn't go back to her original house because it had been taken over by other people during the violence. I don't know how she lasted so long: it's a scary, filthy place and I know I'd be very frightened to sleep here, but Lucia looks at me with her usual soft expression. She doesn't tell her story with any sense of gravity. She continues to seem almost excited to show me around.

In the end it wasn't the conditions that were the biggest problem for her, it was the solitude. After the death of her husband, Lucia needed the support of her daughters, Nokuthula and Puleng. They returned after staying with relatives in KwaZulu-Natal.

'Nokuthula, she was a girl with wishes, she was everything to me. I was very proud of her. She was like a sister to me, they were both sisters to me. She was a business-minded child, she used to sell sweets at school, she even opened an account at the post office. I was a housewife, a mother of six kids, but she is the one who taught me how to budget. She was only young at that time, but I am what I am now because of her. She used to buy nice, strong things, she was a mother-minded somebody.'

Life in Johannesburg was full of temptation after the seclusion of rural KwaZulu-Natal, and Nokuthula became pregnant to her first boyfriend when she was only fifteen. Bongani was born in 1994 and a year later Nokuthula was pregnant again, giving birth to another son, Bobo. Nokuthula left school and got a temporary job at a plastics factory in the nearby suburb of Wynberg, but she was struggling to keep up with the other workers on the factory floor, and was exhausted as she tried to look after Bobo and Bongani. She started noticing small white sores on her skin.

'In 1999, May, it was before the vote. Nokuthula had a flu, just a flu, they called it the 1999 flu, everybody was having it. She went to the hospital. They took blood from her. In June, Nokuthula got worse. I remember on the second of June we were going to vote.

She said, "Mama, I will go with you." I took her, we went there to the polling station. We went back home. She was sick, she starting to have sores on her skin. On July, she passed away. It was short time, only five weeks.'

It happened so quickly. Nokuthula spent the weekend in hospital, and when Lucia came back to visit her on Monday morning she was gone – literally gone.

'When I came back, she was not even there. I found somebody else in her bed. There was a white lady, an old lady in her bed. I said, "Where is Nokuthula?" Her friend in the next bed said, "They took her." I said, "Where?" She didn't answer. She just took a blanket and covered her face. I thought, Nokuthula is dead.

'She passed away about half-past seven in the morning. She was there in the big plastic bag, wrapped, the mortuary thing. I just touched her.'

I feel very sad for Lucia that she found out about Nokuthula's death in that way. She just shrugs her shoulders, as if to say there was nothing she could do. She doesn't show any residual anger, only sad acceptance.

Nokuthula never admitted she was HIV-positive, even to her own mother. AIDS was still surrounded by ignorance and carried a stigma in South Africa, even though the nation was well on its way to having the largest HIV-positive population in the world. The virus was being passed on from partner to partner, mother to child, by people in a state of complete denial; despite the increasing number of funerals of the young every Saturday in Alexandra, HIV/AIDS wasn't spoken of. The undertakers put up the striped tents outside the same houses again and again as AIDS took a husband, then a wife, and often the children as well. Lucia and other grieving mothers explained away the deaths of their adult children as simple illnesses.

'I just said she had flu and that was it. People, they did suspect. When somebody was saying the word AIDS I just open my ears and say they are talking about me, they are talking about my kids. I was afraid of saying my daughter was HIV-positive because it means that she was bad and it means that I am a bad mother. HIV at that time was so secretive. Everybody was afraid of it.

'In May the following year, Puleng started getting sick. She was married, her husband was a soldier, she was working at the same factory as Nokuthula. When Puleng did start getting sick, I did see the signs. She was coughing, sweating, having short breath, I thought, uh-uh, these are the same signs. She came here in May 2000 with her husband. She was very sick by that time. The husband said, "Oh, Mama, will you please look after my wife." I said no problem.

'I started opening the secret box that I was having. I told her about Nokuthula. I said Nokuthula was HIV-positive but I didn't tell anybody, even you. I was afraid. I took Puleng to the clinic. They took the blood tests and it was positive. Nokuthula passed away July 1999 and then Puleng went in November 2000.'

Two daughters, two funerals, in less than two years. Lucia has photographs of Nokuthula and Puleng on the wall of the living room, and when I look at them I'm struck by how young they are. Puleng is wearing tartan shorts and showing off her long legs; she looks cheeky as she poses on a staircase. Nokuthula is cradling Bongani when he was baby. Each of Lucia's daughters died before they reached their twenty-sixth birthday.

In 2000, the AIDS epidemic was still shrouded in denial in South Africa. Health Minister Dr Manto Tshabalala-Msimang was questioning whether HIV even caused AIDS, despite the fact more than 4 million South Africans were already infected. I remember when I arrived in May 2000, it took several weeks to find a family who would allow us to film at an AIDS funeral, even though there were hundreds of such burials every Saturday. In some cemeteries there were so many funerals and the graves were packed so closely together that families gathered at neighbouring gravesites would have to start singing the same hymns, because they were disturbing each other.

People upheld the ridiculous story that young people were simply dying of flu or headache, even though the death column of *The Sowetan* newspaper was filled with pictures of people aged in their twenties and thirties. Black friends would arrive at work on Monday mornings exhausted because they'd been to all-night funeral prayer vigils on Friday and then at dawn on Saturday started preparations for the burial later in the day. The local staff in the office building where I worked went to a funeral almost every weekend.

By 2000, even though AIDS was still being avoided in conversation, it was difficult to miss in day-to-day life. I started noticing the young driveway attendants at my local petrol station. They were only aged in their teens or early twenties, but very quickly I noticed one of them getting sick. His muscular frame started to thin; his hair would thin out, too, and become fluffy like a child's; then the sores would start in his mouth and face; then he would miss work for a day or two or a week or two; and then he would disappear.

AIDS just wasn't talked about.

'Where's your friend, Umfowethu, the one who looks after my car?'

'He's gone, Madam. It was flu.'

You can imagine the fear, when it was estimated that up to one in four adults in South Africa was HIV-positive. Many people didn't know how to protect themselves or how to care for family members who were already dying. Lucia was trying to nurse Nokuthula and Bongani without knowing whether she was also putting herself in danger.

'I was afraid. I can say that. I sometimes worried that maybe I was having it and it was growing inside of me. We didn't know at that time. I was afraid of using Nokuthula's things, I was thinking I was going to get it too. I was not educated and I was afraid for myself. But it was funny. I wasn't afraid of Bongani. I was staying with him, sleeping near him, hugging him, bathing him, eating with the same spoon. When I fed him I took the spoon, put in my mouth, put in his mouth. I was just doing like that. I wasn't afraid. But I was afraid of Nokuthula, I don't know why, that makes me feel like I was rejecting my daughter.

'Now, everybody is afraid. Everybody is afraid. If somebody

passes away, they say, "Woo, did you hear so-and-so was HIV-positive? Who is going to be next?" Everybody is asking the very same question. Who is going to be next? We are all afraid. We are afraid of this thing. There are so many funerals. Sometimes you can't even attend the funeral of your friend because your relative has a funeral on the same day. You just send a message and say sorry.'

Many of the gogos, the grandmothers in Alexandra, don't belong to bowls teams or bridge clubs: instead there are so many funerals, they have set up burial societies. The women pay money into an account every month and when they have a funeral in their family, the society gives them a payout; it's like a home-made insurance policy. The members of the society also do the cooking and cleaning for the after-funeral lunch, they wear matching outfits and berets and lead the singing if there aren't enough mourners. Lucia and her friends started their own burial society in 1999.

'I remember it was the fourth of June because it was my birthday. We were only seven ladies. The name of the society is Ikageng: it means building ourselves, it's in siSotho. We are now twenty women; when there is a funeral we will not leave your house until everything is right. The yard, we even sweep. That is our job. It's nice. When Bongani died they came and I had a lot of support. I can say, everything it came from them. Everything. I'm still asking where those funeral cars were from, because I saw a stream of cars. I don't have a car. I don't even have a friend who has a car.'

Older women in the townships have taken on the terrible burden of burying their children and grandchildren. I remember a cameraman friend from Soweto saying to me, 'It's the gogos, they do everything. When we're young they spoil us. When we grow up and we don't have money they help us and now when we die, they bury us.'

Lucia nods when I re-tell the story.

'The men don't do anything, never. It's up to the gogos. Even the death of their own parents, they just give the money to their sisters. Have you seen a woman who has lost her husband? She sits there with a big blanket, she cries. But the husband will never do that, he will just sit there on the chair. I don't know why we have this kind of culture and I don't like it.'

Lucia is the breadwinner in her house and when Bongani was sick she worked at his school selling sweets and snacks. Sometimes when he was too ill to stay in the classroom, he would sit with Lucia in the tuckshop. His hollow, tired eyes watched the other children who were full of energy as they pushed each other to reach the front of the queue. On the really bad days he would take a blanket and lie on the sofa in the staffroom, looking exhausted as he lay there with the blanket tucked up over his chest.

Lucia prayed for one thing: Bongani's tenth birthday.

'He liked birthdays and even if I didn't have money I still buy a cake. I wanted to make him a big tenth birthday. I wanted to make something nice for him. I think God listened to me. I did make the big birthday for him. Everybody came to the party, even the old people; it was small but to us it was big. There was music out there, people were singing traditional songs. The girls were fighting to sit next to him. I was happy but I was sad, it was a farewell, inside me I was having that bad feeling, I came inside here and prayed.'

Just after his tenth birthday, Bongani received sponsorship from a charity group offering anti-retroviral medication for HIV-positive children. It was the break Lucia had been wishing for; she couldn't afford the drugs herself, but she knew they could dramatically prolong Bongani's life. Despite promises to provide them, the South African Government had failed to start rolling out the drugs in most parts of the country. Lucia was ecstatic the charity had chosen Bongani as one of several AIDS orphans in Alexandra to receive treatment.

'I was so happy. I said, "At last, at last he is going to live long."'

But only a week after starting the treatment, Bongani started changing. He began talking rapidly, struggling to concentrate and becoming confused. He was weak and the medication was extremely strong.

'He was crazy, he started talking strange things and about ancestors. I was cross with him, but I didn't show that I was cross. He was talking fast, this and that, then when he stopped, his eyes would turn like this. I went back to the hospital a week later and they said it is a side effect, he will become right. The tablets were very powerful. Two weeks after, he started getting fat, I thought maybe it was swelling. I took him back to the hospital, they said the tablets do this. It was strange. He was doing funny things. I wished to stop giving him the medicine, but I remembered the workshop I went to they told us that if you are even five minutes late in giving the medication, you could be taking the life of the person. So I thought if I stopped he would die.'

Lucia withdrew Bongani from school for several weeks because his behaviour was disturbing the other students. But by June he was physically well enough to go to a Sunday school camp and by July he was back at school, thrilled to play with his friends again. After only two weeks, he got an infection.

'Tuesday night he cried the whole night with pain; on Wednesday morning, he was crawling. I took him to the clinic, they said he had pneumonia. He was admitted to hospital, I stayed there the whole day. On Thursday he woke up well, I stayed with him. Late Thursday, he said, "Mama, go home and please bring my clean pyjamas." I said okay.

'I came home but I didn't sleep, thinking of him. On Friday morning I woke up and rushed to the hospital; when I got there, Bongani was not right. I was holding his hand and I said, "Are you okay?" He moved his fingers. I asked if he wanted something to eat. He didn't respond, I just held his hand and took the Bible. He was not looking well.

'He never opened his eyes until three in the afternoon. I was holding his hand all the time. Bongani just pulled his hand from me and looked like that. That was then. Everything stopped. I just screamed, "Sister, sister, help me. Bongani, not now." It happened so fast. He passed away at exactly quarter-past three. I could see that Bongani was dead and I just asked for a few minutes to pray. I don't even know what I was saying to God, I was just wishing that he could come back. I think I was mad.'

I remember my phone rang just before four o'clock that afternoon. It was Lucia.

'Bongani is passed away.'

She sounded so frightened, as if she wanted quickly to find a way to bring him back before it was permanent.

I was overseas on a work trip and Lucia had phoned me as I was checking out of the hotel ready to catch a late afternoon flight. I was waiting behind a group of elderly American tourists and I remember looking at them and thinking, why don't each of you just give up a year and give it to Bongani? I resented their wealth and health and age.

When I got back to South Africa, the striped funeral tent was already being put up outside Lucia's house, ready for Bongani's service. Inside the house, the living room was full of gogos drinking tea, reading the Bible and eating tiny biscuits; it was warm with chatter and cooking. Lucia was propped up in the bedroom, wearing a traditional blanket from Lesotho; she'd been in bed most of the day as visitors came in and sat with her. Relatives from Lesotho sat on chairs in the bedroom and held Lucia's hand when she cried. She showed me a frayed photo album full of pictures of Bongani, and she touched the photographs longingly while she told the anecdotes to go with each one. I didn't know what to say to her. We'd talked so many times about how she feared losing Bongani and usually she couldn't even finish her sentences for fear it would actually happen. Now it had, I guess she'd mentally been preparing for it. She looked so cosy with a blanket wrapped around her shoulders and the bedspread pulled up to her waist to keep out the winter cold. I thought, what a lovely idea, rather than putting on your best clothes and trying to greet guests, why not get into your warm bed and sit there surrounded by the ones you love the most?

Lucia had nursed and lost Puleng, Nokuthula, Nokuthula's husband and now Bongani to AIDS. Four family members in less than five years.

'I have seen people dying before, but Bongani's death was so difficult. It is something, I can't even talk about it. I was frightened, I was scared and I was angry. I was angry with Nokuthula and her husband. Bongani was just a kid, he was having his dreams, but, because of them, he suffered a lot. They didn't suffer like Bongani because they didn't get sick for so long. They just got sick and then died. Bongani suffered from day one until he was ten. It's a long time for a child to suffer, not knowing what is happening to him. How could we tell him that he had this from his parents? We were all afraid of telling him that because we thought he was going to be cross with his parents and I didn't like that.'

Bongani's funeral was on a cold, clear Johannesburg winter morning. The striped funeral tent was almost full; one of the women from the burial society led me to a spare seat near the back. I could see Lucia sitting up the front next to the coffin, wearing a beanie to keep warm and her blanket fastened with a shiny silver safety pin. Bongani's classmates were standing in rows at the side. Most of the children looked nervous, their eyes scanning the scene. A small boy in front of me turned around and spent the entire service staring at me. I was the only white person there, I was also one of the few young adults – the tent was full of children and old people. AIDS had taken most of the rest. Bongani's grandparents and elderly relatives led the service in siSotho and English and an old lady next to me translated the parts I couldn't understand.

For one young man it was all too much; he passed out on the lawn near the fruit tree in front of Lucia's house, with a bottle alongside him – it was his escape from the grieving. One of Bongani's classmates read a handwritten eulogy and told how he and Bongani had found a rat in the classroom one morning, and some of the other children giggled with delight as he described the chase to catch it. He paused and in his best schoolboy English he said Bongani was a 'jolly somebody'. The words made me cry.

The children sang Bongani's song.

There is a race, that I must run.
There are victories to be won.
Give me power.
Give me power, every hour to be strong.

Lucia squinted as she came out of the funeral tent and stood in the morning sun. I could see her looking at the crowd but I don't think she noticed them in the tent, she was tucked away inside her grief. Outside, she could see Bongani's schoolfriends hoisting a home-made banner into the air.

'It had Bongani's photo and all those words on the flag. It made me happy, really. I was feeling like he was a king. Woo. It was nice, I can say it was nice.'

The children lined the street as the hearse carried the coffin; some small children from nearby houses waved and clapped as the procession passed, as if it were a parade. They didn't seem to know the car was carrying the body of a boy not much older than them. The ladies from the burial society shooed them out of the way as they ran alongside the hearse, singing and dancing with their hands in the air. The big-hipped women were almost out of breath when they reached the end of the street.

The hearse turned towards the main road and the cemetery on the other side of the valley, as mourners tried to cram into cars following the procession. Six women squeezed into my car. Only 100 metres up the street there was a funeral tent in front of another house where the mourners had already left for the cemetery. The women from a different burial society were the only ones left behind and they peered out from behind the house as they prepared big pots of stew, vegetables and maize meal for the wake.

When we arrived at the cemetery there was a smaller striped tent set up near the grave. Lucia sat down with Bobo at her feet. She patted the spare seat next to her and asked me to sit with her under the tent. I didn't know what to do to comfort her, so I just put my hand on her back and rubbed it backwards and forwards. Lucia sat staring blankly ahead, occasionally dipping her chin into the top of the blanket wrapped around her shoulders. She started to cry.

'The worst part was when Bongani was going down. Yoh. It was then that I saw that he is going. I will never see him again and I don't like this thing of putting the soil on top. I feel like it's going to stop him breathing. I don't know. I hate that part. I hate it when the coffin goes down, it's the worst part. I don't like it, really.'

Bobo was leaning against Lucia's legs, and as the coffin was lowered into the grave, I looked at him and wondered what was it like for him to lose his sick brother, knowing he might be next. I didn't see him cry; he just looked up at Lucia, searching for a glance of reassurance, and eventually he sat on her lap. The women stepped back and all the men in the congregation came forward to fill in the grave, taking turns using shovels to cover the coffin in dirt, and moving quickly and quietly as a mark of respect.

The men used their shovels to smooth the top of the grave and decorate it with some rocks. The mourners stood around the edge singing their last goodbyes. There were so many people, Lucia couldn't see what was happening from where she was sitting. When the crowd cleared, she took Bobo by the hand and stood at the graveside. They both talked quietly; Lucia asked Bongani to send blessings.

After the funeral, the mourners went back to Lucia's house, where the ladies from the burial society had set up tables, big pots and hundreds of plates. It's a tradition for families to provide food after a burial, but it's become an expensive exercise for those hit by AIDS. I wasn't hungry and I felt guilty about the cost of the food, but it would have been rude to refuse. The burial society ladies piled my plate with rice, beetroot and stew, and when I finished, one of Bongani's classmates asked for my plate and fork so he could also queue with the hundreds of mourners lined up in the street.

By mid-afternoon the burial ladies had cleaned up, washed up and packed up, swept the floors and swept the yard and the funeral tent had been taken down. It was all over. Lucia's little house on the corner of the street was almost back to normal. The mourners were gone, their stomachs filled. Lucia looked relieved but tired; she had dark rings under her eyes and her voice was flatter than usual. Life without Bongani was beginning.

The routine of the house changed. After ten years of nursing Bongani, he was gone and Lucia found herself still accidentally serving a meal for him each night.

'I was having a problem of dishing up food, I used to dish eight plates. And I said, "Oh God, he's not here." I just made a joke of it and say he's going to eat it late tonight and I leave it there. Sometimes I just put mine aside and take Bongani's plate. I'm using Bongani's plate now. It makes me feel like he is here because when I left his plate I felt like I'm putting him out of my family.'

Now Bongani's picture is on the living room wall, below those of Nokuthula and Puleng. Lucia straightens the photographs when they're crooked, but sometimes that's not enough to make her feel settled. She keeps a large white candle covered in AIDS ribbons on top of the kitchen cupboard: she calls it Bongani's candle.

'Sometimes I come back from work and my heart is not right, so I just light that candle. I sit here and I talk to it. I used to sit with him, but most of the time I'm alone now. I really, really miss him. I just put it here, talk to the candle like I'm talking to Bongani and pray. Sometimes I have it for an hour and then I put it back. I like it, it makes me feel like he is there. It's a nice thing, I can say.'

Once a month, Lucia walks to a small clinic near the river, a meeting place for grandmothers in Alex who are caring for their orphaned grandchildren. Some of the gogos are big and round, others are thin and frail, and many of the grandchildren already have the spindly limbs, the swollen glands and fluffy, thin hair of the AIDS victim. The gogos gather in a sunny room inside the clinic to cook and talk together; some chop vegetables into big plastic containers, others fry chicken in a pan full of oil, and some stir pots of rice and maize meal on the stove. There's a feeling that's warm and welcoming when the gogos cook; often they sing and swing their heavy hips in unison – if nothing else, it breaks the isolation. In between the chatter, they talk in quiet voices about their grandchildren and the week-to-week battles to hold off the sickness.

After lunch the gogos wash the dishes before sitting in a circle, with their grandchildren at their feet. This circle is what the meeting is all about: it's quiet time, a chance to talk softly about private struggles against AIDS in their families. When this group started more than two years ago, the gogos didn't talk, they were too afraid to tell the truth even in front of each other. Instead they sat in silence or filled the silences with small talk because it was too painful to open up. The group was set up by a local nurse, Sister Rose Letwaba, and she sat patiently waiting for the gogos to talk, week after week. Eventually the first half-finished sentences were spoken; the carefully guarded words delivered from one gogo and then the next.

This group is the only support many of the gogos and their grandchildren have. I remember the first time I came here, to do a television story. I leaned against a table near the back of the room as the gogos sat in the circle and talked, some of them just sobbing with pure exhaustion. I remember one skinny gogo who sat with her hand on her walking stick with her granddaughter sitting obediently at her feet. The girl had long braids and big eyes and she looked up as her grandmother broke down in tears. The gogo was much older than most of the others. She wore thick glasses and a woollen hat, her health was deteriorating and she was so afraid her granddaughter would be alone if she were unable to care for her or if she died. Her tears splashed onto her glasses and ran down her face, and some of the other gogos got up and rubbed her shoulders.

I knew I couldn't help all of the gogos but after I interviewed Lucia for the first time, I decided I would do what I could to help her. When her story was broadcast in Australia, I received several letters from listeners offering help for Lucia. That was the way our friendship started: I got to know her as I delivered the letters from Australia and passed on her replies. Lucia never asked me for anything, and she still hasn't to this day – not a thing.

My friendship with Lucia was a way to balance out all the

times I had to say no to people who asked for help. It was impossible to help every person I interviewed or grant every request scribbled on paper and placed in my hand during visits to refugee camps. While I couldn't help everyone, I knew I could help someone. I remember reading *Emma's War* by Deborah Scroggins, an American journalist who worked in Africa. In the midst of overwhelming suffering in Sudan, she was given simple advice: while she couldn't help everyone she could do *one clear thing*, help one person properly rather than failing to help the masses. It stuck with me. I had often returned from assignments to other parts of Africa feeling utterly weighed down by the desperation and magnitude of what I saw. I could never do enough to change it, all I could do was tell the stories. A South African colleague said to me, 'Once you have got all that sorted in your mind, you can walk anywhere in Africa.' I decided that supporting Lucia would be my *one clear thing*.

Our friendship grew gradually. I like Lucia's shy, cluttered way. She has a messy fridge and a bedroom crowded with bags and suitcases of things. She's warm and modest, almost an accidental role model. I think she would have been happy to let life drag her along – she's never been a woman with rigid plans. If AIDS hadn't come to her family, she might have been just another mother and grandmother in Alexandra, the warm lady who sells snacks at the school. Even in the past three years, I've seen her grow: her cautious, soft sentences have become more definite.

'I never saw myself standing up and talking. Bongani's service was my first time. It makes me feel like I'm telling people something. I'm teaching them something. It makes me feel brave. After this AIDS thing I will be a better person, I think, because if somebody has a problem about AIDS, even if he don't want to tell the parents, he just come to me and say, "Sister Lucia, I'm HIV-positive, please help me." I'm scared, I know I'm scared. I cry when I see somebody suffering. I have nothing but I just wish to do something for them, maybe wash them, clean, do whatever I can. They need love.'

When Lucia and I hug, our bodies don't really fit together:

my limbs are long, Lucia's are rounded and soft. She has had and lost her children and lost her child's child, but my belly hasn't even felt the first bump of a pregnancy. We are opposites, but it's nice, that's the way Lucia puts it. *Nice* is one of her words and *Woo* is the noise she makes when the words are not enough.

'Woo, sometimes I feel like crying, sitting here looking backward. Seeing my problems I feel like crying. Sometimes I ask myself, out of all these people, why me? Why is everything on top of my shoulders? Why? I just want to know. This thing of death keeps me down.

'After Bongani's death, I was tired. I was tired. But when Bobo started getting sick, I got up and started fighting again. I'm most afraid of him dying, but he's strong. He's stronger than his brother so I don't think he's going. He's going to make it. He's going to reach the age of twenty. After Bobo, I'll take care of myself. I'll start taking care of myself. But now I'm afraid because I think if I concentrate on me, he will suffer. I don't want him to suffer.'

Bobo lies on the blanket on the floor while Lucia and I talk, his ribs protruding as his chest rises and falls with each laboured breath. He's lying on the same blanket Bongani used to lie on as he peered out the front door. Bobo's eyes are pleading and tired as Lucia squats next to him and rubs her hand back and forth on his arms. She keeps chatting with me, but I can see she's worried about him. She helps him to the kitchen table and starts feeding him some leftovers. He chews uncomfortably as Lucia feeds him by hand; his body leans against hers and his face grimaces as he swallows.

Lucia nods when I ask her if she wants to take him to the clinic and she goes into the bedroom to get him a fresh change of clothes. Bobo puts on the clean jeans, but they slip down over his skinny hips – a small boy from next door watches carefully and then takes off his belt and offers it to Bobo to hold up his pants. Lucia wraps a towel around her waist and helps Bobo to the car.

We drive to the Alex clinic. It's not a proper hospital, just a place where people can get basic treatment. Lucia carries Bobo inside because he doesn't have the strength to walk; his limp limbs loop around her neck and his feet drag along the ground like a drunken dance partner. He looks tired, and embarrassed to be carried by his grandmother. A group of boys his age arrive at reception, dirty and excited. One of the boys has cut his hand while they were playing. They look at Bobo, staring longer than they should.

The clinic is almost clean, but dirty in the corners. A drunken woman with blood in her hair and cuts in her back staggers in with friends while two stocky policemen, one with a machine gun, bring in a white teenager in handcuffs. Another man is waiting for a wound on his leg to be stitched; he smells of alcohol. His girlfriend looks down when he talks to her and their baby pulls away in fear when he leans over.

This is the clinic where Lucia used to bring Bongani for treatment, sitting patiently next to the drunks and the victims of fights as she waited for Bongani's name to be called by the doctor.

'His medical file was this big. A big pink folder.' She shows me the size with her hands. 'It was so heavy before he died, he came here too many times.'

Eventually, Bobo reaches the front of the queue – it's a Saturday afternoon, so it doesn't take long. The doctor gives him an injection and some tablets, but he's still weak. When we get home he vomits into a towel as Lucia tries to carry him to the toilet. She talks with him quietly and says it's okay, but he looks embarrassed. Lucia says it's lucky we were visiting, so she could go by car to the clinic; otherwise she would have to carry Bobo along the street to catch a minibus taxi, and she can barely lift him on her own. This is what it's been like for Lucia for almost fifteen years, with Nokuthula, then Puleng, Bongani and now Bobo. Lucia is short of breath and makes small grunting noises as she tries to carry Bobo. The visit to the clinic has given me a glimpse of her day-to-day grind.

When there's no-one to give her a ride, Lucia faces the stares and the embarrassment of other passengers shuffling hurriedly out of the way when she carries Bobo in the minibus taxi. The stigma is still there, even though up to a third of the people in the minibus would also be HIV-positive. The official figures are based on test results from pregnant mothers at public hospitals, but many of the other South Africans who are HIV-positive don't know it, because they're too scared to be tested. That's the irony – many of those who perpetuate the stigma are themselves infected. Lucia isn't intimidated now; she wears a T-shirt with a large HIV logo on the front. It still takes a lot of courage to wear it and walk along the streets of Alex, but Lucia doesn't try to hide that she has been affected by AIDS anymore.

'When I was hiding it I was so thin, I was scared. When people were talking, I felt small, I just felt like, woo, they are talking about me. I just felt like fighting all the time, like I hate myself, I hate other people. So, I think being open is a relief, I can put it like that. It's a relief. When you talk, you feel free. You'll never have somebody talking behind your back. You become a person where people say, "Here comes a lady." I now feel like I'm a lady because people say, "Here comes Lucia, she's the one who talks about AIDS. She's the brave lady."'

In March 2006, Lucia was invited to Canada by the United Nations Special Envoy for HIV/AIDS in Africa, Stephen Lewis. She was the guest of honour at the launch of the Grandmothers to Grandmothers campaign to assist AIDS grandmothers in Africa. Lucia gave numerous interviews and speeches, and appeared on Canadian national television. It was her first journey outside Africa.

She returned to Canada in August 2006 to attend the inaugural gathering of Canadian and African grandmothers, organised by the Stephen Lewis Foundation.

Lucia continues to live in Alexandra, South Africa, with Bobo and the rest of her family. She is now a full-time care worker with the Alexandra AIDS Orphans Trust.

CHAPTER 10

NAGWA FOUAD

Belly dancer

EGYPT

Nagwa Fouad escaped an arranged marriage at the age of twelve and ran away to Cairo to become a belly dancer.

She got a job as a telephonist at the city's most famous talent agency, pleaded for a chance to audition, and began belly dancing. She was arrested by the vice squad for being under age, but went on to become one of Egypt's most famous and respected performers.

Nagwa's career as a dancer, movie star and producer has spanned more than 40 years.

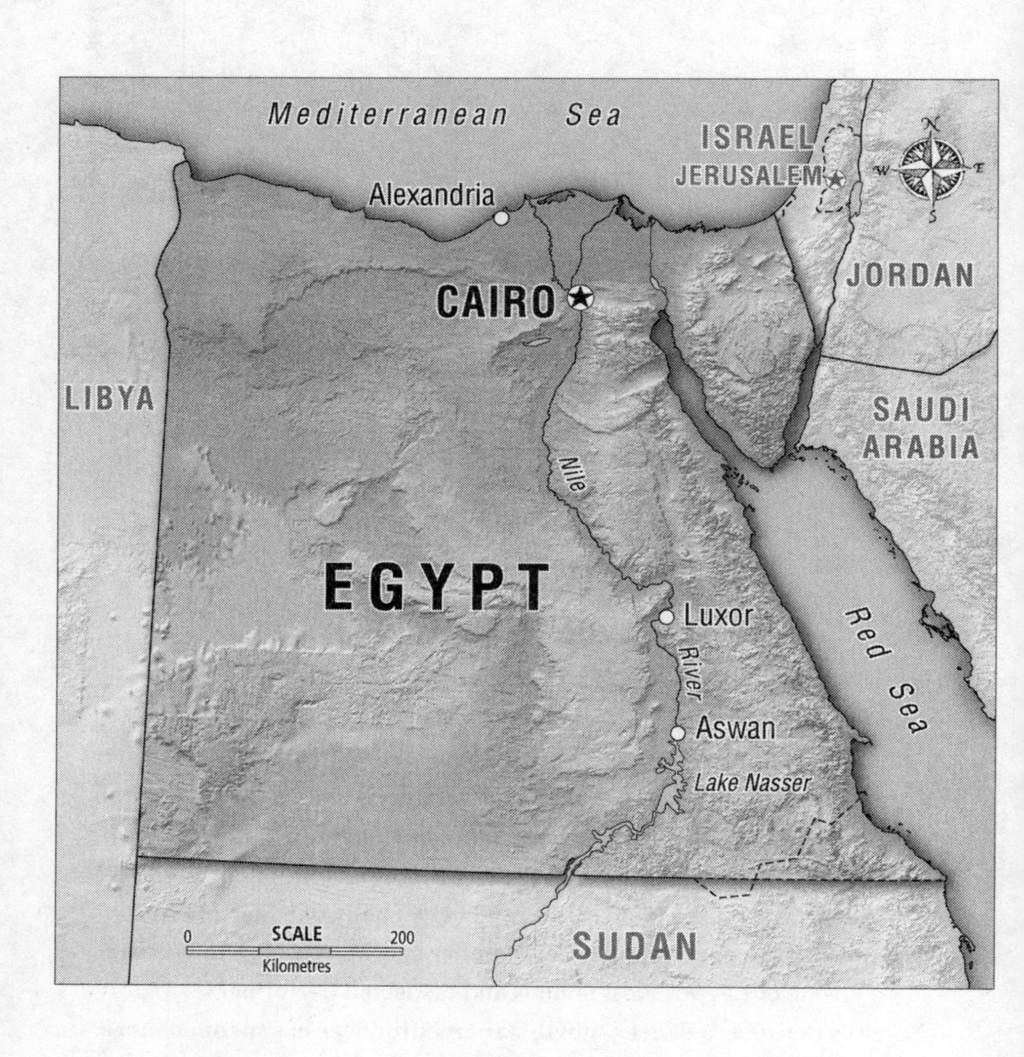
Mediterranean Sea
ISRAEL
JERUSALEM
Alexandria
JORDAN
CAIRO
LIBYA
SAUDI
ARABIA
Nile
EGYPT
Luxor
River
Red Sea
Aswan
Lake Nasser
0
SCALE
200
Kilometres
SUDAN

Every Cairo taxi driver I ask knows her name.

'Nagwa Fouad. Yes, very beautiful.'

They talk about her with a look of familiarity on their faces, as if they are referring to a former girlfriend.

'Mrs Fouad was the number one,' says one driver in a serious tone. He looks into the rear-vision mirror to check that I have heard him.

'Number one belly dancer.'

Nagwa Fouad lives on the banks of the River Nile, where the windows of her apartment look out onto the floating restaurants and the delicious apricot-coloured sky of the Cairo sunset. There are few parks in the city, so couples walk along the Corniche, the riverside promenade, as the traffic buzzes past. Old women with stiff ankles totter in groups of two or three, dressed in black Muslim cloaks and headscarves, gossiping and clasping each other's hands in laughter. The promenade is not really wide enough for all the people who want to stroll, but they politely step around each other and no-one seems to lose their patience.

Cairo is chaotic and full of character. It has its own smell: warm, dry and sandy, the smell of the Middle East. It's loud, too: I have a competition with myself to listen for the longest gap between the sound of car horns; the record so far is only eight seconds and that was in the middle of the night. The car horns, the music, the loud conversations, the markets and the hum of the traffic are the soundtrack of Cairo. It's one of the biggest cities I have ever seen – to be honest, I was dreading coming here, but it has scooped me up in its embrace. It is as if I have left Africa for a while; I see the neon signs of fast-food chains for the first time in almost four months on the road. I feel a bit slow and out of place and I realise my walk has changed. I'm still wandering gently at village pace while Cairo steps and weaves around me. This is Nagwa Fouad's city.

From the outside, her apartment building looks like an old office block. It doesn't seem as if anyone lives here, but inside the foyer there is a marble floor and a grand staircase that curves elegantly into the centre. Two old security guards dressed in blue Arab robes sit inside drinking tea, and when I approach they open the old lift door and press the button for the fifth floor.

Nagwa's apartment has no name at the entrance. The door is almost eight feet tall; it looks heavy and imposing. The interpreter and I ring the bell and a young maid answers, inviting us to come inside and wait. The apartment is large and elegant, decorated like a palace. There are ornate gilt gold chairs with finely upholstered cushions and the tables are polished to a deep brown. But the thing I really notice is that Nagwa has two huge portraits of herself on the wall: big portraits, glamour-style photographs in expensive frames.

The maid brings glasses of freshly squeezed lemon juice as we sit and wait. I look out the window at the spectacular view of the Cairo skyline as I hear Nagwa walking down the staircase in her high heels. She is well groomed and stylish. Her make-up has been carefully applied and her hair blow-dried into place. Nagwa is 60 years old and beautiful. She dresses like a much younger woman, in jeans, a tight green sleeveless top and a see-through blouse. Her belly-dancing figure has softened with age. Her entrance seems planned, as we have been waiting for five or ten minutes since the maid opened the door.

She greets us graciously, but seems a little detached. She is sizing me up and I'm doing the same. Nagwa is elegant and polished; I feel a bit plain and awkward in comparison. She looks politely at the pictures of the other Gogo Mamas, but turns away when I show her the photo of Hellen Lanyom, saying that it is too shocking. I feel offended. Nagwa is very different from the others. Nagwa knows it and so do I. I don't know if this will work; I find it hard to make an initial connection with her.

But the interpreter has sensed what is going on. Her name is also Nagwa. She is energetic, very clever and talkative. She is highly experienced and was the interpreter for Hillary Clinton's visit to Egypt. The two Nagwas have hit it off. They sit on the sofa laughing and chatting; even though they have only known each other for a few minutes, there is an almost instant rapport.

Nagwa sits on the sofa with one of her legs tucked underneath her, surrounded by a nest of plush cushions. She's got a lovely, deep, naughty laugh. As the two Nagwas chatter, I get the feeling Nagwa Fouad is genuinely enjoying a bit of company for the evening.

Nagwa Fouad grew up a long way from the stunning views and manicured lifestyle of a Cairo riverfront apartment. She was born in Alexandria to a Palestinian mother and an Egyptian father; the family lived in a neighbourhood where one building seemed almost to overlap another. Nagwa was only a toddler when her mother was diagnosed with cancer, and the disease had already progressed so rapidly there wasn't much the doctors could do. She returned to Palestine to spend her final months before she died with her family.

Nagwa's father quickly married another woman to take care of her.

'My father remarried a Palestinian woman of Turkish origin. This lady was married previously to an officer. She was barren. She couldn't have any children. He married her to look after me and raise me. At that time I was very young, I was about four years.'

Nagwa's stepmother, Zahra, was a kind and gentle woman. She cared for Nagwa and was a dedicated wife. But Nagwa's father became restless.

'My father wanted to make a family and have other children. At that time women would go and find another wife for their husband. My stepmother was the one who brokered for my father a marriage with his cousin. When he married his cousin he had two sons. He ignored me. Sadness started to appear in me. I started to feel very sad and I wanted to do something for myself.'

Nagwa endured the death of her mother and the loss of love from her father when she was barely old enough to go to school. Her stepmother was at first her only source of security and support, but Nagwa quickly found that she had a talent that would win praise from others. She could dance. Her face changes when she talks about it; she looks off into the distance and then locks on to the gaze of the interpreter.

'It was always in my blood, it was always in me, that talent. Even when I was very young, seven, eight. When there was a wedding at a neighbour's house, when there was a party, they used to ask me to come up and dance. I always attracted attention.

'I wanted to have a personality, a career. I was at school but I used to skip school to go to movies. Whenever I heard music, it was something that made me dance. But I didn't imagine that I would ever become a dancer or a singer or a musician, because my family was very conservative. When my father became very strict, when he not let me have too many things that I wanted, I started to think in a way of how I could provide those things. And that is how it started.'

She grew up next to the crowded neighbourhood of El-Mansheya in Alexandria. The streets were narrow and clogged with market stalls; washing hung from windows above run-down shops. Nagwa and her stepmother lived in a small apartment in the backstreets behind the Ritz cinema, away from the sunny seaside homes along the beach. Nagwa fantasised about escaping the congested alleyways of El-Mansheya. But her father had his own plans for her future. He came to the apartment one evening and announced that Nagwa would be married off to an ageing relative.

'I was twelve years old and my father decided to make me get married to my cousin, who was named Yehia. That cousin of mine was almost the age of my father. I couldn't imagine why he would make me do this. I don't know why he wanted that. Maybe he wanted to get rid of the responsibility. Maybe he didn't want to sponsor me anymore. I told my father, "I cannot marry Yehia."'

As soon as her father left, she started packing her clothes to catch the last train to Cairo. As Nagwa's stepmother was unable to talk her out of it, she reluctantly agreed to go with her. Nagwa was buoyant. It was late at night, she was twelve years old and on her way to one of the most chaotic cities in the world.

'I felt daring !'

'My stepmother tried to convince me to stay. I said, "No, it's over. I am not going to marry Yehia. I will get any job, even if I have to sell chewing gum in the street." My stepmother was a very devoted lady. She brought all that she had saved in her life, it was 50 pounds.

'I broke the rules. I made a decision and I wanted to go. I didn't think of the consequences. I expected that they would kill me. But I made the decision. I said I would go, I will proceed. I will look ahead.

'I always felt I was right. Nobody has the right to deprive me. I felt I was going to be killed. Even if I was married to my cousin who was my father's age, I am going to be dead. I would be dead in my mind. So I went for what I wanted because I felt I had made the right decision.'

Nagwa claps her hands and laughs as she remembers her escape. The more she talks, the more she seems to let her guard down. Her upright posture has softened from when she first walked down the stairs to greet us. She agrees to take part in another interview next week. She will be busy for a few days, so I decide to use the time to visit Alexandria and re-trace her journey to Cairo.

Alexandria is several hours north-west of Cairo, on the coast of the Mediterranean. At first glimpse it looks like a resort town with high-rise buildings towering above the white sand and the sparkling, calm waters. But many of the buildings are run-down, the paint is peeling, the floors are worn. Washing hanging from the windows flutters in the narrow spaces between the apartment blocks. I find my way to Nagwa's old neighbourhood of El-Mansheya. An elderly man with the ring finger missing from his left hand appoints himself as my guide. He takes me to several buildings and swears that each one was Nagwa Fouad's childhood home; the doormen nod in agreement; then someone else overhears the conversation and I'm taken to yet more buildings.

El-Mansheya is the kind of place you would visit if you had to buy a Christmas present for someone you don't like. The market is stocked with gaudy gifts of flashing-light clocks, bunches of plastic flowers, and cheap coloured bras. Every now and then there is a rush of activity, as illegal sellers push trolleys and drag tarpaulins down side streets at high speed every time there is a whisper that inspectors are coming.

It's not far from the market to the train station. I follow the same path that Nagwa and her stepmother took on their way to Cairo. The station is big and grand, and the engine of the train hums as it sits at the platform. Tired-looking businessmen stand on the platform savouring their last cigarette before the journey starts. A warm breeze sends the smoke in a gentle dance until it dilutes into the air. The men shuffle onto the train and slouch into the heavy leather seats.

The train pulls out of the station and rattles along the edge of the city. A steward with a maroon tunic and a thin moustache serves tea and coffee as the buildings thin out to reveal the countryside. He looks like a Monty Python character, and does his job with more elegance and seriousness than the old train and the passengers deserve.

The view from the window of the train looks like something from a geography book. Farmers dressed in smocks work in the fields; small plots that are barely the size of a tennis court are tended by hand. Donkeys pull carts of produce along the roads near the canal, where groups of boys sit on the banks with fishing lines dangling into the dirty water. Women huddle in groups gossiping and laughing as they wash their cooking pots in the canal.

Many of the farmers work in the evening until the sun sinks below the horizon. Others squat under trees, brewing coffee to finish the day. I expect the small fields to open up to bigger farms as the train travels further away from Alexandria, but the countryside is crowded. After a couple of hours the view changes; the canals are narrower and the roads wider. Instead of date palms there are chimneys that look like giant cigarettes blowing smoke into the sky.

Darkness comes as the train approaches Cairo. The lights inside the carriage make it difficult to see outside. I can't distinguish buildings or cars, there are just flashes of streetlights and neon signs. The businessmen in the carriage who have slept most of the way start to stir. Some put on their jackets, others smooth their hair to cover bald patches.

The train pulls into the station and some of the passengers step off before it stops, jumping onto the platform and running for a few steps to keep their balance. The station is crowded and busy; to me it feels like a sped-up version of real life. I walk quickly and try to look like I know where I'm going, even though I don't. I wonder what it was like for Nagwa to arrive here as a twelve-year-old. I walk out of the station and into the warm Cairo night. The traffic is chaotic and the footpaths are full of people; car horns toot and taxi drivers try to grab my wrist as I walk past. I'm trying to see, smell and listen to what is going on around me, but I think I'm only picking up about 10 per cent of what's happening.

Nagwa and her stepmother also arrived at night. They had nowhere to stay and little idea of where to go, but Nagwa took the lead. They found their way into the city and rented a furnished room. However, they knew that their savings would soon run out.

'A week later I started to look for a job. There was a little kiosk that had like a newspaper stall. I used to go and look for jobs. I found one for a very famous impresario called Orabi. He wanted a girl to just answer the telephones. He didn't want a secretary or anything like that. At that time I had my primary school. I could read, but little. I remember very vividly.'

It was 1957. Mr Orabi's office was one of the most important showbiz addresses in Cairo, and some of the biggest stars in Egypt swooshed in and out of his doorway. Nagwa got the job as Mr Orabi's switchboard operator, a turn of fate which would change her life. Purely by good luck, she was answering the phones at the most famous star agency in the country.

'It was something from God. Always when there is something good that God wants to happen for you, he makes a venue for it. It's heavenly, it's God.'

Nagwa was still a child and she was more interested in watching the celebrities who came to meet with Mr Orabi than she was in operating the switchboard. She was full of excitement and wonder.

'I was very impressed when I went to the office. When I was working, those people used to come in and out. I recall Shoukuku was a very comical actor and singer. He had a special hat he used to wear. When I saw Shoukuku, I actually fainted. I once bought a statue of him for two piastres and then here I was seeing him face to face.

'Orabi came and said, "What happened to you?" I told him I just can never imagine, I love art also. He said, "You love art?" I said yes. He asked me what I could do. So I told him anything, anything. I told him I could sing.'

Mr Orabi didn't know that Nagwa wasn't even in her teens yet. He was amused, but also impressed by her bravado. He decided to see if she had any talent.

'Next to the office of Orabi there was a very famous singer called Mohamed Abd el Wahab. Orabi said, "Okay, I will give him a call, maybe I can introduce you."'

A meeting was arranged. Nagwa couldn't sing, but she was

about to have an audition with one of the most acclaimed performers in Egypt. Mohamed Abd el Wahab was expecting to meet a talented songstress.

'He thought he would see a pop star. He said, "Kid, do you know how to sing?" I told him yes. I sang a very famous song of his called, "Ana we al azab we hawak", which means, "Me and my suffering with your love". I started to sing it in the way of a child. He looked at me and said, "Kid, here, take a pound, go and have lunch. Go."

'I started to cry. I wanted to dance. He asked me, "What do you want to do? What kind of career?" He was a very famous music player. He played a very famous song called "Zeina Zeina". I danced. He said, "Damn you. You are so good. You are such a dancer."'

Nagwa had never received any training but her talent was obvious. Mohamed Abd el Wahab knew she had the potential to go on the stage, although Nagwa was afraid to pursue her passion.

'I said, "My family is so conservative: how can I do this? How could I sort it out with my stepmother?" He said, "No, no. We will sort it out. I will take you somewhere remote."'

Remote, it was. Nagwa's first performance was at a wedding on a plantation. She had never performed on stage; her only experience was as a little girl dancing at her own family gatherings. She didn't have a costume or a routine. Mr Orabi decided to help.

'He rented a costume for 25 piastres – 25 piastres then was a fortune.

'I went onto the stage and people were cheering and whistling and throwing money on me. When they were throwing the money I thought they wanted to get rid of me. So I went inside the curtains but Orabi used to push me back. I went back on the stage and it happened again. Finally I kept dancing for one hour and a half. People were so happy. When I ended that, he hugged me and told me a star is born. And that is how it started.'

Mr Orabi gave Nagwa five pounds and bought her a kebab for dinner. She felt like she had hit the big time and rushed home to tell her stepmother. Mr Orabi arranged a contract for her to join a belly-dancing show. She travelled back and forth to the venue with its catering staff, because she was too young to go on her own. Most of the belly-dancing shows didn't start until after midnight, but this show was designed for tourists and didn't finish as late as those others. Nagwa Fouad's career had begun.

'Deep inside of me I knew I would excel. There was a very, very famous tent at that time. It was at the base of the pyramids, called Sahara City. Most of the tourist groups and the tourist buses would see a show down there. He told me I would work down there and I would work very early. I used to go with the cooks who used to cook dinner down there, at three o'clock. I would return with them at 1 am.'

Nagwa was now the breadwinner. Her stepmother gradually accepted her profession and sometimes accompanied her to the shows. Nagwa was the youngest member of the troupe, but she was already attracting attention.

'I was doing very fine and having lots of success. A guy called Wadee who used to have a nightclub, he saw me and he told Orabi, "I want to take this girl to work for me." Orabi said, "It's impossible, she is under age." But Wadee told him, "We can work it out. We can make her a certificate that she is a few years older." They did that. Even now I have a passport with four years added.'

Nagwa started dancing at Wadee's nightclub. The pay was better and it was a step forward from performing for tourists. But she was only half the age of most of the dancers and some of them were not happy about having a younger rival.

'I was under age. You had to be seventeen or eighteen to be able to work. Anyway, I started to work. There was a lot of jealousy. There was another dancer who was very jealous of me. So she went to the police vice squad. She reported on me. The vice squad police came and they took me. I was horrified, I went to the police station.'

She was taken to the office of the vice squad commander, who sat at his desk and examined her fake work permit. He knew she was under age, but decided to let her go with a warning.

'There was a general called Mohammed Abbas. He said, "Go,

kid, and work but remember you will have lots of problems in that career. Even if you excel you will have lots of problems. But go and keep on working." I remember him very well. He passed away but his children and grandchildren still call me.'

Nagwa pauses self-consciously, realising she has become absorbed in her own story. She clasps her hands and apologises; she is running late to meet a friend.

'Please excuse me. I will see you tomorrow evening.'

Despite her retirement, Nagwa Fouad still keeps belly-dancer hours. She sleeps during the day and socialises at night. So I use the daytime to explore Cairo.

The next morning I take a taxi to the Giza pyramids to see where Nagwa started her career – like almost every other tourist I expect to make a long trek into the desert to get to Giza. But the pyramids are only a 30-minute drive away.

'Giza, madam,' says the driver. He points ahead. I can see the pyramids in the distance before we have even left the suburbs: their peaks break the skyline of roughly built apartment blocks and the bouquets of white satellite dishes that sit on the rooftops.

We stop at a stable that is a combined souvenir shop and camel-hire emporium. I have no idea what the going rate is for a rental camel but I barter with the owner until he drops the price. He returns with my ship of the desert, a bored, crusty-looking beast with bad teeth. It glances at me and groans.

'This is Michael Jackson,' says the owner proudly. 'Your camel.'

Michael Jackson groans again as he is ordered to kneel down. I climb on.

'Lean forward,' barks the owner.

I'm not sure if he's talking to me or the camel. Michael Jackson lunges upwards and I almost fall off. I try to look relaxed and experienced as we pass tourist buses at window height but there's no denying that it's extremely uncomfortable. The frame of the saddle is wooden; riding Michael Jackson is like sitting on an upside-down bar stool.

My guide talks in jumbled English. I can't really understand what he's saying, but I nod and smile when he looks back to check on me. Michael Jackson hisses and complains each time the guide orders him to kneel down so I can get off for a photograph.

The road to Giza is lined with luxury hotels, nightclubs and restaurants. This is where package tour groups get their bite-size experience of the pyramids, like some kind of Sphinx Vegas. It's been one of the most well-trodden stretches of Egypt's tourist trail for decades, even when Nagwa was performing here as a teenager. She caught the attention of one of Egypt's most respected orchestral conductors, Ahmed Fouad Hassan, who was the leader of a musical group, Sahara City. Nagwa was thirteen years old.

'He was my senior, [by] nineteen years. He met me, he fell in love with me and he married me. When he married me he was very protective. He put a close shield on me.

'He brought culture to me. He was so respectful of me. He gave me respect and protection. I was in need of him. I was in need of a father, a brother, somebody to protect me. He was an academic man. He was a composer. He was so famous. I was in need of him to protect me in the long hard passageway I was going through.'

Nagwa's father and relatives were still looking for her. They heard she had become a dancer, and uncles and cousins were sent to Cairo to search for her. Her father wanted her dead. She had disobeyed him and disgraced the family by running away. But now that she was married, she had some protection.

'I thought I was going to be killed. They searched and searched for me. After I got married to Ahmed Fouad Hassan, a month later my uncle came. He wanted to kill me. Ahmed told him to walk away, that I was now married. He said, "You cannot do anything to her now. She is under my protection."'

Her career was starting to accelerate. Nagwa's performances in the clubs were drawing the attention of producers and promoters, and she was offered a role on the big screen in a movie called *Devil and Angel*. But as her career soared, her marriage was starting to falter. Nagwa was becoming successful, independent and self-assured. She didn't want to give up her career to start having children, which she knew would take her away from the stage. She and Ahmed divorced in 1965.

'Ahmed Fouad Hassan was an only child and he wanted to have a child. He really wanted that. I knew that if a dancer is pregnant, she will have a child for a year and then she would spend another year for herself to work out and regain her posture. At that time there was no gym and no fitness room. At that time it was a very big sacrifice.

'I had a lot of love and esteem for Ahmed Fouad Hassan. I sat with him and I told him, "I owe you a lot of things, I have a lot of respect for you. I understand your need, you want to have a family, you want to have an offspring. But at the same time, you made me, you brought me to that fame. Do not deprive me out of it. Let's split while we are friends. You go on your way and I go on my way." That is how the marriage broke.'

Nagwa was now twenty years old, famous, successful and single. She was an acclaimed dancer and was receiving offers to appear in more movies. After the divorce she felt free.

I ask my interpreter to find some footage of Nagwa's earlier career. The next day she arrives with two DVDs and I load one into my laptop. The opening titles are in Arabic and quick-tempo belly-dancing music starts up in the background. It begins with Nagwa arriving at the Meridian Hotel in a BMW. She steps out like a movie star. Wearing a white mink stole, she waves to her fans as she walks inside.

The performance begins. Nagwa is serenaded by a group of dodgy-looking male dancers wearing tuxedos and fezzes. She smiles and tantalises them with her pulsating hips. They hold up a large green cloth and she bursts through it like a football star running onto the field.

Each act has a different costume, including one that looks like something from *I Dream of Jeannie*. The back-up dancers put

Nagwa on a giant spinning disk reminiscent of a lazy Susan. They spin her around as she smiles at the camera. They are careful not to touch her thighs accidentally as she whizzes past.

After the final song, Nagwa and her dancers bow to the crowd. The camera follows her as she walks back out to her luxury car. She almost shuts her fur coat in the door, but she rectifies this without losing her smile. Both the DVDs end with her at home, sitting on the sofa until the lights fade to black.

This was Nagwa at the height of her career, when she was attracting the attention of stars she had admired as a child. As she moved on from her divorce, she took a turn away from the seriousness and caution of her early years in Cairo.

'It was like adolescence. It was reckless. At that time I was in a movie with a very famous actor called Ahmed Ramzi. He was older than me. He started to act in the 1950s. He had a daughter who was almost my age. It was a movie entitled *A Marriage in Danger*. I was fascinated by Ahmed Ramzi, I used to like him a lot. At that time he had a lot of family problems, he divorced his wife.

'I was attracted to him. He said, "Listen, shall we get married?" I said yeah. I just had a divorce four months ago. We went. We were drunk. We went to The Auberge, which was a very famous nightclub. We got married.'

The day after she got married, Nagwa was invited to go to New York City to perform in an Egyptian promotion for TWA airlines; it was a chance to earn some money and enjoy a free trip to the United States. When she came back, Nagwa found that Ahmed Ramzi had reconciled with his former wife, and her short marriage was over.

'This was a stage of recklessness. We were married for eighteen days.'

Nagwa laughs heartily and her hands move back and forth as she retells the story of the short-lived relationship. She doesn't speak with any embarrassment or regret. She's happy, too, that I've watched a couple of her belly-dancing videos.

'If you really want to understand the dance, you must meet

Madame Raqia. She is the best teacher in Cairo; she has been dancing forever, more than 30 years.'

Madame Raqia lives in an apartment building not far from the city centre. It's a quiet neighbourhood, which gives no hint of a belly-dancing school in its midst.

Madame Raqia opens the door wearing slippers and short pyjamas: she is a portly woman aged in her fifties. Her eyebrows are drawn on with a thick pencil and her hair is in a ponytail.

She is gracious and welcoming. Her white fluffy dog fusses at her feet while we watch one of her training videos. In it she is wearing bright green Lycra tights and a T-shirt tied at the waist. Her round belly wobbles gently to the music.

Madame Raqia has travelled the world teaching belly dancing, all the way from Australia to the United States. One of her students, an American dancer, Astryd, arrives for a lesson. She comes from Oregon but in Cairo she is often mistaken for a local, with her dark eyes and long dark hair. We follow her into the rehearsal studio in the apartment next door. There are mirrors on the walls and a CD player in the corner.

Astryd wears tights and a tank top, with a scarf tied around her waist and rings on her toes. Madame Raqia comes in still wearing her pyjamas. They look like an odd pair, one young and elegant and the other round and motherly. The music starts and they dance in tandem; their eyes are fixed on each other as they count the beat and practise the steps. They spend almost an hour perfecting just one small part of the routine, going over it again and again. Madame Raqia says it's a painstaking art.

'The belly dance. It is not easy. It is more difficult than acting. Because with acting you have a story and words you can tell. But this, it's music. Just music. The music have meaning.'

Other dancers come in and out of the studio to make appointments for their next lesson. A petite Japanese woman, an Australian dancer and a Russian with a doll-like face come and go. Madame Raqia works with many foreigners who have been drawn to Cairo by belly dancing.

'The foreigners have to stay with us a lot to take the feeling.

Because without feeling here, the people no respect. When you dance without feeling, it is like you make sport. We have the feeling. This is culture. When you have a baby, when they are just two years, you put music and you find they start to move with music. Nobody teach them. It is inside our blood. It is our culture. This is Egyptian dance.'

I talk with some of the other dancers at the rehearsal studio. They all have stories of leaving jobs and families in their homelands to follow their passion, and it's an unforgiving business for those who are trying to work their way up. The pay is modest and the dancers have to buy their own costumes. Some also invest in breast enlargements and other cosmetic surgery; it is highly competitive.

The dance is quite mesmerising to watch. Astryd and Madame Raqia move their bellies in perfect time, back and forth, in and out, up and down. They turn and slide in unison. I ask Madame Raqia about the best dancers in the business. She says Nagwa Fouad was number one.

'She put you in dream. When you see her show, you feel like you are in dream. Nagwa, she was the best in her time. She was the first-class one. How many years, 40? Forty years famous, nobody come beside her.'

By 1970, Nagwa Fouad was the number one belly dancer in Egypt and attracted a swathe of admirers. Men regularly waited for her at the stage door after she finished her show. It had been five years since her brief marriage to Ahmed Ramzi, and she was looking for a more serious relationship when she fell in love with the famous Egyptian choreographer Kamal Naeem. They had only been married for three years when Egypt went to war against Israel.

'When the 1973 war happened they summoned him as a reserve officer. He was crossing the canal when he was hurt. He jumped off into the canal. His ID fell in the water. A policeman found it and took it to me. He told me that my husband had passed away.

'I was horrified. We had a funeral. We had the Koran being

recited. It was a very big funeral. They even announced the funeral in the newspaper. He comes from a very prominent family. It was very big. His family used to live in Shobra. At that time it was a very famous place. It was the place where the leader used to live. The house of his father was next to Omar Sharif 's house.'

Two days after the funeral there was further news from the army. Kamal was not dead.

'A second officer came and told me, "Your husband is in hospital. He is injured." I couldn't believe it. I jumped off and went to the hospital to see him. I brought him back to the armed forces hospital here. He was injured in his leg. He was a choreographer and he was so emotionally hurt out of his injury.'

Kamal was deeply traumatised and the injury to his leg would make it difficult for him to continue working in dance and choreography. He wanted to leave the country and start a new life in Europe, but Nagwa didn't want to go – she'd just got a contract after being out of work because of injury and she had no plans to give it up. Again she chose her career over marriage.

'Yes, it was a very painful decision. But I was very successful. I had just signed a contract with the Sheraton. After I worked with [the] Hilton, I was sick for some time. I had pain in my leg, I couldn't move properly. They had a contract with another belly dancer. At that time I couldn't find work. I was just dancing in weddings. In the summer I would go to Beirut and Syria. I was so happy to find a contract. It was a very long one, for four to five years.'

The next decade saw a procession of husbands and admirers. Nagwa married hotel manager Sami El Zoghby; they were together for seven years and she describes it as the happiest period of her life. She was in love with Sami, and was the top-billed artist at the Sheraton Hotel in Cairo, but the marriage eventually broke down when he fell in love with another woman.

'He divorced me in absentia. Until now I still don't know what happened.'

She seems sad and embarrassed when she talks about it, and hurries through her sentences to tell the story as quickly as possible. Unlike her other relationship break-ups, in this instance she was the one who was left behind. She not only lost Sami but her lifestyle and tenure at the Sheraton. She moved back into her apartment on the Nile and decided the best way to move forward was to throw herself even deeper into her career.

Nagwa won herself some high-profile fans. US Secretary of State Henry Kissinger heard about her show, and when he arrived in Cairo for a series of meetings he asked the Egyptian President's office if arrangements could be made for him to see Nagwa Fouad perform. She was in Alexandria taking part in a charity concert, but the President's office arranged to bring her back to Cairo.

'They sent two choppers, two helicopters to bring me with the performers. I came here by eleven, eleven thirty. This was the first time I met Kissinger.

Jimmy Carter when he came, he went to the Presidency and said, "I want to see the one that Kissinger was so fond of." They reserved the hall for him. It was a private show. Flowers, security and everything. He complimented me.'

I decide it's also time for me finally to see a belly-dancing show. Nagwa recommends I book tickets for a performance by Cairo's top dancer, named Dina. The show doesn't start until the early hours of Monday morning so I catch a taxi just after 1 am and arrive at the InterContinental Hotel, where the foyer is almost deserted. Cleaners are washing the floor and I wonder if I've got mixed up and come on the wrong night. But, no, the doorman guides me upstairs to the nightclub.

The maitre d' checks my name at the door and takes me inside. I sit at the back, at a table for one. There are crisp white tablecloths and on the maroon ceiling there are lines of lights. It looks like the interior of the Love Boat. I'm the only foreign woman in the audience. A fat Arab man in a white safari suit sits in front of me, blowing cigar smoke into the air and winking in my direction. I pretend not to see him and look at the ceiling.

A waiter arrives and hands me a menu, and I choose a fish dish. But then the waiter opens up the menu to reveal page upon page of choices. A four-course meal is included in the ticket price.

One after another, the courses arrive. It is a convenient distraction as the man in the white safari suit escalates his winking campaign.

It's now 2.30 in the morning and still no belly dancing. The Arab band is playing set after set and I've almost run out of courses to eat. Then the curtains close and I can hear musicians warming up. Suddenly spotlights are turned on from the back and the curtains open. There is a full orchestra on the stage; the musicians are dressed in dark suits and look like characters from an old movie. Then, from the corner of the stage, Dina emerges. She is wearing a black bikini top, a G-string and a shiny silver skirt and she shimmies into the spotlight.

Dina has a nonstop smile and large breasts that cheat gravity. They are enormous: the biggest breasts I have ever seen. She bends over, tucks in her elbows and shows off her cleavage to the men in the front row. She goes offstage to change her costume every two songs. One of the costumes is a gladiator outfit, complete with a solid metallic bra. The male members of the audience are captivated, but the members of the band have seen it all before. The piano accordion player has a dull, sleepy expression, which only lifts when Dina turns around with her back to the audience and her front to the band and adjusts her bra.

Different singers come out to perform each song, including a group of men wearing long robes and turbans. The crowd cheers and the music is loud and fast. Dina dances her last number. Members of the audience come up on stage to have their photo taken with her, then she bows and walks off. The curtains close and the lights come on: it's all over. When I get back to my hotel it's almost four in the morning and even the security guards are asleep as I walk up to my room.

When I wake up it's close to midday. I'm officially on belly-dancer time. These are the hours that Nagwa Fouad has kept since she began dancing as a teenager: late nights and short days. She couldn't adjust to a more conventional routine, even when she married the respected General Mohamed El-Sebaie in 1995. They were living in the same house but in different time zones, and her lively evenings and his early mornings weren't compatible.

'He lived for 45 years as a police officer. He would wake up at five o'clock and go to bed at 9 pm. I lived for 40 years waking up at 5 pm and going to bed at 5 am. I came to a realisation: I was not happy, so I told him enough is enough.'

Nagwa was 50 years old, single and nearing the end of her career. The management of the InterContinental Hotel asked her if she wanted to renew her contract. But she decided the moment had come to retire, so she could finish on her own terms and at the top of her profession. Her final performance was the New Year's party in 1996. Instead of going out to celebrate, she worked until after dawn to dismantle all the equipment she had installed in the auditorium.

'I blew the temple. I stayed until 7 am. I tore down the laser and the sound system that I had built myself with my money. I took the costumes, everything. I wanted to do this because I wanted to make a decision to pull out of dance. I didn't want to leave things behind.'

Nagwe's belly-dancing career ended almost 40 years after she ran away to Cairo as a plucky twelve year old. When she looks back now, she is grateful for the support of her stepmother, who came with her and looked after her.

'At the beginning when I was very young I didn't realise the importance and the value of her support. I was very young. When I started to grow, I was around nine or ten. I started to feel the importance of being close to that lady.'

'It was a very big factor pushing me to create and work. If you look at the very big artists like Picasso, there is a sad history in everyone's life, a tragedy that made them create and work. It was a feeling of being lost, just totally left with my stepmother. We were just waiting for the few pounds he threw to us.

'I hope women learn the importance of success. To be achieving something. Not to stop, even if she is a mother, a wife. She should know the value of success. It is not bad to fail. Because failure might lead you to success. But you should have determination. You should have ambition. You should have a goal to achieve.

'I controlled the stage with my art, my show. I had a very big band that was almost 90 people. I had TV screens, I had sound effects. I had music. I impressed people by my shows, my costumes. Thanks to God, I had a very nice figure. Which was true. But I used to like to control with my art, my creativity. The thing that would live long with people is art.'

Throughout her career she was very strict about preventing audience members trying to throw money onto the stage. She felt it was degrading and interrupted the show.

'I used to feel angry. I was the one who worked on banning that in five-star hotels. I felt it was cheap. It was kind of humiliating.

'If I am a performer, if I am doing something good, give me a flower. Send me a gift at the end. Make a photo for me. Do something for me that is meaningful. So for me, I didn't accept money.

'When I am on stage, how could you throw money to me? This change something in my mood. It interrupted the flow. If you throw money, it is like something interrupting the flow of my giving.'

Throughout her 40-year career, she tried to increase her art's respectability. Belly dancing was often a shady form of entertainment for men, but gradually it became accepted as legitimate and decent.

'I made the respect for the belly-dancing art. I was so much in love with it. Families started to love belly dancing. They used to bring their children and their families to watch it.'

Nagwa received many offers to star in movies when she finished belly dancing, which was an affirmation of her fame and talent. But it didn't give her the same sense of satisfaction as dancing had and she lost a lot of creative control over what she was doing. She slipped into several bouts of depression.

'If a movie did not work well, it used to depress me a lot. I would refrain from seeing people for a month and be by myself until I go through that stage of sadness. I was very hard on myself and I always took things very seriously.

'I had a lot of sadness and I still do. I loved that career. I suffered for a year. I could not even change the sort of style of life. For 40 years I was going eleven at night, doing my show coming home late. Now if I have an order for shooting at ten o'clock I can't because I am not used to that style of life. Even my eating habits. When I was performing, my last meal was at three o'clock. I would burn all of that with the show. Now it's different. When I gave up dancing, I was here at home alone. I was not used to that.'

Now she makes a living from starring in Egyptian television shows. I have accidentally seen her on TV several times, when in my hotel room I've flicked through the channels.

'The one that I am playing now is called *The Tree of Koshkhash*. It is about drug dealers. I play an agent for the police, a spy. I pretend to buy drugs from them while I inform the police.'

She laughs with delight when she talks about the soap operas. She enjoys the work and it has maintained her profile: she is still very famous in Egypt and that's the way she likes it.

'I would feel sad if I woke up and people didn't say, "Where is Nagwa Fouad, where are you, we miss you." This makes me feel as if I breathe again.'

At almost every junction in her life, Nagwa Fouad has chosen her career over relationships or family. If she hadn't, she would have been married off to her ageing cousin, just as her father planned. I can't even imagine her as a housewife in the grotty backstreets of El-Mansheya in Alexandria. At twelve years old, she knew she wanted a very different life and that she had the guts and the talent to get it. In 1950s Egypt, disobeying her father and taking up a career as a dancer was an extreme act of defiance. Even now, her independence is out of step with others. On the beachfront in Alexandria, while boys splash in the water, many veiled women only paddle in the shallows, cautiously lifting their long clothing to their ankles.

But her choices have been at a personal cost. She fidgets uncomfortably when I ask whether she wishes she'd had children.

'I had a couple of marriages. I would have had a child from here, a child from there. If I had four or five children, how could I afford for them? I would be a single mother. With the economy and with certain demands that each child could be wanting, I could not afford for them. That would make me unhappy. So I am kind of grateful for what God has planned for me.'

My initial reaction is disbelief. It seems strange to be sitting in a luxury apartment listening to a wealthy celebrity lament that she couldn't afford to have children. Immediately I think of Hellen Lanyom in Uganda, with her hut full of grandchildren and nieces even though she struggles to make sure she can feed them. But, in another way, I understand what Nagwa Fouad is talking about. She knew from the beginning that it was almost impossible to have children and be the very best in her profession. Her long, nocturnal working hours would have left her little time for motherhood. She couldn't have it all, so she chose what she wanted. She followed her dream and for more than a generation became the best belly dancer in Egypt.

'For somebody to persist and linger for 40 years, this is something special.'

Her eyes brighten when she remembers the train ride that brought her to Cairo. She doesn't have any regrets.

'If I went back to my youth, if I returned again as a child I would choose the same path, because this is in me. It is inherent in me. I loved it.'

CHAPTER 11

Juliana Dogbadzi

Former slave

GHANA

Juliana Dogbadzi became a slave at the age of eight. She endured sixteen years of captivity and sexual abuse as a Trokosi slave. Her family gave her to a priest as a sacrifice for crimes committed by an ancestor. Trokosi is a tradition among the Ewe people in southern Ghana, in which thousands of girls are sent into slavery by their own families. The slaves are kept in shrines where they are subjected to forced labour and rape.

Juliana eventually escaped and is working to free thousands of girls and women who are still being held in Trokosi shrines in Ghana. She now has a family of her own.

BURKINA FASO
N
W
E
S
CÔTE D'IVOIRE
BENIN
TOGO
Tamale
GHANA
Lake Volta
Kumasi
Adidome
LOMÉ
PORTO-NOVO
ACCRA
Cape Coast
0
SCALE
300
Kilometres

The entrance to the slave dungeon is dark and makes me feel claustrophobic. I hunch my shoulders and duck my head as I follow the guide into the darkness. Hundreds of years after this dank space was crowded with slaves, their smell is still here. It's a powerful, mouldy smell that has taken the damp corridors of the dungeon captive. The guide uses a dim yellow light to show me a site near the wall where historians have dug down to reveal the original floor.

'Look at this. The floor is buried in almost a foot of this stuff,' he says as he picks up a handful of what looks like dark soil.

'What is it?' I ask.

'This? This is what the slaves left behind. It is human waste. Dirt, skin flakes, hair, excrement and sweat. If you crowd thousands of people into a small space like this for so many years, this is what you get. It is human misery.'

The floor of the slave dungeon is soft with the dark dirt. Now I understand where the smell comes from. This is where the slaves were kept before being loaded on to waiting ships and taken to the Americas. There were no toilets, no lights, no beds and little water, only shallow gutters in the floor to channel the urine and faeces. Their last days and nights in Africa were spent in almost total darkness; only a few spy holes allowed in some light and the unfamiliar sounds of the ocean.

It is difficult to imagine how utterly frightening and confusing it must have been. Most of the slaves who passed through here never saw Africa again. I can only shake my head, there is such a strong sense of sadness and wasted humanity. The guide briefly turns off the lights to give a sense of what it was like. The air is still. I can hear one of the other tourists next to me, sobbing in the darkness. When the lights come on again, I can see her body shuddering as the emotion overwhelms her. After a few minutes, she excuses herself and walks back up the ramp of the dungeon and into the sunshine.

The slave dungeon is deep inside the Cape Coast castle. The white-washed walls and grand turrets belie the misery below. This stunning stretch of West African coastline was at the heart of one of the biggest forced migrations in human history. Despite extraordinary mineral wealth, human beings surpassed gold as the region's biggest export. Now the slave forts are a tourist attraction. Weighty, wealthy African Americans make the pilgrimage on special 'slavery tours' to trace their family history. I watch them carefully, wondering what this experience must be like when there is a possibility that one of their own ancestors passed through here.

The guide takes us from the dungeon to a walkway.

'This is where the slaves were herded towards the boats. These were their final steps in Africa.'

We follow him quietly. Some of the African Americans walk slowly as if to delay each inevitable step until we stop.

'This door was the door of no return. There was no coming back from here, this is where they left their homeland.'

There is silence but, as he opens the door, suddenly we are hit by the sounds of chaos. At first it's difficult to see, because the sunlight is so bright. The doorway looks out onto a beach crowded with old wooden fishing boats and big market women shouting for their share of the catch. Brightly coloured flags flutter from the boats, and muscular teenage boys strain to carry ashore heavy nets in need of repair.

Some of the tourists are squinting as we look out on the scene. In a few seconds, their minds have been jolted from the solemnity of the door of no return to the vibrancy of the beach market. Daily life goes on outside the salty walls of the slave fort.

But, hundreds of years after the Atlantic slave trade, a different form of slavery still exists in Ghana. It's called 'Trokosi'. Its victims are young girls and women who are held captive for life. The 'Trokosi girls' are taken from their families and sent into slavery at local shrines to atone for the sins of other family members. They are told that if they try to escape, their relatives will die, so the girls remain in captivity, enduring rape, hunger, beatings and forced labour. Human rights groups estimate there are still up to 3000 Trokosi girls across Ghana.

That's why I'm here. I'm travelling hundreds of kilometres along the Ghanaian coast to meet a former Trokosi girl who spent most of her life in slavery. Her name is Juliana Dogbadzi and she has been internationally recognised for her work as a human rights activist. She lives in a small village in the Volta region in the far east of Ghana, near the border with Togo. A local journalist, Vincent Azumah, who has also been acclaimed for his determination in the fight against Trokosi, has agreed to be my guide. Vincent has won awards for his investigative reporting on the fate of the Trokosi girls. He and Juliana are long-time friends and colleagues, and both have received numerous death threats because of their courageous campaign to end Trokosi in Ghana.

Vincent and I drive for most of the afternoon from the capital, Accra, along the main highway towards the Volta River. We arrive in the village of Adidome just before sunset. Vincent drives with one hand on the wheel and waves with the other as he greets friends in the village. As we turn off the main street and down a bumpy dirt road near the school, we see a plump woman selling sweets on the side of the road. She turns her head shyly when she sees Vincent's car and then waves at him.

'This is Juliana. We have arrived.'

Juliana giggles as I shake her hand. She is embarrassed and apologises for being unable to speak much English. She's a big, healthy looking woman, aged in her early thirties. Vincent teases her about having put on weight, but she is beautiful. She doesn't wear any make-up or much jewellery and wears a brightly coloured African dress.

Juliana spends each day at her stall near the school. She sells lollies, biscuits and small bags of sugar. When the air is still, Juliana can hear the children and teachers in the classrooms across the soccer field as they recite their times tables and spell out loud. But to her the numbers and letters sound like a jumble. Juliana didn't go to school. She was sent into slavery by her own family, just after her eighth birthday. Her parents took her to a shrine, as payment for a crime committed by one of her ancestors.

'I was only about eight years old when I was sent to the shrine. They took me. My grandfather stole a gold earring from another person. So there needed to be someone to go into to a shrine to make sure that people do not die in the family. I was asked to be that person.'

Thousands of girls in southern Ghana and neighbouring Benin and Togo are sent to shrines as Trokosi slaves. It's a system which relies on fear and ignorance; parents willingly give their daughters to the priest, and the girls are then the property of the priest for the rest of their lives. Juliana didn't understand what was happening. She knew that another girl from the family had died, but she didn't know why. Conversations about the girl's death were brief and whispered.

'She was older than me. Nobody was able to tell me where she died and why she died. So I was a replacement for that girl. My father was a fisherman and they did farming as well. I used to be a happy child. But when I heard that I was being sent somewhere, I became a sad girl. My brothers and sisters told me to run away and escape. Because I was so young I didn't know exactly what was going on. I was confused. I thought maybe I was being sent somewhere to be killed. I was so afraid. I fell ill, perhaps because of fear. I was told if I refuse to go, the whole family would be wiped off the earth. They would all die. So I need to go.'

She said goodbye to her brothers and sisters, and set off with her parents on a long journey by road and river from their village to the shrine in the south of the country. Through it all Juliana sat quietly next to her mother.

'We were in the northern part of Ghana, so it took us three days to travel to southern Ghana; we didn't have our own means of transport. We first went by canoe on the river to where my grandmother was. From there we joined a vehicle to Ho. And another vehicle from there to the village. I stayed with my parents for one week before I was sent to the shrine. I remember that vividly. I was confused. I didn't know what was going on. I was crying. I was missing my parents. Apart from my grandmother, I didn't know anyone else. I was wondering and I was worried and I was sad.'

Juliana followed her grandmother to the shrine and they waited outside until one of the priest's deputies arrived. He was a stern man, who ordered Juliana to take off her clothes. She was terrified.

'I was stripped naked and they covered my waist with a lot of beads. There was a piece of cloth to cover my womanhood. I had beads on my waist, on my ankles, on my knees. I was made to carry a concoction in a calabash. I was also carrying a stool. I was leading the procession into the shrine. We just walked slowly. As soon as I entered the shrine I heard shouts, "New wife, new woman." They mixed some leaves in water to make a concoction which I was washed with. Then I was made to sit by the priest.

'They said a lot of things I couldn't even make head or tail of. After all the ritual performances, the family members, led by my grandmother, went out of the shrine. Initially I thought they would come back. Then I realised they were leaving. So I ran after them, but some elder women came after me. They held me and brought me back to the shrine. They left me without even saying goodbye. From that moment I concluded I was going to be killed.

So I was always crying. There was one woman who would come and put me on her back. Just to console me.'

She was told that every time she entered the shrine, she must take off her clothes and tie a cloth around her waist.

'Before you enter the shrine proper, you cannot wear any dress or shirt. You cannot wear any sandals. You just have cloth around you. Barefooted and bare-chested. It is regarded as a very sacred place that no-one can just get up and go to.'

Inside and outside the shrine there were totem poles made from clay: some had coloured cloth tied at the base, others were soaked in blood from animal sacrifices. It was a horrific sight for an eight-year-old. Juliana thought it was the blood of children.

'There were many things covered with blood. There were all sorts of things scattered in there. That was where they poured most of the sacrificial blood of animals. That was my first experience in the shrine. Anytime I saw a sign of blood and all those things in the shrine, or even think about it, I would start to cry. I had so much fear. But I knew there was nothing I could do to escape.'

Juliana talks quietly and as she tells her story, she tilts her head to the side and looks down shyly. Her beautiful eyes rarely gaze directly at Vincent or me. Her skin is almost flawless except for a small scar on her left cheek and she has the beautiful deep skin colour of West Africa. The back of her neck, which should be wrinkled by the relentless sun, looks smooth and untouched, like baby's skin. She wears gold earrings and her short Afro hair is hidden under a straight black wig.

Juliana lives in Adidome, a small town on the banks of the Volta River not far from Ghana's border with Togo. It feels a bit like a seaside village: the soil is sandy, there are fishing boats and fishing nets and thousands of cockle shells on the ground. Up near the school, there's a mill where the shells are crushed into a powder used for whitewash. The Volta is a strong, dark-looking river with sturdy trees along its banks. Adidome is a crossing point from one bank to the other. River trade, farming and fishing keep the town going; the dirt roads on the outskirts are rippled with tractor tracks and the hoofprints of cattle.

This region is home to the Trokosi tradition. Trokosi shrines are scattered in villages across southern Ghana, especially along the Volta River. Some villages have several shrines, each maintained by a different local family. The shrines are centres of religion and superstition and the priests are extremely powerful; they're consulted when there's a problem or an important matter to be dealt with in the village.

The tradition of Trokosi slaves is a measure of the power of the priests. The slaves are kept, often for their whole lives, simply because of their own fear. There are no walls, no fences to keep them in, they work in the fields unsupervised and could easily run away if they wanted to. But, of course, they believe that if they do, God will kill their relatives. Slaves who arrive at the shrine as young girls grow to become old women, and bear the priests' children. They're not paid for their labour and are expected to find their own food. They are both the workforce and the sexual fodder of the priests.

Juliana was the youngest of the slaves at the shrine. The others were older women who gave her a heavy workload.

'When I went, there were eight other women. They were much, much older than me and some of them had children. I had to wake up at 5 am each morning to fetch water from the stream, which was a bit of a distance. And bring that water to the door of the priest, wake him up. He would use that water to wash his face and mouth, before [we prepared] meals for him. After that they showed me a particular spot in the shrine where I had to sweep every morning. That is what the women were telling me.

'The area they gave me to sweep was quite a large portion of the space. I wasn't used to doing that kind of hard work. When I stopped to rest, they beat me. After sweeping, it was time for going to the farm. They would give me a portion to weed. After that, we would come home in the evening. Nobody is actually responsible to give you food. You need to find food for yourself. If you don't find food, you need to sleep on an empty stomach.

'Food was a major problem. You seldom get any fish or meat. So what happens is you have to go back to the bush after you have come back from the farm, to cut firewood. And then go to the nearby villages and sell firewood. Out of which you raise some money to buy some food. So getting food was very, very difficult. At a very tender age I was made to be going back to the bush to cut firewood and carry on my head and go and sell. Just because I needed to raise money to buy my own food.

'I was already a smallish person when I went into the shrine. Coupled with the malnutrition and the mosquito bites, I was very thin and very weak. I had a lot of sores on my skin because of the mosquito bites.

'We slept in one big room in the shrine. We slept on a mat. The floor was not cemented. It was just a dusty floor. There was not any covering for the doors. There was no covering for the windows. What we did was get some mats to hang on the door. We used to kill scorpions and frogs that entered into the room. We also killed one snake that came into the room through the window.'

As an eight-year-old, Juliana didn't know how to find food for herself and she was exhausted after long days of sweeping the shrine, looking after the priest and working on the farm. One of the slave women, who had several children of her own, took pity on Juliana. Distressed to see her going hungry night after night, she shared some food with her.

'I took her as a mother because she was the only person who was trying [to] console me, any time that I cried. I became weak. At that time she already had four children. Any time she gave food to her children, I would go around and we would eat together. If she didn't have food to give to the children, we would all sleep on an empty stomach. I am very sure that had it not been for the presence of that woman, I would have died in the shrine.

'I got frightened because looking at the women and the number of children they had in the shrine. And then I look at myself. I ask, "Am I going to be here and grow like these women?

And have so many children and not even have enough food to feed ourselves?"

'For me in the shrine, there was nothing like a birthday. There was nothing like a Christmas. When I went to the shrine, I didn't even know my birthday. There was no date for me to celebrate. And even if I knew the date there was nothing for me to use for celebration. My parents were not there. I had no family. I was a total stranger. There were people around the shrine who were celebrating Christmas who had cooked chicken and meat for their children. But we the slave girls had to look on. For us there was no Christmas, no birthday.

'For me, most of the time I felt like I was an orphan. All the time I felt like I didn't have parents. As if my parents were dead. Even though I knew they were still living.'

The slave woman was Juliana's only guardian and she tried to protect her from the priest. He wore white robes and a tall hat. Juliana was scared of him; he was old and unpredictable.

'He was an elderly person. He was about 60 years old when I went into the shrine. At that age when I looked at him it gave me fright. He didn't seem normal to me. At times he spoke to me nicely. But when we had to go to the farm and I said, "I am tired today, I cannot go to the farm" and I ran away to the nearby houses, he would send people after me and they would bring me back to him and he would beat me.'

The priest's tactic of ruling through fear was so effective the slave women became complicit in their own captivity, willingly taking turns in sleeping with him. They treated it as a privilege rather than a violation – in fact, they fought for their chance to have sex with the priest. Juliana watched as the women competed with each other.

'Each woman would sleep with him for five days. Five days rotation for each woman. If you sleep with him, there are some favours that the priest gives you. When you lose that chance you don't get that. The priest also naturally loves some of the women more than others, so that would also bring some jealousy. When it got to the turn of somebody and maybe she has travelled to another village, or maybe to her parents, to get food and come back. So she would not get a chance of going to the priest and then the next person goes in. It means that person has more days than the other women. When she comes back it is like somebody has taken her place. So she is peeved and she talks a lot. At that time there would be a quarrel. They even fight and hurt each other. They thought that if someone is taking your position you might lose the little enjoyment you might have had with the priest. So they would fight and even hurt each other.

'He would give some of the money to the women he loves most. He would tell you to get some corn from his farm and not give it to the others. That means you have more food than the others. Sometimes when I sit back and reflect, it surprises me that those women would end up quarrelling with each other. They were forced to marry that man, and yet they would fight over that man. I don't understand. But what consoles me is those women are no longer in the shrine. They have all left. So I know maybe they have now seen the light.'

Juliana was aware that eventually her turn would come to sleep with the priest. He first tried to rape her when she was twelve years old.

As she reached her teenage years, she felt the sense of expectation as the priest and the other slave women made comments that it was time for her to leave her childhood behind.

'When I was about sixteen years I was asked to start cooking for the priest. Each time I prepare the food I was told to sleep with him. I told them, "I am too young to be sleeping with men. I am not prepared to sleep with the priest." It went on until I was eighteen. One day we were all asleep in the room and he tried to pull me into his room. I started to shout. I didn't know there was a rule that there was a taboo to shout at the priest. One of the other women shouted at me and said I should not shout at the priest like that. But I did not go with him and he left. He would wait for two or three days and repeat the attempt to sleep with me. He took me, carried me into his hut. But I managed to push him off and I ran away. For the rest of the night I had to sleep just behind the room so he didn't know where I was. I knew it was time for me to escape.

'When day broke, he went to call two other priests in the town to come and punish me. So he and the other two priests put me on a table and they were beating me with canes. I got hurt all over. When they finished punishing me, they left the village and went to the farm. I thought if I stayed any longer, they were going to kill me.'

As I listen to Juliana's story, I decide I need to visit the shrine where she was held captive. No matter how vivid her description, I can't really imagine it. I've seen a lot of churches in West Africa, but I don't know what the Trokosi shrines look like. I ask Vincent if it is possible for me to visit. He says the priest who raped Juliana is now elderly, ill and incoherent.

'If we go as visitors to see the old man, they will not suspect us.'

But our arrival the next morning is far from inconspicuous. We manage to get bogged only a few hundred metres from the village, on a muddy track which snakes across a clay pan. Hundreds of children gathered at a sports day on the nearby oval watch as several young men try to dig out the car, which is now submerged up to its axles in mud. It takes almost an hour of engine revving, spinning wheels, tree-branch engineering and pure muscle to get the car out. When it's all over, the men are covered in grey mud and their slippery handprints are all over the bumper bar and the windows. As the grey mud begins to set on the paintwork, it looks like the vehicle has been caught in the middle of a fight between two teams of rival concreters. Vincent puts the car into gear and we slide along the clay into the village like an out-of-control shopping trolley.

Bakpa Kebenu is a small village near the river. There are no proper streets; we just drive in the gaps between the huts, and chickens squawk in protest as they scurry out of the way. The shrine is in a clearing surrounded by huts, where a man sits in a deckchair under a thatched shelter. He wears trousers but no shirt; a white flag flies on a pole above him and the ground is decorated by beer bottles buried nose-down in the dirt. The man is an elder, a gatekeeper for the shrine. The small hut next to him has a thatched screen on the front door so outsiders can't see inside. Alongside it is a circular platform used for animal sacrifices: it has small gutters to allow the blood to drain away.

We greet the man politely and tell him we have heard the priest is ill. The man nods, and we ask if we can visit the priest to wish him good health. He looks at us suspiciously. I feel nervous as other men arrive to ask why we are here. The man reluctantly walks to the shrine to ask the priest. After several minutes, he returns.

'You can go to the shrine but you must take off your top, madam.'

'Sorry?'

'Madam, take off your top.'

I give Vincent a puzzled look. He nods his head. It is the same rule for men and women: all visitors should be bare-chested and barefoot to enter the shrine. The men start taking off their shirts. I feel like I'm on a hidden camera video show to see if I'm prepared to go topless to get the story. But I trust Vincent. I know he's telling the truth and I can't write the chapter without seeing the shrine for myself.

I take off my shirt. I'm wearing a tank top underneath. One of the elders looks at me and says that if I wear my tank top it will be okay. I glance at Vincent with relief. A woman from a nearby hut brings long pieces of red and white cloth for each of us to tie around our waists.

'Come, we go to the shrine now.'

We follow the elder into a neatly swept compound surrounded by a brick wall. This is where Juliana walked as an eight-year-old when she began her life as a Trokosi slave. I try to look down respectfully as we walk behind the elder, but my eyes are darting back and forth. I bow my head as we enter the shrine, a simple building with a concrete floor, tin roof and low brick walls that let the breeze pass through. A tall pillar stands in the middle of the room, coloured cloth is tied around the top and once again there are mini gutters in the concrete to allow the blood to drain from animal sacrifices.

I look up and I can see a small old man sitting on goat skins spread out on an altar at the front of the room. I look at him again. This is the priest who raped Juliana. He is emaciated; the skin on his chest and biceps is limp and withered. He is a small sickly man who looks as if he has lost 15–20 kilograms as he has aged. The priest looks me right in the eyes and smiles. I try to force a smile back at him. He doesn't know I have met with Juliana, he thinks I am just a visitor.

I continue to look at the priest. He is bare-chested with a white sheet tied around his waist and draped over his shoulder. A bucket-shaped white hat sits on his head, tied under his chin with string, and his bony forearms have black rubber bracelets on them. But the thing that stands out the most is his eyes; they are bright blue, sparkly and confused. His gaze is unsteady and disconnected from what is going on around him.

The priest starts welcoming us, as two children followed by two skinny kittens walk inside and sit down in a corner. He babbles chants in a husky voice and then cups his hands in front of his chin, scooping up the air and blowing it towards us. The elders pause for several seconds and then put their hands in front as if to catch the blessing, before making the gesture of throwing it over their shoulder. Vincent copies the elders and I copy Vincent.

One of the elders hands a gin bottle and a wooden cup to the priest, who takes half a swig and then throws the rest at the pillar. The elder repeats the process and hands it on. Eventually the bottle and the cup reach me, and I bring the gin in the cup to my lips, pretend to take a swig and then toss the remainder on the floor in front of me as the elders do. The priest mumbles more blessings at us: it's only mid-morning, but he's already drunk. The elder says it's time for us to go. I bow at the priest and he gives me a goofy smile. We walk out past several huts that have mats up against the doorways, just as Juliana described it.

I still have the hot taste of gin on my lips as we leave the compound. It's the taste Juliana despised when the priest tried to rape her; the scent of alcohol followed him as he forced his way into her hut each night. By the age of eighteen, when she had reached the point of desperation, she planned her escape. She knew her younger sister was staying with a Canadian missionary in a nearby village, so she decided to sneak away from the shrine and search for her.

'I ran away very early in the morning. I had to walk three miles on foot to cross the major road. And then I got a vehicle. I was not carrying a bag or anything to show that I was escaping. I was just in one dress. People saw me and I was afraid they would come after me. But some people liked me in the village. They were not in favour of the way the priest was punishing me. They wanted me to run away but they couldn't tell me. Some of them saw me going.'

Juliana was terrified because she wasn't sure if one of the villagers would rush to tell the priest she was escaping. She was also scared that she would bring death to her family. The rituals of the shrine were powerful; she believed the superstitious warnings she had received from the priest.

'When you first come into the shrine, the rituals are performed. The concoction you are washed with, they tell you if you try to escape or if you do something bad, you will die and your family members will die. So there is that fear of your family members dying or yourself dying that kept most of us for that long.'

Despite the fear, Juliana kept running until she reached the missionary's house.

'My sister was staying with a woman called Sharon. When she saw the way I was bruised from all these beatings, she said, "You can stay with me." So I stayed with them. I was with her for two years. I slept in a nice room on a nice bed. There were no longer mosquitoes and frogs to fight with. And scorpions to kill. I could eat rice every day and good food. I was in freedom and I felt good within myself. Sharon didn't treat me as a slave. She gave me that dignity as a human being. I learned a lesson. I knew there was something positive in the future.'

But Sharon eventually returned to Canada, and Juliana was homeless again. She heard about a training centre for former Trokosi girls, run by an aid group called International Needs. The girls were given shelter and safety and were then trained in job-related skills so they could eventually fend for themselves. Juliana learned dressmaking and baking, but when the course finished she had nowhere to go. Her parents rejected her and she was also shunned by some local villagers, who refused to buy her goods in the market. She was unable to survive on her own and she was still burdened by many of the superstitions from the shrine.

'It was then that I thought about how to finally break the chain of bondage with the shrine. I remember I was told that once another man sleeps with you, the priest can no longer have any sexual contact with you. The only way I thought I could break the chain and the priest would no longer want me back was to have a man sleep with me. So, there was a young man in the area who used to propose to me. So I decided this was my chance. So I agreed to his proposal and I got pregnant. That is how I got my first child. When I left the school I had nowhere to go because my parents wanted me to go back to the shrine. Having nowhere to go and there was this fear. They were continuing to tell me that people in the family would die if I didn't go back.'

Juliana was a young single mother. Her parents ordered her to return to the shrine, telling her she was putting the lives of other family members at risk. It was a distressing decision, but she reluctantly returned to the shrine. She knew she would be punished and, sure enough, when she arrived, the priest and his advisers were waiting for her. He was furious she had run away and had sex with an outsider.

'They said it was a taboo for me to go and sleep with another man. They said I should never ever get close to that man again, otherwise both of us will die. The man had to pay fines to the shrine. Among the things he had to pay to the shrine was two cows, one million cedis – at that time it was a huge sum of money in Ghana – four cartons of schnapps, two kegs of the local brew, a large cloth called calico, some bowls of corn powder and a lot of other things.'

Her self-esteem was shattered: she hated herself for returning to the shrine and she was deeply traumatised by the rejection of her family.

'When I was going back to the shrine I thought that was going to be the end. Even before I escaped, I used to be punished a lot. I thought that was going to be my end. They were going to kill me, so I had given up hope. I thought they would only come for my dead body to go and bury. That is how I felt. I started to think about all the pain I went through. The mosquito bites, the bad food and all the threats from the priest, all the jealousy from the other women. All the fighting. I was going to see all those fighting and insults again. For me it was even more emotional torture than even the physical torture. The question I asked myself was, am I sending myself back to the slaughter, to be slaughtered?

'The most painful part was the rejection. It is so painful and any time I think about it I cry. That explains why I break down in tears now. Because what it showed was my family did not want me back. I was an outcast. Nobody wanted me. I felt like I was useless. That pains me a lot. They told me, "Once we have given you to the shrine you are forever to the shrine. When you return to the family, you are trying to destroy the family. So you need to go back." That is all they kept saying. They didn't care what I said to them.

'I had a right to freedom but I was forced to go and pay for someone's crime. They did not even recognise that. When I said I am in pain and need some respite, they were still pushing me in there and they didn't want me back. So the rejection is painful. I was not responsible for that crime. Why should I pay? Why should I pay for someone's crime?'

Juliana cries when she talks. She puts her chin in the neck hole of her dress and sobs. Being rejected by her family still stirs up a lot of raw emotion for her. Juliana is only in her early thirties and she has spent more time in captivity than freedom. She also seems full of shame that she went back to the shrine.

'I kept thinking of where else I could go to. I was always thinking about what is my next move, what should I do. I knew there were some family members living in Accra. But I didn't know where they were and I didn't even know them. I didn't know how I was going to escape to Accra. All my life at that time in the shrine was thinking and thinking. When I got back, the priest was still there but he had lost three other women. They also escaped elsewhere. He had lost three women so there were only five women in the shrine. They kept beating me. He still wanted to sleep with me. When I tried to fight him, he called his colleagues and they tried to beat me.'

With fewer women in the shrine, there was more pressure on Juliana to sleep with the priest; he kept trying to rape her during the night. Exhausted from her work in the fields, Juliana did her best to fend him off.

'It went on for close to a year. Initially he was trying to take me to his room. But he forced himself on me where I was. It was very late in the night and we were all asleep. The room in which I was sleeping had no door that one could lock. It was just a mat that was hanging. He entered without me hearing. All that I realised was that there was someone trying to carry me. When I pushed him off, he stopped carrying me and all he did was just force himself onto me. And forcibly entered me. I kept shouting and he held my hand. He was even trying to push something into my mouth to stop me from shouting. The other women seemed to have an idea of what was going to happen. For them it was normal so they didn't bother to come and rescue me. After he finished doing what he wanted to do with me, I thought of picking a log or a stick, or something, to hit his head and kill him. But then I thought, what would happen to me when I do that. So I just let it be.

'It happened around 3 am. After that, I went to get water to wash myself and I didn't go to sleep again. I just stayed awake until the following morning. I felt pain in my lower abdomen. I didn't know what I should do. I thought there might be some damage to me biologically. And I also vowed that wouldn't happen to me again. I was very angry. Angry for the fact that he was like my grandfather. I didn't think someone my grandfather's age to have sex with me. I was very angry.'

She was pregnant and battered from the priest and his relatives beating her for trying to refuse his sexual advances.

'My second child was actually the priest's child. I was angry with myself, I was angry with the priest and I was angry with the people who made me come to the shrine. I was angry with myself because I was asking myself, why did I have to come back? I could just have gone anywhere else. Even if I died, that would have been better than to come back to the shrine. And I was angry with the priest because I didn't deserve to be raped by him and I was angry with my family because they had put me in that place.

'There was virtually no food and where we slept was nowhere a human being should be sleeping. My whole life was reduced to that of someone who is useless. It is not something that I can even think about. It is so painful. I cannot even describe it. It dampened my spirits. The confidence I had from Sharon's place was completely eroded. This time I was not only in the shrine. I was also pregnant again. So all the confidence I gathered, all the dignity I gathered from Sharon's place, was completely gone.'

She decided she couldn't continue: the time had come for another escape attempt. Once again, Juliana walked away from the shrine with only the clothes she was wearing because she didn't want to arouse suspicion as she started her journey towards Adidome.

'The second escape was necessary because I was very pregnant. I was hungry. I thought, well, I need to do something. I wasn't healthy. I used to fall ill. I just sat down most of the time without any thoughts. I was angry with myself. I left the shrine and came to this town. I realised that I could still go back to International Needs. They took me back and I stayed with them for a long time. They gave me employment at International Needs training centre. That is how I was able to come back. I never went back to the shrine.'

There were dozens of other former Trokosi girls at the centre.

Some had escaped from the shrines; others had been liberated by humanitarian groups which buy back the slaves from the priests.

'We used to talk a lot about the experience we had in various shrines. We talked about how the priest forced himself on us and all those bitter experiences. We kind of compared notes with each other about who is suffering and where.

'I was happy I was training in skills. Now I could say, "I have a future." I could do something on my own and have my living. I majored in how to make dresses. When I finally knew I could produce bread on my own skills and make dresses, I remember during the graduation ceremony, I was jumping, dancing and singing. I can now use my own skills to take care of myself and my family.'

The more the women talked, the more they became sceptical about the rituals of the shrine. For some, it was the first time they had questioned the beliefs the priests had instilled in them.

'I used to have doubts about the powers the priest professes to have. But I wasn't sure of myself. I changed my mind and I didn't have any fear for them when I came back to International Needs the second time. They used to organise church services for us. We knew there was a God who was more powerful than any other God. So I decided just to move ahead and do what I want to do.'

After we finish the interview with Juliana, Vincent and I visit the International Needs training centre, which is on the outskirts of town, overlooking the river. The classrooms have old-fashioned sewing machines and measuring tapes, and outside there's a clay oven for bread baking. We arrive in the early evening just as a new group of Trokosi girls also arrives. Some of them are so shy it subdues their posture; they walk with their eyes following the ground, and some tilt their head to avoid eye contact, while others simply take the long way around a stranger to evade any interaction.

The girls sit uncomfortably on wooden chairs on the veranda, their knees and ankles folding their legs into clumsy poses. They are frightened and silent. Most of them are dressed in dull, floral dresses. They have come straight from the shrines – it's their first time out of captivity since girlhood. Many have arrived without any possessions, so one of the International Needs staff members hands out plastic dishes, mugs and mosquito nets to the girls, who giggle with excitement.

Juliana decided to use her freedom to help other Trokosi slaves and she began travelling to shrines and talking to the priests, urging them to free the girls and women under their control.

'Initially I took the wrong strategy of trying to confront people head on, confront the priest. So they were hostile to me. Later on I would plan my visits. I normally would go there when the priest would not be in the shrine and the women were available. I would gather the women in the absence of the priest and educate them, tell them why they should not be in that situation and tell them how they can escape, that nothing would happen to them if they escape. I used myself as an example.'

Juliana was one of the first former slaves to start campaigning against Trokosi – it was a dramatic challenge to the local culture. Decades of fear had stopped many people even questioning the Trokosi beliefs and the power of the priests. Juliana's outspoken approach threatened the priests' livelihood and it wasn't long before she started receiving death threats.

'Some of them came to my house here in Adidome to threaten that if I don't stop what I am doing they will kill me. I told them I have gone through this, I have gone through pain. I know the in and out of it. I know that what they are doing is not right and only God can kill me.'

Despite the dangers, she persisted. She travelled from village to village, secretly meeting with Trokosi slaves and sometimes confronting the priests, trying to undo deeply felt traditions. Juliana struggled to convince the slaves that nothing would happen to their families if they left.

'I always have myself as a living testimony. What I usually do is to use myself to show them, well, I have left the shrine for this long and I am still alive. No-one has died in my family and I know some of the deaths were not caused by any power from the priests or the shrine. Most of the time after I spoke to them they sit back and reflect. They know there was some truth in what I was saying. So even if they don't take it wholeheartedly at that time, they also sit back and think about it and later maybe change.'

Juliana's self-confidence grew with her work and she began to feel a strong sense of purpose as she met with the Trokosi girls and helped them to freedom. Many of the girls went on to International Needs, to learn skills to support themselves.

'I felt that I had some work to do. I felt that whatever happens in one's life does not happen as an accident. There is a reason for whatever has happened. So I sat back and told myself, I have been to the shrine and I have suffered this. I had the chance to escape, but other people are in there. So once I am out of the shrine and I have some confidence to talk, people can look at me and relate to the shrine life. It is my duty as an ex-Trokosi woman to get people to know what goes on in the life of a Trokosi woman and how painful it is to be in there. So I took it upon myself, to work hard to prevent other people going through that pain.'

The Ghanaian Government eventually passed legislation to outlaw Trokosi slavery, but it wasn't enforced because most police were too frightened to arrest the priests.

'It hurts to know that after we fought for that law to be passed, the practice still goes on and no-one makes the effort to arrest anyone and prosecute anyone. It's hurtful. I think it is still a matter of fear. Some people fear to even enter the shrine. So that fear is keeping the police at bay.'

Juliana was also starting to repair her own life. After the years of sexual abuse from the priest, she met a local man in Adidome. His name was James and he was a builder.

'After I had my second child and he was about a year old was when I met James. We used to attend the same church, so we met in church. He proposed to me and I told him I would think about it. I considered that he was a nice guy. I agreed that I would marry him. So we got married. I saw that he was a nice person and very peaceful. Not rowdy. So I thought he could make a good husband.

James has done a lot. In many cases, Trokosi women are stigmatised. No-one will want to have a relationship with them. But he took it upon himself to come forward to propose to me. That has brought some respect to me in the community. People know that I am a married woman and they forget I was a Trokosi. That has changed me a lot.

'People fear that when they marry a Trokosi or ex-Trokosi girl they may also have deaths in their family or maybe the priest will make bad things happen to them. So normally they will not have anything to do with an ex-Trokosi girl. That is the major factor. But if you believe there is a bigger God than what the priests worship, and you believe in your Christ, then you can go ahead, meet a Trokosi girl and marry her and nothing will happen. Just as I have with my husband.'

Juliana talks about James with a lot of pride. Without him, she would still be marginalised in the village, but with him she has respect from the surrounding community.

James is a good man. You are very lucky to have a husband like this one.'

Juliana nods and smiles.

It's getting late in the afternoon and I can see Juliana's attention is drifting as her children begin circling, awaiting their evening meal. We arrange to meet the following evening, Juliana says she will cook for us tomorrow night.

'Real Ghanaian food. Some white people can't eat it, but I will cook gently for you.'

The next day we arrive just before sunset so I can take some photographs. Juliana has set up some chairs outside the house. James walks up the path to meet us: he's wearing leopard-skin pants, a bright African shirt and thongs and he smiles brightly as he invites us to sit around a small table. Juliana brings out a bowl of water so we can wash our hands and then she returns with pots of fish stew of tilapia from the Volta River and a big blob of *banku*. This is dough made from cassava and maize flour, and then left to sit for two days until it starts to ferment, giving it a slightly sour flavour. We use our fingers to roll it into small pieces and pick up pieces of fish stew. The tilapia are a minefield of fine bones, but the stew's tasty and we're hungry. The sun disappears quickly and Juliana carefully carries a hurricane lamp from the house and places it on the table.

The children hover in the half-light. The eldest, Wonder, is thirteen years old: he's the son Juliana had to the young man in the village when she was trying to break ties with the priest. Nine-year-old Samuel was fathered by the priest. The next son is five-year-old Edem and last of all there is a daughter, two-year-old Blessing.

Blessing is the centre of attention. She has big deep eyes and a clever grin and her hair is plaited into spirals that flop from side to side when she moves. Her brothers fuss over and carry her without complaint; she tries to be coy, but she seems to relish her role as the youngest. She spends her days with Juliana at the market stall outside the school, playing with the children across the road and coming back to the stall for sweets and bubblegum. Late in the afternoon, Juliana packs up the stall and takes Blessing home, and the boys collect the goods, load them onto the trolley and follow her, pushing the cart all the way home without complaint.

As the sky darkens, bats fly in wild circles above the trees. Juliana sits down next to me and I show her the photographs of the other gogo mamas. The glow of my laptop screen throws light onto her face. She studies the pictures of the women and gently shakes her head in sorrow as she looks at the picture of Hellen Lanyom.

The last traces of the day disappear and the mosquitoes come out. Juliana leads us with the hurricane lamp along the path to the car. Her neighbour is fixing a busted old Datsun by torchlight and he looks up optimistically from the battered engine and wishes us goodnight.

We drive off slowly down the dirt road, and as we turn around a bend we can see Juliana's sons pushing their cart. Wonder is leading, Edem and Samuel are helping. The boys are grinning and chatting in the dark as they carry a large plastic drum full of water on the cart. They've been up since dawn and now, after dark, they are carting water home for the rest of the family, pulling the cart to the side of the road so we can pass.

'I am happy that they are obedient children. Occasionally I sit them down and tell them about the pain I have gone through. I tell them I don't want them to go through such pain. They should be obedient so I can give them the best. I try to give them the best I have. They listen to me.

'I have learned a lot from the pain I went through. I don't want my children or any other child to forfeit the care that he or she is entitled to from the parents. Children are entitled to the care and support from their parents. They deserve that. They need to get that. I know it has also given me some strength and courage to fight pain because I have gone through a lot of pain. Now a lot of things will happen to me that many people, they would start crying. But it has toughened me up and I can go through any other pain.

'The pain that I had and the hatred I have for the priest and my parents was so much I had to actually do special prayers to get it out of me. Some time ago I was actually fasting to ask God to get that thing out of me so I can forget the pain. And just continue with life. Now I don't have it.

'I used to be a shy person and I wouldn't want to speak in public. I remember the very first time I ever met a big crowd of people. It was at the British Council in Accra. I wasn't very confident. So I didn't speak the way I wanted to speak to the people. I was shaking. Now I don't fear anyone. I have confidence. I can talk anywhere, I don't feel intimidated. I can say anything I want to say.'

In 1999, Juliana was nominated for an international human rights award, which was presented to her in the United States.

'When I won the Reebok human rights award and was flown to the USA, it was publicised in Ghana. I was happy. I didn't believe it because I was asking myself, I am going to travel to America. I have never been to school. It was so sweet to believe. Until I was in America I didn't believe I was actually travelling to America to receive the award. People were surprised. They were asking, "She has never been to school, how is she going to America, what is she going to see?"

'I saw many beautiful things. It was very cold. I saw snow. I was feeling cold. I was amazed to see so many tall buildings. So many beautiful things. I was happy, even though I was cold. When I saw those tall buildings, I would tell myself these white people are quite good. They can build these tall buildings. The hotel, I was on the sixth floor. I needed to go up and go down in the lift. I was asking myself, what if the lights go off?'

After the visit to America, Juliana returned to real life. Her husband was struggling to carry heavy loads in his building work; he underwent surgery and the family was left with expensive medical bills.

'Life is not easy now. My husband last year had an operation. He is not that strong to work. A hernia operation. I am selling petty things. I used to produce some local cloth, the tie and dye. It didn't go too well. Things are not that good.'

The next day we go back to Juliana's market stall to do the last interview. The morning is hot and the wind is blowing, and dark clouds gather along the Volta. Juliana knows rain is on the way; she starts packing up the goods onto the cart and then takes them to a friend's house across the road. As the wind grows stronger, goats and dogs sniff the air and people riding bikes are pushed along by the blustering air until eventually the clouds break and the rain tumbles. People peer out from verandas and shops as mother ducks and ducklings splash in puddles. Juliana runs with a towel on her head to keep dry as she rescues the rest of her stock.

Juliana puts her leftover goods on the back seat and we do the interview in the car to keep out of the rain. I ask her what she would like to be doing if I come back to visit in five years' time. She smiles and shakes her head. There's something ridiculous about flirting with the future in Africa: it's so unpredictable. Juliana laughs and then looks off in the distance as she answers the question.

'I am hoping that before you come in the next five years, I should be a richer woman with a nice house to show you and a big shop of my own. I should also be able to establish some skills training and bring back all of those girls I have been able to liberate from the shrine who might be going through worse things than I am going through now.

'We know that the Trokosi practice did not start with taking human beings. They used to take animals like goats to the shrine. A human being is not an animal to be used for sacrifices. You are humiliated. You are treated like an animal. You lose confidence. You are not counted among human beings. You are like an animal and that is a big damage to yourself. We must all fight to stop this. I am going to continue to talk and continue to advocate until it is completely stopped. A human being is a human being born with rights.'

Blessing wriggles on the back seat as Juliana speaks; Juliana strokes her hair to distract her. The rain falls heavily outside and the children in the classrooms are barely visible across the school playing fields.

'I have lost a lot. If I hadn't gone to the shrine I would have been to school. Only God knows who I could have been. Now I cannot read even anything. I now try to struggle to read. I am very old now to begin to learn a lot of the things. I cannot even read the Bible. As much as I wish to read, I cannot. Trokosi has kept me in the dark. I am trying to get out of the dark. It is very, very difficult in this part of the world. I have lost many things.'

She pauses and cradles Blessing on her lap. Juliana's rounded, healthy arms envelop her as she kisses her forehead.

'Now I have my freedom. Freedom means a lot to me. Now I can have the right to choose the man I love and the man I want to marry. That is what I have done. I have the freedom to choose what I want to eat. I have the freedom to choose what I want to wear. I have the freedom to go wherever I want to go without any restriction. So that for me is freedom. It is sweet freedom, very sweet freedom.'

CHAPTER 12

Traoré Fatoumata Touré

Midwife

MALI

Traoré Fatoumata Touré grew up in a village north of Timbuktu on the edge of the Sahara Desert. She was the only girl at her school and fought against tall warrior boys from the Tuareg tribe who brought their spears into the classroom.

She was one of the first nurses to graduate in Mali, which is one of the poorest nations on earth. She has delivered babies in some of the most remote villages in the country. She has also become an outspoken advocate for family planning and has won international human rights awards for her pioneering work.

Taoudenni
SCALE
0
300
Kilometres
ALGERIA
MAURITANIA
MALI
Timbuktu
Niger
Mopti
Bandiagara
Djenné
NIGER
NIAMEY
BAMAKO
OUAGADOUGOU
GUINEA
BURKINA FASO
BENIN
GHANA
N
S
E
W

Mali is famous for Timbuktu and Timbuktu is famous for being one of the most remote places on the planet. The locals pronounce it *Tombouctou*; they shape their mouths as if they are blowing smoke rings when they say it. *Tom-bouc-tou* – it sounds even more exotic. This place name has cast a spell on visitors for centuries. Dozens of European explorers lost their way and their lives trying to reach the mythical golden city. I want to finish this journey in Timbuktu and see the sands of the Sahara before I leave Africa. I've found a woman who grew up in a remote village near Timbuktu and has gone on to become a world-renowned midwife, and she's agreed to talk to me. As for Timbuktu, I've got two weeks to find my way there.

When I arrive in the capital, Bamako, it's so hot the dirt smells as if it's been baked – it's a pottery smell. The city is coated in dust and anything painted white is not quite white, it's powdered with the orange of the earth. The clouds above the city are stubborn and slow; their dark colour promises relief, but it's some of the slowest rain in Africa. It's as if each cloud has been sown by hand – it's excruciating, the heat seems to fight them for hours. Late in the afternoon, the pottery smell slowly disappears and the wind starts blowing. It whistles through gaps in window frames and underneath crooked doors, blowing the curtains in a wild dance. The first raindrops sizzle as they hit the hot road. Plap. Plap. Plap. The raindrops get bigger and faster, then drops turn into showers that fall in diagonal lines set by the wind: it is pure relief.

Bamako is a low-slung city straddling the Niger, a wide, lazy coffee-coloured river with warm waters that give little respite from the heat. I'm sitting in the back of a taxi crossing the Pont des Martyrs, a bridge made from rattling piano-key slabs of concrete. The driver weaves in and out of the green minibuses that clog the road. It's so hot, the buses don't have any glass in their windows, just canvas awnings to keep the sun out, and when they flutter I can see the fat backs of market women sitting inside. There aren't many cars – the rest of the traffic is made up of motorbikes and bicycles.

Madame Traoré's office is on the other side of the river. We've been communicating by email for almost six months. I've studied pictures of her on the internet and read articles about her work as a pioneering midwife in Mali. Her replies to my emails are elegantly written in English speckled with some accidental French; now I want to hear her voice and shake her hand.

Her office is in a white building surrounded by bare orange ground with a large sign above the doorway: ASDAP, Association de Soutien au Développement des Activités de Population. The door opens and Madame Traoré smiles and puts her hands together politely, before shaking mine. She's a short, round, motherly woman with dark eyes and a friendly face; she's dressed in a bright pink and blue kaftan, with a scarf tied around her head like a turban. She leads me into her office: it's neat, plain and organised.

'Welcome, welcome. I apologise, my English . . . you know, it is a little difficult.'

Her English is fine, but she's an articulate woman accustomed to speaking without hesitation. I explain I want to visit Timbuktu, to see where she grew up.

'You will not reach my childhood place; Tombouctou is very far and my village, Rarous, is even further.'

She shakes her head.

'Too far into the desert?'

She looks back at me and pauses.

'Yes, very far.'

Madame Traoré grew up in Rarous, on the edge of the Sahara, beyond Timbuktu. She was small, thin, black and the only girl at the local school. Her family was from the south, and she was much darker than the people in Rarous, who were members of the Tuareg tribe; tall, lighter skinned and strong. All of the other pupils at the school were Tuareg boys, young warriors who brought their weapons to class each day.

'They came to school with spears, they didn't accept people with black skin; they thought they were superior, it was their culture. When I was a child I tried to be like a tomboy, not exactly like a little girl, because in that area, people didn't send their girls to school, but my father sent me to school. So during my childhood I was like a boy, I tried to fight like a boy, be strong like a boy. Since I was the only girl in the school, it was a challenge for me to succeed. I remained there for five years, then another girl came from another area. Then we were two. It really was a challenge for me to succeed.'

She rolls up her sleeves and shows her stocky forearms when I ask her if she fought with the boys.

'Yes, I would fight them. I fought a lot. I was very thin, I didn't have a lot of force because I was very thin, so I used my fingernails to fight like a cat. Even now in Mali, girls and boys are always fighting because boys think they are stronger than a woman.

'It is like something natural in Africa. All this is due to the education in the family, from the time you are born, parents try to make boys stronger than girls. So this has consequences even at school. Men always try to show they are stronger than women. When women don't like this there will always be trouble. Now there is some democracy, women are trying to fight to get some rights for the small girls so the men will understand. People should have the same rights, there is nobody who is stronger than the other. I was much supported by my father. My father was intellectual, he understood the importance of school and culture.'

Madame Traoré's father was a tax collector, one of the most important men in Rarous, just a step below the white French colonial officials. But in many ways he was a traditional man. He had two wives: they shared the same name, husband and house.

'It was part of the culture. He would spend two days here and two days with the other one; the mothers understood each other, there was no tension because the other wife was the cousin of my father. So my mother considered the other wife like a sister-in-law. They had the same name, Pinda Diallo, but one was light and the other one was dark, that was the only difference. People used to call them "the twins".

'The mothers didn't attend school so they had no idea about the importance of school, they had no appreciation of that. My mother wanted me to do the housework first. Washing up, cooking and things like that. That was the traditional education, they let me go to school only after doing the housework.'

The family compound was often crowded with visitors from outlying villages who came to Rarous to pay their taxes. They would camp in the yard for several days while they finalised payment. As children, Madame Traoré and her brothers were fascinated by the strangers who arrived from the desert and set up camp.

'We had a tent. When they came they had all the things they need. They would cook for themselves. We had a lot of curiosity about these people. They would pay the taxes in cash. Each community had a chief, so the chief came and paid the money for the whole group, they would spend several days and then they went back.'

Madame Traoré's mother and stepmother had the help of an old woman from the village who cooked, cleaned and took care of the compound. She wasn't a Tuareg, but a member of an impoverished ethnic group.

'It was very hard. This ethnic group, we called them Bella. It was pitiful for me to be with the children of this old woman who came to do the housework, she did it just to get something to eat. I always remember that.'

In some ways, not much has changed – the heat, dust and isolation give little reward for hard work, and poverty is almost inescapable. Mali is landlocked in one of the harshest parts of West Africa, in a neighbourhood of troubled, forgotten countries. But the local people speak of Mali's goings-on with such immediacy, as if I would automatically know the details without any explanation. They don't seem to realise that few people in other parts of the world would even know where this place is. Mali sits in the Sahel, a ribbon of land between the Sahara and the rest of Africa, going right across from Mauritania in the west to Somalia in the east. It's the frontier between the last dusty acres of farming land and the unforgiving sands of the Sahara, where farmers wrap seeds in the flimsiest of soils. It is one of the most impoverished regions on earth.

Up to 65 per cent of Mali's land is desert and without the Niger River it would be almost uninhabitable. The Niger is the biggest river in West Africa and snakes its way through the Sahara to the Gulf of Guinea. It's a source of survival rather than riches. Up to a third of all Malian children under the age of five are stunted and underweight because they can't get enough to eat. Mali is still a young nation: it gained independence in 1960 after decades as a French colony. Its ten million citizens have endured vote rigging, attempted coups and regional rebellions in their first 45 years of nationhood.

When I walk into the city centre, I'm followed by a rowdy dust cloud of street boys, phone-card sellers, money changers and hawkers who each squawk at me in French. Some are holding just a single item they are trying to sell – a clock or a pocket knife, a tool set in a limp cardboard box. Other hawkers join in along the way, and each day I count them. My biggest entourage so far has been nineteen. They follow me as I walk to the few English-speaking travel agents in search of a ticket to Timbuktu. The agents put me on waiting lists, but all of the flights are booked. One agent tells me that a new local airline is starting next Wednesday – well, hopefully next Wednesday, but it could be a week later.

'Is it good for me to be one of the first passengers on a new airline flying to Timbuktu?'

The travel agent shuffles a pile of business cards, trying to avoid eye contact.

'No, madam. Sometimes, new airlines in Africa fly before they are ready. It is better you find a driver and go by road, the river is also too slow.'

The drivers gather on the footpath across the road from one of the five-star hotels. They polish their four-wheel drive vehicles to relieve their boredom. I start negotiating with one of the bosses and we sit inside a Land Cruiser writing prices on the back of an envelope until we reach agreement. He introduces me to the driver, Abdoulay.

'Abdoulay will take you Tombouctou.'

'Does he speak English?' I ask.

'No.'

Abdoulay is young, thin and neatly dressed. He smiles and shakes my hand, and, for whatever first impressions are worth, I trust him. The boss has another driver who speaks English, but I don't feel as comfortable with him.

'Yes, I will go with Abdoulay.'

I ask the boss to show me the tool kit, jack, spare tyre and registration.

'Abdoulay and I will take this car, yes?'

I apologise to the boss for being cautious, but I've had dodgy car rentals elsewhere in Africa when I've signed for a vehicle and had a broken-down jalopy turn up in its place. One taxi driver in Sudan promised to bring a 4x4, but arrived with a packet of videotapes instead. 'You see, madam, 4x4,' he said, reading proudly from the cover of the four 60-minute tapes. I felt like I was going to have a Basil Fawlty explosion as he placed the videotapes in my hand and bowed. But he smiled so sincerely that all I could do was say thank you.

Abdoulay looks at me with a similar eager expression. Sometimes the drivers can sit waiting for work for several weeks. To get a job with a foreigner is highly sought after; it's the kind of good news that will be passed around Abdoulay's family when he gets home tonight. We shake hands and agree to depart in three days, after I've finished some more interviews with Madame Traoré.

The next morning I take the taxi ride across the bridge to Madame Traoré's office. She has asked me to meet her early, before her day is at its busiest. She nods when I tell her about the difficulty of making arrangements to get to Timbuktu, but tells me it is much easier now than it was when she was growing up in Rarous. Getting from the village to Bamako – that could take more than a week.

'It was difficult. We took the plane, then we took a bus, from there we used the traditional boat to cross the river. The transportation was only camels, horses and donkeys. At that time there were only two cars in all of Rarous that belonged to the French people, the chief and his assistant. It was difficult to reach Rarous. So that made the living conditions very hard.'

Madame Traoré's chubby fingers follow the route of the river on the map in my guide book. The river boats would bring much-needed fresh fruit and vegetables when the river was high from August to November. The boats were met by large crowds waiting on the riverbanks, even in the middle of the night.

'I remember well. When the boat arrived it was like a celebration. A feast. The boat used to be there at midnight, but all the people were near the river waiting. It was just for three months. But during this time the boat would arrive two times in a week. People were very happy because in the boat there were vegetables and fruit. All the families made stock for the children. As the time passed, there was no other alternative to get the fruit like oranges, bananas and things like that. We used the local fruits.'

While the villagers waited for the boats during the high river season, she noticed a woman amongst the crowd, dressed in a crisp white uniform – she was the district nurse. As a young girl, Madame Traoré was fascinated by her.

'When I saw her in her white clothes, I was excited. I wanted to become a nurse. I was seven years old. I was wondering whether the nurse would accept me. So I asked my father to introduce me first. The woman said okay. She was happy to see me because I was the only girl at school. I first started by asking her if I could come and learn how to sew. The nurse said, "That's okay, you can come." This is how I became closer to her.

'I thought it was an important job and also wearing the uniform. It was very exciting. When there was a new baby in the family, she came and cleaned the baby. I was impressed to see this. I was really curious to see all these things. I observed everything. I was really excited to see it. The nurse understood me. She used to say, "Do you want to become like me?" And I said yes. I had only one wish. Even at school when they would ask about jobs, I used to say a nurse. It was my only ambition.'

Madame Traoré looks at me with conviction, then shrugs her shoulders and smiles to dissolve her stare.

'It was nursing or nothing?' I ask.

'Yes, of course,' she replies.

There was no nursing school in Mali, so Madame Traoré had to travel to neighbouring Guinea to do her training and in her third year she led a successful campaign to set up a nursing course in Mali. She was in the first group of nurses to graduate in Mali; a source of great pride for her father, who had defended her right to study since she was a little girl in Rarous.

'When I succeeded he killed a sheep, he invited friends and relatives and neighbours. It was a feast in the family.'

At last Madame Traoré had the white uniform and responsibilities of a qualified nurse. Even during her student years, she knew she wanted to specialise and be a midwife. She was fascinated by the wonder of birth.

'I got really emotional because it was my first time. It was a little bit hard to look at the birth. But we were trained to assist and look at it. By assisting the midwife and doing this work of birth,

I was excited. If a woman comes to you who is suffering because of her stomach and you make her free, by giving life in the free world, that makes a midwife happy. It gave me a new inspiration. I loved it. I loved becoming a nurse, a midwife.

'But my first time to see someone dying was a pregnant woman, she couldn't give birth to the baby. We did an operation. I was at this time in my first year. I was the one who had to take care of the woman. When the woman started to deteriorate I was afraid. I called a second-year student. She said, "Don't touch her, she is dying, she is passing away." I was really afraid but I couldn't run away, I had to stay there and see the woman dying. That really marked me. I was really afraid because it was my first time to see someone passing away. It is hard to forget about it. It is almost impossible to forget about it. I could just forget for a while and then I would think about her. It was very emotional.'

Having a baby is one of the most dangerous things a Malian woman can do. In many parts of the country there is a one-in-ten chance she will die in childbirth, and most women give birth without any medical help. The majority of girls in Mali are married before they reach the age of eighteen and up to nine out of ten can't read and haven't been to school. By the time they reach their twenties they are already in middle age; on average they are only likely to live until their forties. It's a shocking set of statistics, but it's the reality for the young women of Mali and part of the reason Madame Traoré became a nurse. She was one of the few girls given an education, while she saw other girls her own age in Rarous falling into the dangerous cycle of early marriage and pregnancy.

I explain to Madame Traoré that my mother is also a nurse: she nods in approval. My mum wanted to be a nurse from when she was only three or four years old. I remember her telling me how she always would look upwards when she walked past the Children's Hospital in Adelaide, just to get a glimpse of a nurse walking by a window. Madame Traoré smiles.

'Yes, yes,' she says. 'All nurses are the same, they know from when they are very small.'

As a student, Madame Traoré caught the attention of a bright, outspoken young student leader, Mamadou Traoré. He was passionate about politics; she was passionate about nursing. They fell in love and she followed him to the USSR, where he won a scholarship to study economics.

'When I finished I got married and went to Moscow to study gynaecology. I was very impressed by Moscow. It was a developed place. I remember there was Metro and the tramway, there were also high buildings that didn't exist in Mali. All these things impressed me. They had the ability to live with black people. Almost all African countries used to send their people there to study. I spent only one year. I didn't like the climate there. Sometimes it was minus thirty below. It was so cold you couldn't even touch your nose because you would fear it would break.'

She laughs as she looks at the red dirt and hot wind blowing the dust outside. Her secretary knocks on the door; the first appointment of the day has arrived. Madame Traoré clasps her hands politely, as a signal that my time has finished. She wishes me well for my trip to Timbuktu and we arrange to meet when I return next week.

'Good luck.'

The journey to and from Timbuktu is measured in days and seasons, not kilometres. I don't know for sure if I'll be able to get through. The distance is only part of the equation – the real measures are the level of the river, the condition of the road, the likelihood of bad weather. Sometimes the road is impassable after big rains and the river narrows during the tail end of the dry season.

The next morning, my driver, Abdoulay, arrives just before dawn. As we leave Bamako, people are walking into the city in search of work. The sweaty sunrise brings the heat and the bright yellow light of day. The recent rain has left a thin carpet of green grass covering the red dirt on the side of the road, but it only lasts for a few kilometres outside of town; after that, the country is parched. I soon realise that, despite its dusty appearance, Bamako is a comparatively kind corner of the country. The further we go, the hotter and drier it gets. The trees are so spindly, they look as if they have been drawn rather than grown; their pencil-thin branches hold almost no greenery.

It's an eight-hour drive from Bamako to the river town of Mopti. All the way, there are two roads, one for the cars, and a smaller one alongside for the donkey carts and foot traffic. The donkey road is where the real action is. Families bounce along in carts full of farming tools or produce, and their dogs trot underneath to make the most of the shade. The women are dressed in brightly coloured cloth, their eyes squint against the dust as they peek out between the folds of the fabric.

Abdoulay raises his palms in playful outrage every time one of the dogs from the donkey road strays into our path. We don't have enough shared words to make any conversation, but he chatters in French anyway and we seem to understand each other. He drives well and looks at me with great pride as he plays his cassette library of local music – wild Malian pop, French ballads and reggae. He explains the lyrics to me with gestures and broken words, and he adjusts the volume depending on whether I seem to like it or not.

I doze on and off, keeping an eye on the happenings of the donkey track every time I wake. As we get closer to Mopti, the soil starts to change colour, the red dirt of Bamako blending into the light-coloured clay of the river country. I look on the map: Timbuktu is still more than a day's drive away on rough roads. Mopti is an unofficial halfway point; it's a market town. Women arrive in the morning carrying heavy bundles of goods on their heads, and hope to leave with money in their hands by the end of the day. We arrive late in the afternoon as the market is starting to subside. A teenager carrying postcards paces outside the guesthouse and he introduces himself as soon as I walk outside the gates.

'Hello, my name is Agali, Mr Very Good Price. I will be your guide. Welcome to Mopti.'

Agali smiles at me warmly and I'm too tired to say no or beat down the price. He's young and lean, dressed in combat pants, sneakers and a shiny basketball T-shirt, the unofficial uniform of the hip-hop diaspora. He listens to American music on pirated tapes and recites the lyrics of songs about ghettoes, gangsters and girls in faraway cities.

'I would like to go to USA,' he says.

'Americans are very fat. Eating, eating all day. Why do you want to go there?' I tease him. He laughs as I stretch out my T-shirt in a false belly.

'Yes, America very fat. But very good,' he says with certainty.

We take an old yellow taxi to the market, which is perched on the steep banks of the river. The market women look tired – some have dozing babies tied to their backs and the babies' heads flop with exhaustion. There seems to be almost communal fatigue; flies squabble over slimy lettuces and buzz in and out of the eyes of the women who half-heartedly try to swoosh them away. I can smell the stagnant muddy riverbank mixed with the cluttered scents of the market.

Agali takes me on a guided tour. At one end of the market, there are slabs of salt from Timbuktu, bundles of firewood, cloth, batteries, carved calabashes, dried fish and home-made soap. The soap is shaped into white balls that look like peeled oranges; they are bumpy with the thumbprints left behind by whoever made them. The market women keep their money tucked under woven mats, hoping for a few more sales before the afternoon disappears. Even in the late afternoon the temperature is still well over 40 degrees Celsius. When I get back to the guesthouse, I decide to cool off in the swimming pool, but the water is so hot it's like swimming in a giant cup of tea.

'Tomorrow, we take a boat?' Agali asks from the other side of the fence.

'No, my brother, tomorrow I must go. I'm going to Bandigara and then Timbuktu.'

'Tombouctou? Good luck.'

The next morning I get up early and go for a run along the riverbank. It is unnaturally quiet, almost silent – the whole scene only breathes a few decibels of sound. A young mother washes clothes on the edge of the river, fishermen in wooden canoes gently push themselves along with long wooden poles. My heels sink into the soft river sand as I follow the foot track used by the market women walking to and from a nearby fishing village. Even my footsteps are muffled by the soft sand. I can hear my own breathing and little else. It's exquisitely peaceful and remote. But the early morning is already hot and people are searching for shade while the sun is still making its way above the horizon.

We leave early to drive to Bandigara, where Madame Traoré worked as a young nurse. It's the last big town on the rocky road to the remote Dogon region. As we drive slowly along the main street, young tourist guides crowd around the car windows and hands reach inside to greet Abdoulay. One of the guides greets him warmly, he's young, fit, has glistening black skin and is dressed in jeans and a bright orange hip-hop T-shirt.

'Hello, my name is Baby,' he says in a deep voice.

'Hi, Baby.'

I giggle a bit as I say his name, but Abdoulay puts his hand over his heart and gives the thumbs up to tell me Baby is trustworthy.

'How did you get your name?'

'It is from my mother, she said I was very sweet. I was her favourite, her Baby. I will be your guide if you wish, I am good friend of Abdoulay. We can go to Dogon, I will make a tour for you, we will eat with my friends and sleep in the village.'

Bandigara is a flat, dusty town which is a staging post for tourists going to the Dogon. The Dogon is a World Heritage site and is renowned as one of the most spectacular regions in West Africa, a magical place where people live in stone villages built into a spectacular cliff face. This is where Madame Traoré started her career and she could hardly have chosen a more rugged place to work as a midwife. The hospital at Bandigara was her first posting after she returned from the USSR in 1964.

The yellow buildings of the hospital are surrounded by a bare red dirt compound. It looks like a typical African bush hospital: a herd of goats tussle for shade space under a prickly bush while patients and relatives sit in any shade they can find, waiting stoically, clutching medical files. I phone Madame Traoré to check we are in the right place.

'Yes, yes,' she says as I describe it to her. Her voice is full of warmth and excitement that we have reached Bandigara. She asks me many questions about the condition of the hospital and our journey so far. I tell her the hospital looks run-down and she sighs in agreement.

'Not only in Bandigara but in all the rural area, people live very hard and there is extreme poverty. But they are really courageous. I noticed that women even when they are pregnant take a basket of tomatoes or other vegetables coming from a far village and sell it in the market in Bandigara and then go back again.

'The road was very long from villages to Bandigara. Pregnant women had to be examined in Bandigara. If they needed surgery they would be taken to Mopti. That is very far. Sometimes they died on the way, they also died on the operating table.'

Many of the Dogon women lived in tiny stone huts, high in the cliffs. In the 1960s the medical facilities were basic, transport was almost nonexistent and sometimes it took more than a day for Madame Traoré to reach isolated patients.

'It was very hard to get the pregnant women to the hospital. Sometimes they used the bicycle to let the midwife know there is an emergency. Then the midwife could take a vehicle and come and even to reach the woman was very hard. Especially in Sanga with the hills. We used to tie the women with rope on a stretcher and come down very slowly until we reached the vehicle.'

As we drive from Sanga down the tight, winding road to the Dogon villages, I start to understand what she's talking about. The escarpment is hundreds of metres high: villages and caves are carved high into the cliff. Baby tells me the locals believe their ancestors either had wings or used vines to climb to some of the highest caves. I have never seen villages like it. Everything is made from rock – crumbling huts, stone fences, stone walls and small granaries the size and shape of an outdoor dunny.

The villages are set at the base of the cliff and look over an endless plain, where crops are sown. It is like another world, one of the most fascinating regions in Africa. I follow Baby along the rocky paths between the huts and granaries. He takes me to the meeting hut, where some of the village men are sitting quietly. The roof made from sticks is just over a metre tall and the men can only crouch because it's too low to stand. I ask Baby why it's built like that.

'So they can't get angry,' he says, as if it's obvious. He mimics how the men bend over when they're inside. 'They can't stand up and shout at the chief when they bend over like this, they will hit their head on the roof. It means they cannot be angry when they are inside.'

The men invite us to enter; I crouch and crawl underneath the low roof. They sit with their shoes off and their legs stretched out in front of them, conversing in murmurs as they look out over the plains below. It's extremely peaceful. Baby points at the granaries, explaining that the large ones are for men, the smaller ones are for wives – they're clustered into family groups. The pointy roofs sit above the crumbling walls. The granary doors are decorated with pictures of crocodiles and tortoises.

'The people believe the tortoise is very wise. The woman must feed the tortoise before she gives the food to her family. If the tortoise refuses three meals in one day, it means something bad will happen to the family.'

It's brutally hot and I can almost feel the heat pressing down on my head. I don't know what the temperature is, but it feels well above the mid forties; one of the hottest days I've ever experienced. It's difficult to look at the ground, because the sun glares back from the light-coloured rock.

'Are you too hot, Miss Sally?'

'No, Baby, I'm fine.' I still smile when I say his name. 'Are you okay, Baby?'

'Yes, but we will rest here, it is too hot for walking. You

can sleep for some hours and we will begin the afternoon again later.'

We shelter in a large hut, in which one of Baby's friends has set out makeshift beds covered in dirty cloths. When I lie down, I look up at the rough beams of the roof covered in spider webs and dust; it looks like the inside of a bunker. The men are sleeping at the other end of the hut, so I pull up the bottom part of my T-shirt for a while to cool off, but only a few hot sighs of air make their way through the window. Baby has given me some sort of home-made swat, which looks like a sawn-off whip, to keep the flies off. I lie on the old bed swatting the flies back and forth, as my sweat soaks into the mattress where countless other tourists have passed the time during an enforced nap. When the hottest part of the afternoon passes, we return to the main village and sit on the roof of the guesthouse drinking bottles of water and beer. The view is spectacular. Despite the heat, it's been one of the most interesting and enjoyable days of the whole *Gogo Mama* trip; Baby has been an excellent guide and I've never seen anything like the Dogon.

We face our chairs to the west so we can watch the sun go down above the escarpment, which towers hundreds of metres above us. The top of the cliff is so high, the people in the village above look tiny from a distance – I can only just make out their arms and legs. I can see the silhouettes of three children sitting under a boab tree and women walking carrying buckets of water on their heads, while the hot orange sky rages behind them.

The villagers return after working in the fields. Some arrive in a flurry on board out-of-control donkeys, but the women walk quietly in lines, carrying their tools and their babies. The men and boys drive the cows and goats back up the hillside into their stone pens. It's very quiet and when darkness takes over from the sun-set, I can hear the thud of women pounding grain for the evening meal. None of the houses in the village has any lights; there is only the small glow of cooking fires.

I drink one bottle of water after the next, feeling quite dehydrated. I've drunk more than 3 litres of water, but haven't urinated all day and keep feeling thirsty. It's still extremely hot.

Baby takes off his T-shirt and Abdoulay the driver takes off his shoes. We're all hungry and eventually the owner of the guesthouse brings us a big bowl of macaroni and onions. One of Baby's friends from the village sits with us fidgeting and looking shyly at the ground until we offer him some food – he's hungry.

After dinner, he sits hunched in conversation with Baby.

'Miss Sally, my friend wants to ask you a question. He has heard about this AIDS thing. He wants to know if it is real.'

I try not to look surprised.

'Yes, my brother, AIDS is real, even here. You must use condoms, be careful.'

Baby relays the message and his friend nods. The young man looks embarrassed, but satisfied to get an answer. The remoteness Madame Traoré encountered in the Dogon in the 1960s still lingers. Most of the people in the villages can't read and few can afford batteries for radios, so it's very difficult to deliver health information. It's an isolated region locked inside an isolated nation.

The men set up mattresses and mosquito nets on the roof. I'm offered a space too but several of the men are Muslim and they seem extremely uncomfortable about the idea of me sleeping nearby. Abdoulay looks relieved when I politely decline. I'm given a small room downstairs with no windows; late in the evening its mud walls are still warm from the heat of the day. It's one of the few nights when it's genuinely too hot to sleep. The room is stifling and my body is wet with sweat. I drink another 3 litres of water during the night.

In the early hours of the morning, the wind starts to blow wildly and I can smell rain off in the distance. Within minutes the first droplets hit the ground, then it starts pouring. The men scramble off the roof as their bedding is soaked.

When dawn arrives, the water outside the guesthouse is ankle-deep. The men squat on the veranda brewing tea on a coal stove and watching the rain fall.

'No Tombouctou,' says Abdoulay and he splashes the water with his toes. It's too wet for us to reach Timbuktu; the journey could take several days and it would mean I would miss my final interviews with Madame Traoré back in Bamako. We're not even sure if we'll be able to reach the top of the escarpment because the rain has washed parts of the road away and trees have fallen over. We sit down and study the map and Baby points to the historic town of Djenné.

'Today is market day in Djenné, there will be many people. Tomorrow you can start driving back to Bamako. The rain will make it too slow to go to Tombouctou.'

I feel disappointed. Timbuktu has been my goal for the end of the trip for months, but I can't lose my chance to finish the interviews with Madame Traoré before I'm scheduled to fly out of Mali.

The rain keeps falling as we drive out of the village and the ground is alive with thousands of coin-size brown frogs like jumping jacks in the puddles. The windows of the car fog up as we drive carefully up the winding road. We stop several times to clear fallen trees and wait almost an hour for the river to subside between Sanga and Bandigara. The water is rushing over the flood barriers in a wild swirling froth and I feel nervous as we drive through and it splashes at the doors of the car. When we reach Bandigara, we drop Baby off near his home and shake hands to say goodbye before Abdoulay and I continue the journey.

We make slow progress. It's well into the afternoon before we reach the ferry to Djenné. Teenage boys with long wooden poles steer it across the shallow water. Djenné is an island, not just in geography: it's a place of its own time and making. It's pronounced 'Jenny', a swampy island in the middle of nowhere where daily life has changed little over more than 500 years. It's fascinating but filthy, one of the dirtiest places I've visited. The edges of the island are covered in rubbish and open drains run through the back alleys.

The island is home to the largest mud mosque in the world – a beautiful, sandcastle-like building with rounded walls, a simple construction with wooden beams sticking out of its towers. Once a year, the men of Djenné gather to repair and strengthen the mud walls. It's one of the most unusual buildings I've seen. Around the mosque is the chaotic, crowded maze of the Monday market. People from surrounding villages bring their produce to Djenné and buy goods to take home. The lanes between the stalls are so narrow, and the Monday market crowds so large, it is difficult to walk. Most people shuffle.

Djenné is all about mud. The mosque is made from mud, the houses are made from mud, young boys use mud to copy the Koran onto wooden tablets as they squat outside religious schools in the alleyways, and local artists use mud to dye cloth into different shades of brown, black and grey. It's a flat-roofed town that looks like it's in the Middle East. There are no cars in the back alleys of Djenné, just horses, livestock, bicycles, and farmers in long purple robes and pointy wizard hats driving cattle through the narrow streets, leaving hoofprints in the muddy clay.

The next day we take a dirt road from Djenné to Ségou. Abdoulay tries to convince me in his best French sign language that it's a good short cut. We drive through tiny villages with mini mud mosques and flat mud houses. Abdoulay laughs at how small some of the mosques are; they look only big enough for a dozen people to pray in.

'Petite mosquée.'

'Très petite!' I reply.

But soon the mosque jokes subside and I notice his eyes looking at the fuel gauge – it's running low. At each village he stops to ask directions and I get the feeling we're lost. We follow a soldier riding a moped: he wears a beret and aviator sunglasses and has a machine-gun slung over his shoulder. His directions lead us to a larger town with a market where we can buy fuel. Out of the crowded market, a blind teenage girl stumbles towards our four-wheel drive, begging for food and money. She stops and listens before she crosses the road and then puts her hands out to guide her to the vehicle, feeling her way from window to window, knocking and talking. She can't see there is no-one sitting inside. The garage man pushes her out of the way as he pours fuel into the tank with a funnel. She walks over to a minibus, hoping for some generosity from the passengers, but she hits her head on the driver's side window. She gets up, tilts her head to listen for the traffic and crosses the road back into the market again, scurrying with her hands in front of her. It's horrible to watch her floundering in solitary darkness; there's no sympathy for her here. I look away. The locals use silence to avoid her and surprise to frighten her.

Outside the town we stop at a dusty intersection, surrounded by nothingness. Abdoulay looks confused – we're lost again. We can see a young woman walking alone near the roadside. Abdoulay drives slowly to go and ask her directions, but she looks up, sees the vehicle and starts running. She runs at full speed, with absolute terror, zig-zagging through the saltbush like a rabbit. She's frightened because we're strangers. Abdoulay stops and calls out to reassure her and I get out of the vehicle so she can see me, but she's gone.

We drive all afternoon and reach Bamako just before sunset to fight our way through the evening peak-hour traffic. The next morning we drive across the bridge to Madame Traoré's office. She greets us warmly when we arrive and asks many questions about the journey. I tell her about the young woman running away at the intersection and she shakes her head knowingly before explaining how vulnerable and uneducated many of the young rural women are.

'In the villages, women get married very early. Sometimes their bodies can't permit them to give life to a baby, they are thirteen or fourteen. It is common to have eight children per woman. Some have fifteen.'

Married off when they were barely in their teens, girls were having their first children when they were still children themselves and, in the absence of contraception, they were having a large number of them. Madame Traoré started travelling from village to village to educate young women.

'I was one of the first to talk about family planning, to space the births. I did it because I noticed that women were the ones who had the consequences of having a lot of children. The knowledge of contraception and family planning was very low. I worked to give them the information. They had to know the importance of birth spacing.'

'I used the theory that they know. These women grow plants like millet, at a certain stage they pull out some of the plants to thin them out. I said to them, "Why do you do that?" They said, "Because if there is a space they can grow stronger." I said, "Yes, it is exactly the same for you and your children, so that they will be strong and you too will be healthy."

'I could do two or three villages per day on motorbike. Some people were really sceptical. When I came to the community I would contact the chief and try to convince him by example. We have a saying in Bambara, "The child who drinks a lot from the breast of the mother will be stronger than those who don't drink a lot." I told him, in order to have milk from the mother there needs to be spaces between. This really made the chief of the family laugh but it also worked.'

Madame Traoré also encountered many myths in the local beliefs and there was very little understanding of medicine amongst the villagers.

'In one village I asked people about how they got malaria. Some said by eating some kind of fruit. They didn't know that it is mosquitoes that give malaria. And women used to tie things around her body thinking that this could prevent her from having a new baby. It wasn't a cultural problem; it was just a problem of information. They didn't have access to information. These women in the rural zone trust hospitals, they believe that all the information coming from the hospital is good information, but they just don't get enough of it because they are so remote.'

Madame Traoré became well known in Bandigara and the Dogon villages. She travelled the rough roads of the escarpment delivering her message about birth control. The young women started putting the information into practice and the older women started noticing the difference.

'They noticed that the other women look younger and stronger than them. Giving birth made them very tired and family planning for them came too late. From that time I made a decision to help these women. I was excited to help them and to promote family planning.'

In 1975 Madame Traoré became director of a maternity hospital in the rural area of Katibougou. Several thousand students also attended the local tertiary college and many of its female students and other local women had unwanted pregnancies.

'I worked to prevent undesired pregnancy among students and people. That would also permit them to avoid abortion. Women thought it was almost impossible. I arrived to convince them. I could read the distress in the eyes of these young women who had unwanted pregnancies. I would just talk to them and say, "Please avoid abortion. Don't do it in an illegal way, it will kill you." I tried to convince them to do family planning in order to avoid unwanted pregnancies. That would allow them to finish their studies without any risk of pregnancy.'

As well as helping the students, Madame Traoré wanted to help the other local women reach their full potential. Unlike her, most hadn't been to school, and didn't have the basic skills to get a job or start a business.

'I taught them to be literate. Most of them didn't know how to write, to read or to count. Before I left, almost all these women knew about writing and reading and even generating income. There was a woman called Connie. She didn't know anything and she didn't believe it was possible to learn how to read, write and count and be successful. Today this woman is a chicken seller and a fresh fish seller. Now she is very happy.'

'I got a great satisfaction from doing that. If you make a comparison between their former situation and today, these women are trying to be the leaders of associations. From time to time I go to see how they are doing. I am really pleased to see them succeeding in their different way. They were really strong, the problem was they didn't know they had potential, they had low self-esteem. We taught them to understand they can do something.'

She set up a family planning program in Katibougou, which gradually spread across the country, village by village. She trained male health workers to deliver the message to men in the village and female health workers to deliver the message to women. In 1982 she was invited to a community leadership conference in Bamako. The participants were asked to put together a proposal for a neighbourhood project, including a detailed budget.

'This conference was very important for me. Some others, their budget was around 40 million CFA francs. But for me it was just two million. The reason was I knew what I would do. It was really designed for community women to give services and information to the community.'

Madame Traoré's vision was clear but simple: her proposal for a family planning program stood out because it was cost effective and detailed. She was chosen to go to an international conference in Washington, DC.

'I understood what I would do with the minimum budget, that is why I was invited to Washington. It wasn't because I didn't like money. It was because I knew what I would do. Some doctors and other nurses thought I would not succeed because there was no family planning project in the rural areas. The main problem was that the men always want to have a lot of children, but I thought the problem is that people don't have access to information. The more they thought I wouldn't succeed, the more I had courage to do it.'

It was a low-budget approach that worked. Health workers were trained in groups and sent out by foot, bicycle, motorbike, bus and boat. They took the message of family planning to villages where people didn't have access to newspapers or radios. In the beginning, national surveys showed only a small number of people had any knowledge of family planning.

'The national number was 1 per cent. Only 1 per cent of people knew about family planning. But the percentage grew; after four years it went from 1 to 57 per cent. Now we cover more than one thousand villages. When I began, people said, "No, you cannot do it, they have not ears to hear." But, when I saw I could do it I was very, very satisfied. I was always determined.'

In 2004, Madame Traoré won the Perdita Huston Human Rights Award, an international prize recognising the work of outstanding advocates for women's rights in the third world. She travelled to Washington and delivered a speech on Capitol Hill. The national newspapers in Mali featured articles celebrating the win.

'I was emotional and I was honoured to get this prize. Especially when I read about Perdita. I understand from this that we were like twins. The way Perdita tried to help women, that is exactly the way I try to help women. I was really proud when I went to Washington from Mali. I was very excited. There were a lot of people, including the Mali ambassador. That made me proud. It's really been important at a national level. It permits women who didn't think it was possible to make progress because they are not schooled, [to realise] they have potential. Women understand that by themselves they can do something important. Now we have more than seven thousand associations working for women.'

But the challenges are still enormous. Almost two-thirds of Malian girls are married by the time they are eighteen and 95 per cent of them have no access to modern contraceptives. The lack of reproductive rights contributes to the large number of maternal deaths and unplanned children. The most important transactions of many Malian women's lives are carried out when they are only teenagers and they don't have a voice equal to those of their parents and adult husbands. The majority of Malian girls undergo female genital mutilation, and become married and pregnant, long before they reach adulthood and can choose for themselves. The women's basic right to survival is closely tied to their right to survive pregnancy and childbirth. That's why Madame Traoré is fighting so hard for family planning; it's not a luxury, it's a way to save the lives of thousands of women in Mali.

She pulls out a scrapbook from one of the cupboards in her office and shows me the newspaper articles. I look at one of the photographs of her in Washington.

'It's a long way from the back of Timbuktu to America,' I joke with her.

She laughs and nods.

'Nobody can know the future, but when I succeed I always think about the past. I always thank my father for sending me to school. My father had a friend whose wife always invited me to have tea with her, they were in Timbuktu. Each time I came she would give me tea and advise me not to go to school: "A girl is not designed for school, stay home." When I went back I would tell that to my father, we would just laugh and I continued to go to school.

'I am a normal woman, I am not extraordinary. I like fighting. I like succeeding. This is the only reason. Otherwise I am a normal woman. Every day at five past seven I am here in my office. It is very important for a woman to know she has potential. To know that she is able to do something. In Mali we have many women who have determination and courage to succeed in life. A lot of women are fighters.

'I don't make any distinction between poor woman and rich woman, all the women are the same for nurses. I really love this job. I can spend a night with a sick woman, assisting her, it doesn't matter for me, just to make the woman happy. The work is hard but I have to do it.'

Madame Traoré shakes my hand as we say goodbye. I catch a taxi and cross the Pont des Martyrs over the Niger, as the red dust coats the morning traffic. When I get back to the hotel, I start packing my backpack ready to fly to Ghana, on to London and eventually home to Australia. I haven't seen my friends or family since Kate Peyton's memorial service almost five months ago. I'm homesick and excited to be finishing the journey even though I didn't make it all the way to Timbuktu. The drivers outside the hotel are still touting for business.

'Madaaaaaaame! Tombouctou. We go. Road is good now.'

When I check out of the hotel, the receptionist types my name, occupation and business card into one long, jumbled title on my receipt, *Mrs Author/Correspondent of Africa Sally Jane Sara*. He bows his head as he hands it to me.

'Thank you, Mrs Author. We will see you again.'

'One day, my brother.'

EPILOGUE

ACCRA AIRPORT, GHANA
6 July 2005

These are my last few hours in Africa. Tomorrow morning I'll be waking up in London. I have been dreading this farewell and my eyes fill up when I think about leaving but, after five years, it's time to go.

Africa has changed me. It has imprinted itself on my values; a bit like being parented all over again. I have learned a different way to see the world. Africa has shocked and infuriated me, but I have also learned to look for kindness in its darkest corners. While in some ways it has been a very long and solitary journey, my memories are in the shared custody of so many companions who have guided me, and those travelling friendships have been the pieces of gold along the way.

The twelve women in this book have taught me about hope. During the many months of travel and interviews, I've tried to understand what has kept them going in their lives, when they had every reason to give up. Most of the women have focused on three things: children, religion and the pursuit of education. Children have been the reason many of the women have pushed on, religion has been a way to explain unexplainable hardships, and education has been an unwavering goal for the women and their offspring. But, for some of the other women, childbearing and religion have been sources of oppression.

During the journey I have been forced to confront my own spirituality for the first time in my life, and this was unexpected. The questions of faith linger, even though I try to push them away. It's difficult to spend so much time with women such as Hellen and Eugenie and walk away unchallenged. I don't share their faith, but I have tried to understand it and this has unsettled some of my own beliefs.

Kate Peyton's death also shook my confidence in myself and in Africa. Initially it made me reluctant to continue this long journey on my own. I was angry at Africa for taking her life. The deliberateness and randomness of Kate's murder remain in my thoughts and yet it has also deepened my understanding.

I think sometimes I assumed that my observer status as a journalist somehow gave me protection from harm. I had immersed myself in Africa, become streetwise and remained determined not to shut myself off or fall into the easy trap of cynicism. It's a decision which paid off again and again in rich experiences, but it came at a price. It is very difficult as a journalist to set the right distance between your subject and yourself: to get in close enough to be able to tell the story with empathy, but also to retain the clarity that outside eyes can bring.

Distance has often been used as a way to dilute the humanness of Africa's troubles. As a result, stories are often told about the millions and the masses, rather than the individual. But women are women, regardless of where they live, and that universality is the key to understanding and further action. The time has come for women in developed countries to stop, look over their shoulders and see that many women in poor countries have been left far behind. While much of the focus has been on narrowing the inequality between men and women in wealthy nations, the real gap is *among* women. The chasm between women in wealthy and poor countries is often far greater than that between men and women *within* wealthy countries. I wonder whether we have forgotten the real battle lines and become too caught up in our own concerns of glass ceilings, childcare and family, while women in faraway places have been all but forgotten.

Feminism must be a movement for the advancement of *all* women, not just for the already advanced. If it is based on the universality of womanhood, then talents, resources and attention should be shared to overcome the most profound disadvantages.

I'm extremely grateful for the experiences I've had on this journey. Africa has reset my boundaries and priorities, and it will forever be my compass. Gorgeous, gorgeous Africa. *Hamba kahle.* Go well.

ACKNOWLEDGEMENTS

Sincere thanks to the Gogo Mamas and their families for their honesty, friendship and patience.

Thanks to my family for their love and support. Nanna, Poppa, Mum, Dad, Justin, Sally, Tyson, Louise, Emma and Lucy.

Thanks to the organisations, interpreters and fixers who made the journey possible. Peter Ramatseba, Candace Rivett-Carnac and Daniela Ossato in South Africa, Ally Saleh and Mariam Mohamed Hamdani in Zanzibar, Resom Habte and Grace Aba from Catholic Relief Services in Sudan, Philip Lutara in Uganda, Gabriel Gabiro in Rwanda, Robert Chamwami in the Democratic Republic of Congo, Martha Getachew in Ethiopia, Nagwa M. El-Hamzawi in Egypt, Vincent Azumah in Ghana, Abdoulay Diarisso, Habibou 'Bebe' Tembely and Diaffé Bagayoko in Mali, Ivan Giesbrecht from Samaritan's Purse, Rosie Schaack, Kendell and Bev Kauffeldt in Liberia for their assistance and extremely generous hospitality.

Thanks also to Fiona Inglis from Curtis Brown, Tom Gilliatt and Sarina Rowell from Pan Macmillan, ABC News and Current Affairs, Michaela Andreyev, Patricia Barraclough, Sarah Clarke, Mark Colvin, Pip Courtney, Kate Evans, Marion Frith, Wendy Glamocak, Renata Gombac, Maree Haynes, Jo Jarvis, Katerina Lawler, Dr Cath Long, Heather Mahar, Chelsea McCarthy, Paula McKay, Lisa Millar, Catherine Nikkerud, Kathryn Paige, Alex Sloan, Gillian Vale, Susan Watson, Mark Willacy.

Finally, special thanks to my sister-in-law, Sally Anne Michell Sara, for so much encouragement and feedback during many long phone calls over the past four years. Sal, I'm honoured you've shared the journey from the very beginning.

BIBLIOGRAPHY

Books

Juma Aley Aley, *Zanzibar Series: Enduring Links*, Union Printing Press, Dubai, 1994.

Philip Gourevitch, *We wish to inform you that tomorrow we will be killed with our families*, Picador, London, 2000.

Anthony Mockler, *Haile Selassie's War: The Italian – Ethiopian Campaign 1935–1941*, Random House, New York, 1984.

Thomas Pakenham, *The Scramble for Africa*, Phoenix Press, London, 2001.

Anthony Sattin, *The Gates of Africa – Death, Discovery and the Search for Timbuktu*, Harper Perennial, London, 2004.

Deborah Scroggins, *Emma's War*, HarperCollins, London, 2003.

Abdul Sheriff and Ed Ferguson, *Zanzibar Under Colonial Rule*, James Currey, London, 1991.

Els De Temmerman, *Aboke Girls – children abducted in northern Uganda*, Fountain Publishers, Kampala, 2001.

Other Publications

Amnesty International, *Liberia: Submission to Truth and Reconciliation Commission*, London, 2006.

— *Marked for Death: rape survivors living with HIV/AIDS in Rwanda*, London, 2004.

— *Liberia : The Promise of Peace for 21,000 Child Soldiers*, London, 2004.

Giliane Cherubin-Doumbia, *African commitments to Human Rights: a review of 8 NEPAD countries*, African Human Security Initiative, 2004.

Coalition to stop the use of Child Soldiers, *Child Soldiers Disarmament, Demobilization, Rehabilitation and Reintegration in West Africa*, London, 2006.

Rene Degni-Segui, Special Rapporteur of the Commission on Human Rights, *Report on the Human Rights situation in Rwanda*, United Nations, New York, 1995.

Human Rights Watch, *Famine in Sudan 1998*, New York, 1999.

— *World report 1993: Sudan*, New York, 1993.

— *Stolen Children: Abduction and Recruitment in Northern Uganda*, New York, 2003.

IRIN, Integrated Regional Information Networks, *Minorities Under Siege: Pygmies today in Africa*, United Nations Office for the Coordination of Humanitarian Affairs, 2006.

Jerome Lewis, *The Batwa Pygmies of the Great Lakes Region*, Minority Rights Group International, London, 2000.

Dr Richard Pankhurst, *The Ethiopian Patriots: The Lone Struggle 1936–1940*, Ethiopia Observer 13, 40–56, Addis Ababa, 1970.

— *The Patriots join hands with the British, Africa Quarterly*, 10, 355–74, 1971.

— *The Emperor rides back in triumph*, *Africa Quarterly*, 11, 43–62, 1971.

Refugees International, *Forgotten People: The Batwa 'Pygmy' of the Great Lakes Region of Africa*, Washington DC, 2003.

Save the Children, *Mothers' Index and State of the World's Mothers report*, Westport, 2006.

The Centre for Reproductive Rights, *Claiming Our Rights: surviving pregnancy and childbirth in Mali*, New York, 2003.

— *Female Genital Mutilation: A Matter of Human Rights*, New York, 2003.

UNAIDS, *UNAIDS/WHO AIDS Epidemic update: December 2006, Fact sheet: Sub-Saharan Africa 06*, Geneva, 2006.

UNICEF, *At a glance: Mali statistics*, New York, September 2005.

United Nations Development Programme, *Mali Country Assessment*, New York, 2000.

Photo credits

Bi Kidude performing at Durban, South Africa, 2004, courtesy of Busara Promotions, Zanzibar.